"THE QUEEN IS AN ACE! *As the star of the 4-person softball team called 'The Queen and Her Court,' the 5-foot-9-inch Rosie Black has 16 or 17 pitches that she throws with alarming effectiveness. And that's not counting the trick pitches—behind the back, between the legs, blindfolded and pitching from second base.*"

—New York Times

"*Rosie Black has been called the most feared pitcher in the world. And not without reason. She has struck out an average of 2 batters per inning for an amazing career total of 38,891 (more than the all-time major league pitchers combined.)*"

—Athletes in Action

"*She's a pitching prodigy, a female Feigner, an undisputed Queen of Diamonds. Her brand of softball is so exemplary she tours the U.S. and Canada, using only her catcher, a first baseman, and a shortstop, challenging, and beating, state championship teams, both men's and women's.*"

—California Living

"*Bowing before the Queen. The heat from her fastball could launch a rocket.*"

—Fellowship of Christian Athletes

Diamond in the Rough. The queen of diamonds is awesome. For most of Rosie's games, the headline for the next day is already written; 'The Queen Reigns. Long Live the Queen!' The sportswriter has only to add the winning margin.

—Karen Drollinger, Profiles of Faith
and Courage in the Lives of Top
Woman Athletes

"It didn't sound like a strike!"

—Billy Crystal, after being struck out by Rosie Black on the *Mike Douglas Show*

"A foul tip is a homerun off her!"

—Burt Convy, after hitting a foul tip on the *Johnny Carson Show*

"She's doing it with mirrors!"

—Jay Leno after being struck out by Rosie

"Behind the Queen's Smile *is a masterpiece. In this riveting memoir, Rosie Black Schoepf artfully highlights her career in professional sports while allowing us to see the physical and mental abuse she suffered behind the scenes. Just as Rosie Black Schoepf worked to excel in sports, she was able to work through the trauma to excel in life too. This book shows exactly how she did it.*"

—Erik Seversen, Bestselling Author of *Ordinary to Extraordinary*

BEHIND THE
QUEEN'S
SMILE

BEHIND THE
QUEEN'S
SMILE

A Professional Athlete's Journey of Success,
Abuse, and Healing From the Inside Out

A Memoir

ROSIE BLACK SCHOEPF

THIN LEAF PRESS | LOS ANGELES

This book is based on the author's true story. The events and characters are real, but liberties have been taken to condense the telling for clarity. The names of some characters have been changed to protect their privacy. The conversations related within the story have been drawn from the author's best recollections of those discussions. The author has made every effort to ensure the completeness and accuracy of information contained in this book. She assumes no responsibility for errors, omissions, inaccuracies, or inconsistencies herein.

All scripture quotations unless otherwise noted are from the New King James Version of the Bible. Copyright © 1979, 1980, 1982 by Thomas Nelson, Inc. Used by permission. All rights reserved.

Scripture quotations marked (TLB) are taken from The Living Bible copyright © 1971. Used by permission of Tyndale House Publishers, Inc., Carol Stream, Illinois 60177. All rights reserved.

Scripture quotations from THE MESSAGE. Copyright © by Eugene H. Peterson 1993, 1994, 1995, 1996, 2000, 2001, 2002. Used by permission of Tyndale House Publishers, Inc.

Library of Congress Cataloging-in-Publication Data
Names: Author, Black Schoepf, Rosie
Title: *Behind the Queen's Smile: A Professional Athlete's Journey of Success, Abuse, and Healing from the Inside Out*
LCCN 2022923440

ISBN 978-1-953183-24-8 (hardcover) | 978-1-953183-25-5 (paperback)
ISBN 978-1-953183-26-2 (eBook) | 978-1-953183-27-9 (audiobook)
Memoir, Professional Sports, Christianity, Self Help, Abuse

Editor: Erik Seversen
Cover Design: 100 Covers
Interior Design: Formatted Books
Thin Leaf Press
Los Angeles

THIN
LEAF

To my Lord and Savior Jesus Christ who has held me close, sustained and strengthened me, I dedicate not only this book, but my life.

—

And to my sister Eileen...my teammate, counselor, business partner, and best sister in the whole wide world! This book wouldn't have happened without you. You're a blessing and gift from God! I wouldn't want to navigate this life without you.

CONTENTS

FOREWORD

By Eileen Francabandera
Rosie Black Schoepf's sister and catcher
on The Queen and Her Court

"Having a sister is like having a best friend you can't get rid
of. You know whatever you do, they'll still be there."
—Amy Li

For as long as I can remember, my sister Rosie and I have been referred
to as "The Sisters." The title was securely established when we became
the pitcher/catcher duo for "The Queen and Her Court" at the tender
ages of 9 and 12. Decades of traveling and performing together tethered
that bond, and a half century later, we are still inseparable. No matter
what activity we are engaged in, people still greet us with "Are you The
Sisters?"

After hanging up our softball gloves, Rosie and I partnered in doubles tennis, line dancing, ministry of life counseling, foster parenting,
business, vacations, leading GriefShare, teaching after-school Release
Time programs, and doing public speaking engagements together. No
matter where we were or what we were doing, we were always "The
Sisters."

However, when Rosie informed me she was thinking of writing a
book detailing our young family life and adventures as a professional

exhibition softball team, I thought, *You're on your own for this one.* The idea of this seemed a daunting, and quite frankly, impossible task to encapsulate and accurately detail that journey which was composed of 25 years of ball games, complicated relationships, surprising exploits, and crazy stories. More than that, I realized that a book about our life couldn't be written without digging up some buried episodes from our life. I didn't know if I wanted to relive, let alone share, the mental and physical abuse we suffered. *Did Rosie really want to bring these things up,* I questioned?

After a few weeks, Rosie brought me a chapter she had written, and I was amazed at her ability to describe our lives with transparency, vulnerability, and honesty. I realized that regardless the pain, our story needed to be written. "The Sisters" were suddenly on a new adventure again in the production of the book, *Behind the Queen's Smile.* Our mission in this book is to highlight the positive side of our professional sports career and even reveal some funny, behind-the-scenes moments, but equally important is to reveal some of the trauma that we tried so desperately to hide for many years.

It is our hope that the sports enthusiast enjoys the narratives but also that this book finds a way to touch anyone in a current or past abusive situation. It is our desire that, through Rosie's example, this book shows others that no situation is hopeless. A new beginning is possible through faith in Jesus Christ and a willingness to work through the pain. Both Rosie and I are now dedicated to counseling others who are suffering the abuses of life alone. Now, with our lives on display, we endeavor to use our difficulties, struggles, and trauma to bring hope to those in similar situations.

INTRODUCTION

I was born into an extended family of great smilers. You could spot our "Beaird" smile in any crowd. My cousins broke into show business with their talent and beautiful smiles doing commercials, television shows like *Leave it to Beaver,* and movies with Kurt Russell and Elvis Presley.

My dad had a dream to follow suit with his family, even though we didn't quite know what that dream would look like. He began our preparation and training early on and was eager to present us to the public...always with a smile. I can't tell you how many publicity photos I've taken in my lifetime.

Whenever my siblings and I wanted to laugh until our sides split, we would start repeating our dad's instructions to each other on how far to part our lips...not forgetting to manufacture a little spit, strategically placed to show our pearly whites with the maximum glistening effect for each photo.

While my siblings and I were being set up for public exposure, never in my wildest dreams could I ever have conjured up the life that I ended up living. Our family found our place in professional sports as well as the entertainment business. We ended up as a touring fastpitch softball team, and our accomplishments have remained unmatched. No female athlete in the history of fastpitch softball has been able to replicate the success and longevity of The Queen and Her Court. Let me explain.

The Queen and Her Court is what people began calling our unique fastpitch softball team. The team consisted of only four players—a pitcher, catcher, first base, and shortstop—and our tiny team traveled around challenging any nine-member male or female team in the world. Since I was the pitcher, I was given the regal title of "Queen." With my grand status, I was placed into the limelight from 1965 through 1989. While this provided many perks, it also came with extra pressures and responsibilities of representing our team as well. The pressure was compounded by an expected perfection of our team's performance that would launch us to the top in the sports world.

As it turned out, our phenomenal achievements included a ninety six percent winning record, and I racked up over 52,000 strikeouts over almost twenty-five years. While those statistics alone would have been enviable for any professional pitcher, there was an unexpected icing on the cake since all of this was occurring during the upstart of the women's liberation movement in the late sixties and seventies. Since the media was in high demand for stories of women who were competing with men, and coming out on top, the media attention collided with the peak of my career.

Even though I was not the hard core "women's libber" that everyone assumed I would be, I represented the picture of a powerful woman achieving great success in a man's world. I chuckled the day I appeared on a talk show with Helen Reddy, the singer who popularized the women's lib anthem, "I am Woman" ... hear me roar!

At our team's peak, we were in high media demand, appearing on almost every national talk show that you could think of during this time period. We were on shows hosted by Steve Allen, Mike Douglas, Merv Griffin, John Davidson, Dick Cavett, *Good Morning America*; and realizing the dream of every Hollywood celebrity and sport's figure, we appeared on *The Tonight Show*, striking out the legendary Johnny Carson as well as the then leading home run hitter for the Los Angeles Dodger, Jimmy Wynn. After this performance, there was a sense that The Queen and Her Court had "finally arrived."

One night, following a game, an adoring teenage girl seeking my autograph gushed as she said, "You are the luckiest person in the world...I wish I could be you."

As she heaped an overflow of flattery upon me, I knew I should be embracing her words of admiration. But, an internal war of words was simmering underneath the surface, threatening to expose my real feelings to this young woman. Instead of revealing how extremely tough my life was, I didn't miss a beat, responding with my perfect words and my perfect smile. As she walked away, silent utterances exploded in my head, *I doubt you'd want my life if you really knew me.* How could she or anyone else really know me? I kept all the family secrets like a good daughter, even as I could feel myself sinking into a deep, dark hole of despair. Thank God, the story doesn't end there.

My story is one of healing, restoration, and redemption from the inside out. In this book, I break our family code of silence in the most honest way I can, describing some of my happenings, my struggles, and my successes. My desire is to share how I was pulled from the pit, making sense of subjects like abuse, depression, suicide, forgiveness, relationships, guilt, and shame.

While I do share many personal, behind the scenes stories (that have never been in print) that are humorous and entertaining, my supreme purpose is to encourage and bring light to any person who has ever felt stuck or without hope for their future. If you are one of those people, there is a way out...just hold on!

Whenever I am praying for someone when it seems everything is stacked against them, I pray this prayer, *"God, be merciful. Help them, like you helped me. Even if they're wearing a fake smile, like I did for so many years, You know what they are going through...You know their sufferings... and You can help!"*

May this writing honor God, and may you, the reader, be immensely blessed.

CHAPTER 1

THE NIGHTMARE

*"Be sober, be vigilant; because your adversary the devil walks
about like a roaring lion, seeking whom he may devour. Resist
him, steadfast in the faith, knowing that the same sufferings
are experienced by your brotherhood in the world."*

I PETER 5: 8-9

◇◇◇◇◇◇◇◇◇◇

Tap, tap, tap. Once again…I heard the faint sound of the tap, tap, tapping.

All my senses strained to decipher what I was hearing and where the rhythmic sounds were coming from.

At first, the taps seemed weak, coming from a distance; gradually, they increased in volume, getting louder and louder.

What was wrong with me? It was a sound so familiar, and yet I could not seem to solve the mystery. My mind was draped in a thick fog. I couldn't even see an inch in front of my face, making it completely impossible to detect my whereabouts.

Unexpectedly, the tapping turned into a knocking, forming a familiar pattern, reminding me how my family and teammates would knock on my hotel door with a special code, so I would know it was safe to open the door—knock, knock, knock, knock, knock—a pause—knock, knock.

Was I on tour? I knew I needed to snap to attention and answer that door, but my mind and body wouldn't cooperate. I was so lethargic and disoriented. It felt like one of my slow-motion dreams, playing over and over throughout the night like a broken record. *That's it! I must be dreaming.*

As the loud knocking began again, my body jolted upright as if a lightning bolt had surged through my frame. Instantly, I woke from my deep sleep, straining to focus my eyes in the darkness of my bedroom, trying to assess what was happening. Quickly, I glanced over to my nightstand where the bright red numbers on my digital clock indicated that it was 3:30 a.m.

As thoughts returned, I chastised myself for falling asleep because I had vowed to remain awake in an all-night prayer vigil interceding on behalf of my dad...spiritually wrestling with God until He answered.

I was startled as the loud knocking commenced. My body tightened, as I comprehended that the sounds I heard were not part of a dream—they were very real.

Adrenaline coursed through my veins as I realized that someone I knew had walked around to the back of my house and was using our team code-knock on the sliding glass door of my bedroom. My heart felt like it was pounding as loudly as the knocking. Even though the next details happened very quickly, a slow motion of events was about to transpire and change the rest of my life.

I rushed to the dangling white cords, tugging hard. The blinds retracted to reveal my sister, Eileen, and her husband, Gregg, standing expressionless behind the sheet of glass.

As our eyes met, I instinctively knew why they were there. A flood of emotions consumed my soul as I realized that God had heard my prayers. Two weeks earlier, the Spirit of God led me into a very specific prayer and now I was certain the next words spoken aloud would be

His answer. Because of the palpable somberness that pierced our stares through the glass, I sensed His answer was not the one I would have chosen or hoped for.

Moments before opening the sliding door, before any words were exchanged, I felt a deep sense of peace and an unmistakable calm that God was with me. Little did I know that in the days ahead, I would need every ounce of His presence to see me through each day.

Eileen and Gregg stepped inside my room. In a very tender and calm manner, Eileen said, "Daddy is dead."

Tears flowed from our faces as we embraced one another. In the midst of our sadness, I lifted my hands up to the heavens as an act of acknowledging God's presence and faithfulness to hear our prayers. With my hands extended high above my head, I began speaking forth audible praises and thanks to God. My daddy was finally out of his suffering and pain...in heaven with Jesus.

In the midst of praising God, I glanced to my sister and brother-in-law who stood silently. Eileen had an unrecognizable look of dread on her face. My praise ceased as I waited for her next sentence... "Rosie, Daddy took his own life."

The piercing pain shot through my body like a dagger to the soul. All praise ended. It felt as if all the air and lifeblood was sucked out of me. I gulped for breath. "What are you saying? What do you mean?"

Eileen repeated her pronouncement, adding additional details that fell on my incoherent ears.

My body collapsed as I fell to my knees and started pounding my clenched fist on the top of my bed. Every fiber of my being, writhed in pain, as I began screaming at the top of my voice, "no, no, no, no, why, why, why, why"—over and over again. Minutes passed, but it seemed like an eternity.

In vain, Eileen and Gregg pulled me up and tried to console me. I willed myself to calm down, grabbing a few articles of clothes, and we drove together to Daddy's home in Rolling Hills Estates.

My thoughts were whirling as I stared blankly out of the back seat window. *How can I possibly bear the pain of this, Lord? Haven't I suffered enough for one lifetime?*

Before my negative thoughts took me under, I opted for an alternate behavior, slipping into my finely honed and perfected childhood survival mechanism, tuning out most everything and everyone around me.

I was naïve to think the worst was behind me. The real nightmare had begun.

CHAPTER 2

THE LEGACY

"Strength and honor are her clothing; She shall rejoice in time to come. She opens her mouth with wisdom, and on her tongue is the law of kindness. She watches over the ways of her household, and does not eat the bread of idleness. Her children rise up and call her blessed."

PROVERBS 31: 25-28

A number of years ago, my mother wrote an eight page autobiography called "Memories of My Life" and gave it to each one of her five children, along with a few pictures. This cherished Christmas present was filled with priceless stories from her childhood that started out on a small farm in Bennington, Nebraska, just outside of Omaha.

Four boys were born to Henry and Della Palke, one of whom died after just a few weeks, and then came the long-awaited "only daughter"—my mom, Jeryldene Mae, Jeri for short.

When I first received this gift of her memories, I huddled in a quiet corner, removing myself from our family's Christmas chatter, intent on no interruptions. I was excited to read about this woman whom I so deeply loved and cherished.

My jaws were aching from the big smile that I had on my face as Mom recalled one comical story after another. I loved reading about her carefree childhood. The short autobiography took me on her journey from her early years to adulthood.

My reading quickened, as I was anxious to see her feelings and reflections concerning our childhood. My anticipation was mounting. After all these years, I couldn't wait to see what she would have to say about our family happenings and the secrets that bonded us together for a lifetime.

Finally, the last page was before me, and her story ended with an abruptness that took me by surprise. Her last words were sad and unsettling.

Mom wrote, *"After this point, many of my memories are unhappy ones and serve no good purpose to put them into print. Many times I wondered, did I really listen to God's voice and follow His plan, or did I just pursue my own desires? Often my faith grew weak and I questioned…Why? But God remained faithful!"*

Mom continued to list many of the blessings God had bestowed on her over the years…including our loving step-dad, Jerry, financial provision, the luxury of travel, and good health.

She ended with this, *"My crowning glory are my five special children, who have given me much joy. I have watched them grow and mature as they learned to deal with scars of the past and be victorious over life's battles through Christ!"*

I sat in silence as I absorbed each of her heartfelt words to my siblings and me.

It was true. Over the years, I had labored hard to find answers and inner peace dealing with hurts and scars, always in a quest to resolve the haunting memories of my past.

Once I returned to my home, I pulled out Mom's abbreviated account of her life. Even though her words stopped short, leaving me hanging, and wondering about many of our shared experiences, I was sure that knowing her early years would give me a better insight into who I was, so I re-read her pages again and again.

With each new story, I began to understand the incredible gift that had been handed down to me. As Mom recounted the legacy her parents bestowed upon her...especially a desire for spiritual things, the importance of personal faith in Jesus Christ, and an appreciation of the blessing of close family ties, I knew that my mom had also bestowed these upon me.

Mom imparted her personal thoughts to each one of her children. *"My greatest desire would be to share this legacy with you and that you, my beloved children, would, in turn, Pass It On! In this way, our life will not have been in vain and a part of us will always live on."*

After reading this, a flood of emotions followed. Not only was I grateful as I read how this generational gift had touched my life, but I also felt a new determination to do whatever it would take to live out her words of wisdom.

I mouthed silently in response, *"Mama, with God's help, I will pass on this hope and legacy. Even though it will be difficult, I do believe it will serve an important purpose to put into print some of the hardship that we have lived through. I've discovered that secrets and lies exposed lose their momentum and power to destroy our very souls. There is a great strength and bond that comes from knowing that our experiences are no different than others who have struggled with pain and suffering and are now victorious. Somehow it gives me courage to know we're not alone. Part of God's plan of healing and restoration takes place when truth sheds light in the dark places."*

As I recall my mother's roots and legacy that has helped mold me into the best part of who I am today, I am especially drawn to the sections of her writing where she described her thankfulness for a family that passed down such a strong spiritual heritage of the truth of salvation through Jesus Christ.

My mother had a very sensitive heart for God at a very early age. Around four or five years old, Mom's first recollection of feeling sorry for sin happened as she was playing a childish game of rhyming words with letters up and down the alphabet—bod, cod, dod, fod, and then she said, *"God."* In her little heart she thought surely, she had taken the Lord's name in vain. She felt very repentant, and her mother said if she would just ask Jesus, He would come into her heart and would forgive her. My mom believes that was the moment she was saved.

On the humorous side, Mom remembers a plaque on the wall that simply read, "PRESS ON." For days, she wondered if it meant to push…as a button, and what mysterious, magical thing might happen if she did.

One day she worked up the courage to get on a chair and with a little fear and great anticipation, she pushed the spot. To her disappointment or relief, nothing happened, and she had to assume it must have some spiritual meaning like "Keep on trying."

On June 25th, 1939, Mom (nine years old) gave a public affirmation of her faith in Jesus Christ as her Lord and Savior at Benson Baptist Church.

Life on a farm in Nebraska was filled with hard work, fun, and family gatherings almost every Sunday after church. Grandparents, aunts, uncles, and cousins by the dozens gathered for dinner at my Grandma Palke's house for great food, singing around the old pump organ, and reading from the Bible. Birthdays, Christmas, and other holidays were also a good reason to get together with delicious home-baked goodies or maybe some ice cream—the kind you churned by hand in an ice cream freezer.

Mom recalls that gifts were never a very big part of the celebrations, but it didn't seem to matter. Furthermore, she can never remember discussing diets, calories, or fat grams. No one ever heard of Weight Watchers or Jennie Craig!

Even though Mom never felt she missed out on things or felt inferior, in 1940, Grandpa and Grandma auctioned off the farm. They decided to make a big life move, following other relatives in pursuit of "the good life" in sunny Southern California.

Besides the tears of missing her old friends, the hardest adjustment was the awkwardness of being the younger new girl in a big California junior high school. She was three years younger than any of the other kids. The substantial age difference between Mom and the other kids happened because there was no kindergarten in her small Nebraska town. Mom started first grade in a little one-room schoolhouse at four years old. Despite the fact that there was only one teacher doing her best to teach sixteen to twenty students from grades one through eight, little Jeri excelled on her own and completed the first and second grade workbooks that year, moving straight through to the third grade in the fall.

With the new move to California, my bewildered ten-year old mother started seventh grade, mid-term, at Horace Mann Jr. High, only blocks from the corner of Florence and Normandie in South Central Los Angeles. It was quite a change for this little pigtailed farm girl, being thrown in with her thirteen-year-old classmates.

Even with all the obstacles and awkwardness, Mom breezed through junior high and high school with flying colors and was ready for college. She prayed about what her next steps would be, and it seemed like a three-year General Bible course at Biola was the place where God would show her what to do with her life. She thought, *I may even meet the man of my dreams!* To her disappointment, her application was denied because of her age. Biola had never encountered a fifteen-year-old applicant before, so they suggested that she wait until mid-term when she would be sixteen. With great excitement, Mom was allowed to enter Biola in January, 1947. She was privileged to have some excellent Bible teachers such as Dr. J. Vernon McGee—everyone's favorite.

With school and a part-time job, Mom was pretty much self-supporting from age sixteen on, paying for her own education expenses, clothing, etc. In her second year at Biola, she was smitten with her first real heartthrob. He was out-going, popular, and sang in the Biola quartet. There were a few dates, but as she puts it, "My dreams were crushed—I got dumped for someone else."

During this time, Mom was still pondering over God's will for her life. Many times, she was challenged by missionary speakers to consider a foreign field, but that didn't seem like a fit. About this time, she met another personable young man, Royal, who was about to change the course of her life. He was already preaching at a tiny Baptist church in Walteria, California, and he invited her to come to a service with him.

Mom was completely impressed with his style, fervor, and his winning personality! She thought, *Could this finally be the direction God is leading me?* Soon after, a proposal of marriage came from Royal worded like this, "How would you like to spend the rest of your life as a preacher's wife?"

Mom thought, *this must be God's answer for me.* Her reply was *"Yes."* She completed her three years at Biola in January, 1950, and in February, my mother became Mrs. Royal Beaird.

CHAPTER 3

THE PREACHER

*"For whoever calls upon the name of the Lord shall be saved. How
then shall they call on Him in whom they have not believed? And how
shall they believe in Him of whom they have not heard? And how
shall they hear without a preacher? And how shall they preach unless
they are sent? As it is written: 'How beautiful are the feet of those who
preach the gospel of peace, who bring glad tidings of good things.'"*

ROMANS 10: 13-15

◇◇◇◇◇◇◇◇◇◇◇◇

A number of years ago, my sister, Eileen, was completing the
final credits she needed to graduate with a Bachelor of Arts
degree in Psychology at Vanguard University in Irvine,
California. As a transferable elective, she signed up for an in-depth
class on I Corinthians at Calvary Chapel Bible College in Torrance.

When she mentioned the class to me, I jumped at the idea of doing
a couple of my favorite things in life—getting to know the heart of God
just a little bit better and spending time with my sweet sister.

Within the first couple of weeks, we were given an exercise that
greatly impacted my life.

Most of the class centered around the teachings and tremendous influence the Apostle Paul had on the lives of the people in the city of Corinth. In conjunction with this theme, the professor had the class answer five questions. Afterward, we were separated into small groups to discuss our answers.

The first question was: "Other than Jesus Christ, who has been the greatest influence of your life?"

That sounded like such an easy question, but after giving it a little thought, I became greatly agitated. My easy answer wasn't coming to mind...so I proceeded on. Within minutes I breezed through the other questions, coming full circle to that first question again.

I scrolled through my mental list of possibilities and just kept coming back to the one name that I so desperately resisted acknowledging on paper. I could feel my cheeks flushing with emotion. Out of the blue, anger was welling up within me. If I was truthful, I had to write down the name of the one person who had caused so much pain, hurt, misery, and confusion in my life.

As the professor gave the "one minute" warning to finish, I refused to think about the depths of this question, jotting down what I considered to be the truth. The greatest influence on my life was the "preacher man" who proposed to my dear mother... my daddy, Royal Beaird.

As we formed our small groups to disclose our answers, I pre-determined to gloss over that question without much explanation. I wasn't up for anyone seeing the raw emotion that was lying dormant in my heart.

Eileen went first, and I was shocked that she had written down the same answer. I was taken so off guard that I forgot my former vow of nonchalance. Instead, I blurted out, "Eileen, how could we both have chosen Daddy as our greatest influence when he was the one person who caused us so much pain?"

Because Eileen continued the discussion with openness and vulnerability, my natural inclination to keep my unexposed feelings hidden started to melt away. Somehow, a heavy weight was being lifted. I was learning that moving past hurts and wounds, caused by others, could be healed if I would be honest. I could be healed by refusing to run from the haunting memories of my past.

I had been taking little baby steps for years, struggling to move forward toward wholeness. That night, I realized that if I wanted to make peace with my past, I had to continue along this path of honesty—asking the hard questions and opening myself up to revisit painful situations.

Maybe you're thinking—that certainly doesn't seem like sound wisdom. What person in their right mind would choose to talk about and experience more pain to get out of pain? That sounds ridiculous!

I agree. It is ridiculous, if you do this on your own. Instead, I invited the One who loves and cares for you and me more than we could ever fathom to participate in my journey of going back. I chose to work with The Spirit of God, who is our Great Counselor. He took me by the hand and led me back through the difficult seasons in my life. He wept when I wept. His comfort was authentic, reaching the deepest recesses of my heart like no one else could. He handled every emotion that I felt, no matter how vile or raw; and He remained faithfully by my side, loving me with an everlasting love that was beyond my comprehension.

As I entered adulthood, I knew I was facing a pivotal place in my life, but I didn't have to take on my past alone. I could shrink back or be courageous, moving forward in this process of healing. I had the freedom to choose! Two things helped me in my process of reconciling the pain in my life. The first was acknowledging the truth—my dad had influenced me greatly. Slowly, healing came when I began to separate and recognize that he was instrumental in bringing both good and bad influences into my life, and figuring out how to distinguish between the two.

I know that for some of your cases, looking for anything good will take every bit of creative imagination you can possibly muster.

Truthfully, it might come down to the idea that Dad and/or Mom were simply the sperm and egg donors that God used to create the absolutely, one-of-a kind, magnificent you!

In my case, after my mental sifting process, I chose to hold onto the good influences in me and be proud of the traits that positively reflected Daddy. At the other end of the spectrum, what incredible freedom God gave me when I realized I could turn from the lies and negative patterns that my dad spoke into my life. These lies threatened to suck the very life out of me, seeking to control and destroy everything God had intended me to be.

The second step of healing came as I looked back at Daddy's life with a softer, more compassionate heart. I can honestly say that I haven't gotten all the answers I've needed to reconcile some of his behavior. But through God's strength, I can forgive, and not validate my dad's behavior at the same time. Also, I will admit that as I have gotten older and have fallen and failed in many areas that I never thought I would, I am much more empathetic with my dad's struggles and sins. Being humbled by my own sin has given me a maturity that didn't exist when I was younger.

In my new quest for truth and healing, I determined to uncover as many details about the man who had such a profound influence over my life. What insights would history give me? While I looked deeply into my father's life, I would find out.

My dad was born on June 13, 1929. He was the sixth son and the baby of ten children in his family. After reading my Grandma Beaird's account of her life, I was amazed at how many times my dad's family moved. At three months old, Daddy and the Beaird clan left Vernal, Utah for the lone star state of Texas. In a span of about ten years, they proceeded to move almost a dozen times while in Texas.

One of my grandma's recollections was of staying on a little run-down farm just outside of Carrizo Springs, where she wrote, "It was one of the worst little shacks on this farm—so many cracks—cold, wind blew through and Dallas [my uncle] got the croup and almost died. Terrible struggle in those days, but the precious Lord surely watches over His own."

When Daddy was around five or six years old, his dad and all his brothers, except Dallas, left Texas and headed to California to make more money building houses in the booming construction business. Eventually, Grandma Beaird, Uncle Dallas, and Daddy made their way out to California also.

Daddy never saw his father, except for one short duration of time, living in a small trailer with his dad and brother, Dallas.

Recently, I talked to my Uncle Dallas and asked him to describe my dad since he was the closest brother. I asked, *"Why was my dad so angry, intense, controlling, and jealous? How could he be such an influential person in so many people's lives and then kill himself? Was he insecure because he didn't grow up with a dad? Was he driven to succeed at all costs because he felt poor?"* I'm sure I bombarded my uncle with many unanswerable questions, but our conversation together yielded a unique comfort to my soul, despite the lack of answers.

Uncle Dallas described Daddy as a bit spoiled and undisciplined as the baby—a single boy with a single mom. Often, he was disrespectful and bullied his little five-foot mother. As my uncle spoke, I also recalled a memory when I was about seven years old. Our family went to Grandma Beaird's house, and I remember thinking, *Daddy is talking meanly to his mom. If I talked that way, I'd be spanked.*

I do believe the absence of my dad's father left a gap that is necessary in helping to discipline and train boys to respect and honor the women in their life. That pattern of bullying and abuse carried on with my mom and his very own girls.

My uncle said that he and my dad got along most of the time, but that Daddy might have felt like a tag along among his brothers. "For some reason Royal was always making enemies and guys would come to fight him. Uncle Dallas continued, "Our dad never really taught him how to fight, so every day I'd have to help Royal fight off these boys in town."

I said, "That sounds like my brother, Marv. It's like he had a chip on his shoulder; and he was always trying to prove his worth. For some reason, he'd always end up in fights with people."

"There are two things that are true about Royal," my uncle declared, with certainty and confidence. "All his life, he wanted to serve the Lord, and all his life, he was troubled and tormented by Satan."

I had heard my uncle say this before, and I have witnessed the truth to both of those statements. Just hearing him describe Daddy's life like that made me feel a little numb and quietly somber.

Upon more reflection, I also felt great fear because, similar to my dad, I knew that my greatest passion in life was to love and serve God, while I too, had entertained deeply troubling thoughts, being supernaturally tormented at times in my life.

It was a wake-up call for me. I could live in some of the same self-defeating patterns that could actually lead to death, or I could learn how to live in the newness that Christ offered and be different from my own Daddy. The choice was mine.

Dear Daddy,

If you were here, I would tell you that I greatly admired your charismatic and confident leadership abilities. As a little girl, I was always blown away while watching you speak to crowds with such convincing and persuasive words. I witnessed how you could make friends with anyone. Everyone loved being around you, and even though I tired of hearing the same stories and jokes that you told with that certain "Royal Beaird" flair, I sure wish you were here to tell them one more time.

I envied how you had such incredible dreams and set goals. I was amazed how you worked with great certainty and a singleness of mind until your dreams came to fruition. The best part was getting to witness your gift of sharing the good news of Jesus Christ and watching as many people accepted the Lord because of your words. I loved how your Bible was all highlighted, ragged, and worn from studying it so much. I remember how you offered me a quarter if I would memorize John 3:16–17. It was the first scriptures I actually put to memory.

You forgot and never paid up, but I have not forgotten. Those words are forever written in my heart and soul, and my passion is to share those words of eternal life with others.

Oh, "Preacher Man," your words for Christ have profoundly influenced my life. I have chosen to live out the best part of your impact on my life. For that, I say, "Thank you."

CHAPTER 4

THE SOVEREIGN ONE

"You made all the delicate, inner parts of my body, and knit them together in my mother's womb. Thank you for making me so wonderfully complex! It is amazing to think about. Your workmanship is marvelous—and how well I know it. You were there while I was being formed in utter seclusion! You saw me before I was born and scheduled each day of my life before I began to breathe. Every day was recorded in your Book!"

PSALMS 139:13-16

◇◇◇◇◇◇◇◇◇◇◇

My parents were married February 24, 1950; one month after Mom graduated from Biola. Signs of Mom's whirlwind life with Royal began on the night they were married at Calvary Baptist Tabernacle, the small church in Walteria, California.

The beautiful nineteen-year-old bride, who had dreams of a new life with her handsome pastor husband, didn't know that the day of her wedding would include a bet that would cause a major eye-opening conflict and a continued abusive pattern that would escalate for the rest of her married life.

One of my dad's closest buddies jokingly made a wager, betting that he, my dad's friend, was going to kiss my mom at the wedding. Daddy warned Mom ahead of time not to let this happen. But when the long line of guests formed to greet the new bride and groom, sure enough, my dad's friend quickly snuck a kiss on her cheek.

In good humor, everyone was all smiles and laughter as Daddy's buddy bragged he had won the bet.

The phony merriment lasted until my mom and dad were alone later that night. Daddy got so upset about the kiss that he continued to harass Mom all night. Her beautifully imagined wedding night turned into hours and hours of interrogation on how many boyfriends she had had previously, and how many kisses she had given away before she met him.

Mom said, "What he had, he had to control."

In the following days and weeks, the constant questions and verbal abuse was never-ending. Daddy went through Mom's closet throwing anything away that seemed threatening to him—pictures, records of her old boyfriend, Cliff singing in his quartet, and a pair of beautiful red shoes that Mom loved.

Everyday was nerve racking and tense, and Mom couldn't understand why Daddy was so angry and untrusting all the time. The naïve young country girl, who had honored God all her life and earned the love, respect, and trust of everyone, was now being treated like a loose woman with a sordid, evil past. It didn't make sense.

One day, about three months into their marriage, Daddy started in again, with all his routine questioning about Mom's past relationships.

Recently, Mom confided to me, "I just didn't want to answer all the same old questions again, so I told him, I want to see my mom. I didn't necessarily want to leave him. I suppose I was trying to call his bluff. Really, I just wanted him to stop with all the same questions and be normal."

Mom continued, "Without missing a beat, your dad said, "Okay, I'll take you to your mom." Not a word was spoken as he packed my things and dropped me off. Mom was sure that Daddy would call within a day or so and say how sorry he was for his behavior, but three months passed without a word.

Without the constant harassment from Daddy, the peace and tranquility of everyday life returned. Emotionally, it was a very sad time for her, and she felt like a failure, like somehow it was her fault.

Mom's heart's desire was to live a life that was pleasing to God, but there didn't seem to be a clear-cut answer or direction that would slice through the dark cloud of confusion. Mom didn't want a divorce, but she couldn't live with such an angry, jealous, and insecure man. What to do?

Once during my mom and dad's courtship, Mom returned home. She was crying after a spat and apparent break-up with Daddy. My sweet grandma wanted to make things better, so she called my dad and said "there's an awfully sad little girl over here." Grandma encouraged Daddy and Mom to talk things out and get back together—and they did. As my mom recounted that story to me, she chuckled aloud and said, "Gee, thanks, Mom!"

However, this time around, there were no such intercessory talks coming from my grandma, as Mom told her a little of what married life with Royal was really like. As summer was coming to an end, Mom accepted this new life of married, but separated. She didn't know what else to do, so she went out and got a job.

After about a week of working at her new job, a knock at the front door revealed my dad's mom, Grandma Beaird. While Daddy remained in the car, he commissioned his mother to deliver his divorce papers that required Mom's signature.

This was all very shocking and sad to my mother.

When Mom was sharing this most bizarre part of her story with me, I was puzzled to know exactly what Daddy did to win her back and how he talked her into coming home with him. How did things turn around so drastically, especially after he had gone so far as to file for divorce?

The next part of the story is a bit sketchy for Mom, but she had the feeling that she was not supposed to let this happen. She walked outside to Daddy's car door, motioning to roll down the window, "We've got to talk."

Daddy got out, and they walked up and down the street as they talked.

I asked Mom, "Did Daddy ever say he was sorry or ask you to forgive him? Did he ever say anything that indicated a desire to change his behavior?"

Mom said, "I don't remember anything like that. There were no words like I need you back, or I miss you or anything. I came away from hours of talking with the feeling that whatever it was that caused our break-up was my fault. I really wasn't sure about anything, but I thought, I guess we could try again…It would be the right thing to do. When we finished our talk, I remember packing my clothes and peeking my head into my mother's dark bedroom and telling her that I was going back with Royal. I'll never forget the sad look in her eyes."

Things did not get better after the separation. On the contrary, Daddy's behavior seemed worse with an additional rule set in stone for Mom. Daddy said that Grandma Palke was a troublemaker, so Mom was forbidden to see or talk to her own mother.

When I heard this new mandate that Daddy handed down to Mom, I thought it was ludicrous to put my Grandma Palke's name and the phrase troublemaker in the same sentence. She was a sweet, gentle, loving and soft-spoken woman—just like my mother.

It seems crazy now that my dad could get away with that behavior, and I would witness far worse things later on.

This kind of abuse was definitely more prevalent in the 1950's where troubled families were more apt to keep their problems and strife secret. At the time, resources and counseling for abused women was minimal, at best.

My mom's grandmother passed away on July 23, 1951, and Mom finally got to see her own mother again at the funeral. One whole year had passed without a word or visit between them. After the funeral,

Mom was allowed to visit her mother again…mostly due to the fact that everyone had sufficiently learned to put on their best faces and play by Royal Beaird's rules.

In the fall, after Mom returned home with Daddy, she got pregnant for the first time. Sometime during her first trimester, she went to the shed to get the lawn mower. As she pulled it down from the wall, she felt a strange jolt in her stomach. She paused for a moment, then disregarded the twinge from below and continued to mow the lawn.

That night she awoke to discover her body covering a pool of blood on the sheets below her. Quickly, my parents rushed to the hospital to find out the sad news that Mom had miscarried.

Had this baby lived, the dynamic of my birth order would have changed to number two…if indeed, I would have been born at all.

Mom never did know if she would have had a boy or a girl. She never thought to ask. Her mind was preoccupied with other more immediate concerns that took precedence. As I probed Mom for her feelings during this time, she said, "I know I wasn't thinking or feeling emotions that were consistent with a mother losing her child. I was wrapped up in the hardship of marriage and pleasing Royal. As we headed to the hospital with the dread of something being terribly wrong, there was no thought of compassion from your dad toward me, or our unborn baby. Instead, he was obsessed with making sure no men in the hospital attended to me. His clear message was, whatever you do, and no matter what happens, don't let a male doctor look at you. So basically, I survived losing my baby in a robotic, emotionless way without any opportunity to grieve such a great loss. My main focus was following your dad's instructions."

Mom didn't have to say another word. I understood her reaction perfectly, as I fell into that same survival mode growing up.

The following summer, Mom got pregnant again with me. When April 2nd rolled around, my parents had their first of five children. I was named Rosalee Rae Beaird. Daddy named me after a beautiful girl he knew named Rosalee Brown, and my middle name was his middle name…only spelled Rae, instead of Ray.

There is a Proverb from chapter 16, verse one that reads, "We can make our plans, but the final outcome is in God's hands."

Although I have wrestled many years with questions surrounding God's sovereignty, I believe He ordained my birth and life long ago…as revealed in Ephesians 2:10, where God says we are His workmanship, or His poema (poem), created for good works in Christ Jesus, which God prepared beforehand. My future, and when the time comes…even my death, will come as no surprise to God. He knows the day and the hour.

My part in this grand scheme of life has been a matter of choice. God has given me the choice to trust Him completely, even though I didn't and still don't fully understand all His ways; or I can put on my "pretend" Christian face, acting like I trust Him while living with bitterness, fear, anxiety, and doubt.

From experience, I know the latter leads to unspeakable soul torment, as well as addictions, obsessions, and an eventual falling away from God altogether. Choosing to believe the truth that God is in control, even when it doesn't feel like it, has been quite a transforming process that's taken place in my life over many years.

Some days I sigh with regret, wishing I could've taken these strong truths and inner convictions that I have now back to the darkest, most scary days of my childhood. But then again, maybe I am exactly who I should be. Only He knows.

CHAPTER 5

SEEING RED

"A wise man controls his temper. He knows that anger causes mistakes."

PROVERBS 14:29 (LIVING)

◇◇◇◇◇◇◇◇◇◇

U p to this point in my parent's marriage, there had been no physical abuse. But life was about to change as new stresses, financial burdens, and a general sense of Daddy's lack of control was ebbing away with each additional child. Mom's first alarming recollection (*Sorry, Mom, for making you dig up these haunting memories again.*) was Daddy's way of disciplining me as a baby. At night, Mom would put me in my crib, and naturally, I would cry. Daddy said, "Let her cry; she'll stop on her own."

Well, Daddy, so far, so good. I recall my pediatrician giving me almost the same instructions which allowed limited crying for about fifteen to twenty minutes before I went back into my son, Luke's nursery.

Some mothers cannot bear their baby crying, so they use other methods. Mom had no choice, and there was no discussion. She agonized when my crying continued. Daddy resolved to end the crying as he marched back into my room and pushed my little face down into the mattress.

Mom expressed her alarm, *"Royal, you can't do that!"*

With a voice that warned Mom to stay away, he replied, "Let me do the training!" My crying became muffled whimpers and then silence.

Upon hearing this story, I thought, *Ah, success, Daddy, and control in tact* once *again!* Also, I always wondered if this account, and the fact that I'm very claustrophobic in certain situations have anything to do with each other. Nevertheless, it's the excuse I gave my 6' 7" husband, Dan, and my 6' son, Luke, as I begged them to trade seats with me on an airplane flight to Hawaii and back.

I insisted that a panic attack would surely ensue if I didn't get the less confining aisle seat. Both relented like gentlemen, with Luke squished like peanut butter between two slices of bread in the middle seat, and Dan's large frame compressed up against the airplane window! *Sorry, guys! I couldn't help myself.*

You'll get no argument from my mother, or any of my siblings, that my dear brother Marvin received the wrath of Royal far worse than any of us. One year and three months after I was born, my little brother came bounding into this world with what doctor's called an infant hernia. Mom described this condition as nothing to be alarmed about, except that it required him to wear a harness until it healed, causing a perpetual and painful rash. These complications, along with being colicky and always spitting up, meant that Marvin required more attention and care from Mom.

Mom described this time period as "nerve racking… trying to keep a little baby comforted and quiet, so your dad wouldn't get mad and take it out on him." Mom recalls, "Early on, it seemed like your dad had a special dislike for poor Marvin, and I've always wondered if it was just because he was crying and fussing so much, or if it was just because I had to give so much of my attention holding and spending time with the little boy?"

During this time period, we lived in a small rental house in Los Angeles and started attending Athens Baptist Church in Gardena.

Mom said, "We began going there because your dad wanted to be on their fast-pitch softball team. Royal's dream was to be their star pitcher, and he became obsessed with practicing his pitching."

My parent's little rental had a front room that adjoined the dining room creating more length than width, and that's where he trained Mom to catch his practice pitches when it got too dark outside. Mom said, "I was terrified to miss the ball, but since he was firing it as hard as he could, I did miss and there were lots of holes in all the walls from ricocheting pitches."

When it came to holding and pursuing a job, Daddy's priority was softball, attending every game and practice. This took precedence over making sure there was money to pay the rent. Because money became tight, Daddy did allow Mom to take a graveyard shift working at Hughes Aircraft, where she sat at a machine, welding little dots to posts, for eight hours every day.

While Mom worked, she said, "Most nights your dad went to the ball park. Sometimes he had Grandma Beaird watch you, but mostly he took you kids along, or left you at home alone." I remember many hours watching Daddy play softball and playing with other kids under the bleachers.

The only other unsolicited memory I have during this time period of about three years old is accidentally spilling a significant amount of red shoe polish on my little twin bedspread. I was sick to my stomach and knew I'd be in big trouble if Daddy saw it. It wouldn't wash out, so everyday I was filled with dread that Daddy would discover the red mess. Daily, I meticulously tried to camouflage the red polish with clothes and toys. Mom remembers the shoe polish too, and even though it consumed me with worry day and night, we don't remember Daddy ever finding out about this incident. He either didn't notice or didn't care, but the memory of my fear of him finding out stays with me all these years later.

Early in life, I learned that controlling my surroundings with absolute precision, covering up, lying, and trying desperately to be the "perfect child" would serve me well, helping protect and save me from pain. Because this false belief system was so deeply ingrained in me, it took years to recognize and change such destructive patterns.

When my sister, Eileen, was born, our family moved to a house on Menlo Street, just down the road from Grandma Beaird. Daddy asked Grandma to come stay with us to take care of baby Eileen because he couldn't bear the crying of his new infant.

Grandma Beaird said it would be easier if she cared for Eileen in her own home. This is what my grandmother wrote in her memoir concerning this time period. "I lived in this little home for about two and a half years, on Menlo, in Los Angeles, California. While I lived there, I spent most of the time taking care of my grandchildren—especially one. I took her when she was five days old and kept her five weeks. This is Eileen."

When I read Grandma Beaird's account of this, I couldn't help but wonder what my mom would have been feeling to carry her baby for nine months, give birth, and then have her newborn taken away from her for five weeks. I guess you survive something like that by not allowing any feelings at all!

Soon after, we moved from Los Angeles to a cute little house in Gardena on 138th Street. At five years old, I started kindergarten three blocks away at 135th Street School. By six, my brother and I walked by ourselves to school. It didn't feel scary or out of the ordinary like it would be nowadays. Daddy got a steady job working for Knudsen Creamery, which helped the finances and reduced everyone's anxiety with him gone for certain hours of the day.

Marvin, Eileen, and I loved spending days with Grandma Palke when Daddy would take Mom up north to do a job. I felt happy and relaxed, but the anticipation of his return was gut wrenching. My poor little brother, Marvin, would break out crying every time Daddy would return to pick us up. He just couldn't fake it as well as me. Mom would try her best to quiet him before Daddy noticed; but it never worked, and he always got a spanking.

Fourth in our sibling line-up was Karen, named by Daddy after a pretty girl at Athens Baptist Church. Karen was born into this world when Daddy dropped Mom off at the hospital while on his way to play a ball game with his team.

Three years later, Mom had her fifth and last child, my cute little baby brother, Norman. Somehow, I don't remember babysitting Karen at all, but I've always said that my brother, Norm, owes me "big time" for all the hours I spent taking care of him.

I have vivid memories of hearing the laughter and fun of neighborhood kids playing outside. I desperately tried to get little Normie to go to sleep in his crib, so I could go outside with everyone else. I would pat his back and count each bounce of the mattress until I reached one hundred. Then I would slowly remove my hand, glide across the hardwood floor in my lightest, stealth manner, praying he would be asleep. Many times, this method worked but on the days that it didn't, I returned to his crib, starting my counting at one again. Admittedly, the gentle pats on his back probably looked more like baby launching bounces of frustration, but I was doing my best.

Memories of life at the Gardena house centered around pleasing Daddy and accurately reading his moods when he entered a room. I was determined to follow his instructions to perfection, so I could stay on his good side to avoid whippings.

In contrast, Marvin seemed to be cut from an entirely different cloth. He was a spunky, creative little boy who was filled with wonder and excitement over everything new he could get his hands on. Over the years, we watched as his adventurous spirit slowly disappeared into a withdrawn, angry, rebellious teenager.

In my late twenties, out of nowhere, something triggered a very traumatic dream that involved my brother and me. When I woke up, it felt like a movie I had seen; but the more I thought about it, the details seemed real. I called Mom, and she confirmed the details as true.

One day when Marvin and I were about seven and eight years old, we were playing with the neighborhood kids in their front yard. Marvin and I got in an argument over something and started yelling at each other. We didn't know it at the time, but Daddy had driven up and was observing everything. Next thing we knew, he called us into the house and asked us what was going on.

We lied, pretending we weren't mad at each other, blaming it on a neighbor kid. Our response probably made him more upset, plus I can only guess that our argument embarrassed him in front of our neighbors.

Daddy said, "If you want to fight each other, then go for it. Start fighting!"

We both meekly assured him that we didn't want to fight. Instinctively, I think we both knew this confrontation was not going to end anytime soon as we saw our father's temper escalating from zero to ten in a matter of minutes.

We refused to punch each other, so Daddy proceeded to angrily pepper us with punches to the head and the stomach over and over again... intermittently grabbing handfuls of our hair and cracking our heads together.

The unsolicited boxing match from Daddy, along with his screaming, seemed like it would never end. Finally, as we continually begged his forgiveness, promising never to argue again, Daddy's punches ceased. He shoved us to separate corners of the room with our aching, bruised bodies and bloodied faces to the wall.

Before departing, his verbal warning to us was clear. "Unless you want more trouble, don't you move a muscle until I say so."

Although I don't know how long I stood like a statue facing the wall, I knew a lot of time passed as the light in the room turned to darkness, and my eyes were begging for sleep. I was pretty sure daddy had forgotten about us, but I was petrified to move a muscle because I envisioned him right behind me...just waiting to pounce on me if I disobeyed his orders. Marvin and I didn't peep a single word to each other.

The next scene was the part of my scary dream that Mom had recently confirmed as factual. Mom led me to the water basin in our laundry room where she ran lots of cold water over my crusty, matted hair. With my head faced down in the huge sink, I saw swirling pools of seemingly unending red blood going down the drain. This wouldn't be the last time Marvin and I would see red.

While these traumatic episodes created a new resolve in me to be better or at least be more alert to Daddy's whereabouts, it seemed that Marvin wasn't fazed. Part of me admired his daredevil attitude, always pushing the envelope, without any concern for the consequences. Mostly, I was just plain petrified for him.

As adults, humor helped my siblings and me to reduce the pain of the insanity that was a part of our lives. Even though Marvin could spin some of our most horrendous episodes, making us laugh until we cried, I always wished that in addition to humor, he could have opened up and shared the sadness too.

One of my favorite childhood stories was retelling the weekend that our Grandma Beaird was caring for us while Daddy and Mom were away. My precocious seven-year-old brother, Marvin, seemed especially uncooperative, refusing to obey Grandma's wishes to settle down and come inside the house. Instead, he climbed on top of the roof of our newly built rumpus room.

As the older sister, I decided to take the initiative and help Grandma. I volunteered to talk him down.

Marv wouldn't budge from the rooftop, so even though I was afraid of heights, I shakily made my way up to the roof to continue our conversation face to face. With a hand on my hip, and in my most authoritative voice, I said, "Marvin, Grandma wants you to come down right now!"

Without a single word, and in the blink of an eye, Marvin shoved me over the edge. My body catapulted through the air, missing the sidewalk directly below, and landing feet first, like a cat, on our soft green grass. There were no tears, no injuries, and no more words spoken. I proceeded to walk away in an absolute state of shock!

After every retelling of that story, I would laughingly say, "Marvin, what in the world were you thinking? I could have been seriously injured!"

With a snicker forming on his mouth, Marvin insisted that he never thought I would be hurt. He just wanted me to stop talking!

Unfortunately, for most of our life, haunting memories remained tucked away in the recesses of our souls. We could find nothing comical about them.

I especially wish with all my heart that my sweet brother could have found the courage to talk about all his inner torment and suffering. With God's help, I believe that opening up about some of the senseless acts he endured at the hands of our dad might have started him on the path of healing.

Every time I saw my brother's scarred and burned hand, I winced at the thought of my father pouring lighter fluid on his own son's hand, then setting it aflame to teach him not to play with matches.

When I remember Daddy's attempts to train Marvin to stop wetting his bed, by submerging and holding his face down in our toilet bowl, the horror and irrationality of it all makes me sad.

In high school, Marvin chose to dull his pain with drugs. He struggled with his addictions most of his life, landing him in prison. While incarcerated, Mom, Eileen, Norman, and I tried to keep Marvin encouraged, reminding him that he was so very loved. He would regularly respond back with letters, which we passed around to each other, written in his own unique satirical flair. Somehow, he managed to describe his bleak surroundings with humor.

I told Marvin that he should've been a writer, but in my heart, I always knew that it wasn't a lack of talent that stopped him; it was his lack of self worth.

One of my favorite letters was about the time Marvin received a new cellmate, whom he aptly described as this tough, tattooed, skinhead from the Aryan Nation.

Marvin was sitting on his bed, reading his Bible, and casually said something about God. The guy got up in Marvin's face and said, "If you ever say another word about God, I'll kill you!"

Marvin got the message and didn't say another word for months.

One day his cellmate was visibly crushed with some kind of bad news from home about his family. He rescinded his threat to Marvin, asking if he'd pray for him.

Of course, my brother said yes. From that day on, his tough-guy exterior softened. The two became friends, reading and studying the Bible together, which led to Marv's cellmate praying to receive Jesus Christ as his savior.

Shortly after that, the guy was transferred somewhere else. As he left, he thanked Marvin for helping him discover Jesus in his heart.

We had heard in one of Marvin's letters that his release date from prison would be soon, but no one could pinpoint the exact day. I couldn't wait to see him again, feeling especially hopeful for his future after hearing how his faith in God was growing.

My sister, Eileen, will never forget the day she received the shocking news from an unsympathetic voice from the coroner's office. This is a recollection of that day in Eileen's words.

There are only a few memories that I can recall so vividly that it is as though it happened yesterday.

My husband, Gregg and I were in the den laughing and playing with our two-year-old son, Josh, who was swinging from our Stairmaster as though it was his own personal set of monkey bars.

The phone rang, and I still had a huge grin on my face as I answered it.

A lady on the other end asked if I was Marvin Beaird's sister. Immediately, I thought, Oh, no, Marv has had a run-in with the law.

I said, 'Yes, I am.'

Her response was so harsh that I can still feel the anguish as she said, 'He has been in the morgue for ten days, and you need to come down and identify his body.'

The words hit me so hard, my mind wouldn't function properly to retrieve the information from her as to where his body was located.

Gregg saw the horror on my face as I handed him the phone, dissolving into a heap of sobs.

My funny, witty, big brother was dead.

The report stated that Marvin, age 49, had died from a heroin overdose.

One month later, the news exploded around the world, with horrifying pictures of 9/11, the Islamic terrorist's attack on New York's World Trade Center. While the world mourned the tragedy of thousands of lives lost, our family was also grieving the loss of one beloved son and brother.

Amazingly, God comforted us in the midst of such a sorrowful time. A friend from church shared a vision with Eileen and me that God had given her the day after Marvin's death. She saw searing holes riddled throughout his entire body. In an instant, the holes were filled, and he was glowing and shining with joy.

Both of our jaws dropped in astonishment, as we remembered that a couple years earlier, God had individually given Eileen and me almost the same vision of Marvin in heaven…his body brilliant with light.

When I see a picture of Marvin's handsome face, I still mourn his life and premature death, always wishing things could have been different. His life reminds me that I am on a mission to comfort, encourage, and direct as many hurting hearts to God—the God who restored my life and made me whole again. I renew my convictions and courage, because I truly believe that our sufferings are never in vain!

HEARTSONG

I love you, Lord Jesus; In my heart is a song.
It's so true I am weak…Tho Your ways make me strong.
"My will" was a shambles; In your will I belong.
Show me, then tow me, and guide me along.
Afflicted, addicted…Where did I go wrong?
Such mercy and grace, or my future'd be gone.
Now filled with Your Spirit in my heart is a song.
Written by Marvin Charles Beaird, February, 1997

CHAPTER 6

FROM DEATH TO LIFE

*"Jesus said, 'Most assuredly, I say to you, he who hears My word
and believes in Him who sent Me has everlasting life, and shall
not come into judgment, but has passed from death into life.'"*

JOHN 5:24

◇◇◇◇◇◇◇◇◇◇◇◇

As far back as I can remember, my life seemed confusing, uncertain, and definitely off-the-charts scary. Our whole family survived each day living in reaction to my dad's highs and lows, with the goal of keeping him happy and calm so heads wouldn't roll. It seemed like whatever he wanted, he got, so my young thinking was that he must be in God's will, or God would not have allowed some of the things that were going on…Life would surely be different.

No one ever bucked Daddy's plans or system; and if they did, it wasn't ever going to be a pretty outcome. In a way, it all seemed very normal to me as a young girl. I didn't know any different.

When I hear my boys, Luke and Michael, talk about plans and goals for their lives, I'm overwhelmed with mixed emotions. I'm elated to be a part of their growth and independent thinking—I must be doing something right. On the other hand, I feel a heavyhearted melancholy because I can't ever remember having any independent, adventurous dreams or goals of my own. I existed each day inside the pre-ordained box that was chosen by my dad.

As a quiet and introverted little girl, who would cry at the drop of a hat, I secretly hid away in the recesses of my heart the only two goals for my life. I desperately desired to be loved and have a successful marriage, and I wanted to love and serve God.

The early years of life in our house consisted of church and sports. We worshiped at a little church in Gardena called Athens Baptist. I loved going to church each week; we usually went twice on Sunday and at least once during the week.

Sunday mornings I went to a children's class and heard about all the amazing miracles of Jesus. It made me happy to sing songs like "Jesus loves me." The truth of God's word was planted in my heart, and I believed it. I felt joy spring up in my soul knowing that Jesus would love little children so deeply. It seemed easy to love someone like that.

I liked what Jesus said to the disciples in Mark 10:15 when they tried to keep the little children away from Him. He said to them, "Let the little children come to Me, and do not forbid them; for of such is the kingdom of God. Assuredly, I say to you, whoever does not receive the kingdom of God as a little child will by no means enter in." I didn't really understand that in this story Jesus was making a point to the adults who seemed to require lots of miracles, signs, and wonders before believing in Him. Instead, if they wanted to get to heaven, they needed to come with hearts of love and a simple faith like these children who pressed in so closely just to be near him. It made me feel special and loved that Jesus chose little children—maybe like me—to crawl up into His loving and protective arms.

In years to come, doubts, questions, and disillusion wedged their way into my soul. I became unsure and confused concerning my relationship with God, but those formative years, laying this foundation of gold and learning about my loving Savior proved to be one of my most cherished gifts of all time. Through the darkness that was looming in my future, somehow, I knew He still loved me just as He did when I was a little girl—beckoning me to come into His loving arms.

Sunday nights at church, everyone would get together for "A Sing." This was a time of fun, food, and lots of singing. I still remember how handsome Daddy looked in his blue suit coat, matching slacks, white shirt, and tie, as he stood on the podium and led the congregation in song after song. Daddy moved his hand in a triangle-like motion to the beat of each melodic hymn, like he was leading a professional choir. He seemed larger than life, and I was proud that he was my dad.

Every so often, I'll hear some background music of one of these old standards, and without missing a beat, every word comes flooding back to my memory just like it was yesterday.

To navigate our way successfully through this life, each person is faced with a handful of important decisions and choices—What profession to choose, who to marry, where to live, etcetera. But the most important question to be answered is—What did you do with Jesus Christ? This decision is supreme because it affects our life on this earth, as well as in the afterlife.

American Statesman, Daniel Webster said, "Wisdom begins at the end." For the most part, I would have to agree that the older we get, the wiser we become. With age, our knowledge and understanding help guide us in our life choices. Having said that, it strikes me as ironic that I made the most important and wisest decision of my life at the ripe old age of eight years old. Because this decision impacted my life so profoundly, I will detail the testimony that prompted me to make such a decision the night of my conversion so many years ago.

One night Daddy piled our family into the car and headed to a tiny church in Southern California to hear my twenty-two-year-old cousin, Joan, share her testimony.

Even though I was so young, I was mesmerized from start to finish because she was an extremely beautiful Hollywood actress, and the stories she told were so unbelievable. Her life-threatening stories seemed like a larger-than-life movie, where the heroine repeatedly faces death, but somehow manages to escape.

It was hard to fathom how my cousin could endure one incredible set of events after another; but I knew that every story was true, and I hung on every word. I do not remember the order of the stories, so I will share her testimony in chronological order.

My cousin, Joan, was single-minded, hard-working, and headed for the fast track as an actress on the Hollywood scene in the 1950's. The twice primetime Emmy nominated hit show, "77 Sunset Strip" starring Efrem Zimbalist, Jr., Roger Smith (Ann Margaret's handsome husband), and Edd Byrnes, was just around the corner in Joan's future.

In preparation for her bright career, Joan attended the "Hollywood Professional School" three hours a day. The show business pace accelerated so quickly for Joan that for her sixteenth birthday, her dad and mom bought her a beautiful yellow and white 1949 Ford, covered with plush white leather interior and big white wall tires. She was beaming with pride!

Along with her magnificent new ride, Joan's dad gave her his best parental speech on the dos and don'ts of safe driving, with specific roads to take each day to Hollywood.

On a day no different from any other, Joan quickly got dressed and took off in her beautiful birthday car, heading to Hollywood for school. Because of her neophyte driving skills, and her decision to take some unknown back roads, Joan was unfamiliar with the area and didn't see a stop sign. As she headed through an intersection, an approaching vehicle appeared from the left side going full speed. Moments later, the air was filled with screeching brakes and the sound of metal colliding with metal.

Joan's birthday car rolled about four times as glass shattered into a million pieces, slicing Joan's left temple from the front of her hairline to the very back of her hairline. Blood was gushing out of her head at such a rapid pace that her black knit top was drenched in the thick pools of sticky red, and her white leather jacket was completely soaked—now resembling a red leather jacket. Her jet-black hair was caked with blood and glass, and Joan's body rested on a bed of glass as she was slipping in and out of consciousness.

As Joan stared out the rearview mirror hoping to be rescued, curiously, Joan noted that her eyelash curler was laying in the middle of the road...then came the sound of an ambulance.

Joan went into shock and couldn't speak as people were scurrying to get her into the ambulance, but she could hear every word of concern in the voices of those around her...*horrible head injury...so much blood lost... veins shrinking...hard to breathe.*

One of the attendants whispered, "Is she dead?" Joan wanted to scream, but nothing came out, *"No, no, no, I'm not dead!"*

Upon arriving at the hospital, Joan received a much-needed blood transfusion. All family members joined forces in prayer, and God sustained her life.

After months of recovery, Joan returned to normal with a new awareness of the brevity of life and a deep gratitude of God's merciful intervention. Later, Joan sighed a thankful praise of gratitude to God when she found out from news reports that her car landed right where a little boy was playing just minutes earlier. In addition to that, her career got back on track, as there was not even a cut on her face to remind her of the horrible accident. All the stitches were underneath the hair that grew back.

According to Joan, the scariest thing that ever happened to her occurred at nineteen years old on a road trip from California to Fort Carson, Colorado. She was heading down the highway in her black and white, 1957, four-door Chevy. Eager to reach her destination and save an hour of driving time, Joan ignored her Daddy's words, "Don't deviate from the main road".

Before long, Joan started getting nervous. There were no lights and no signs on the lonely road that seemed to go on for miles. With a quivering voice, she tried to remain relaxed as she asked her little traveling companion and poodle, *"Shakespeare, where are we?"*

To calm her frazzled nerves, Joan turned on the radio. Within minutes, a voice broke into the regular program with this announcement that seemed like it was scripted from a thriller movie. Be on ALERT. There are two escaped convicts. They are very dangerous and are suspected to be in such and such vicinity and perhaps on such and such road. The announcement sent shivers up Joan's spine.

A few minutes later, Joan spied the first sign she had seen in miles, and her heart almost melted. This was the road the convicts were suspected to be on!

As she headed up the steep and winding hill, in horror, Joan saw the image of a man standing to the side of the road at the top of the hill. The next few minutes felt like slow motion. Hoping to accelerate and double her speed, unexpectedly, her engine began missing and sputtering. It seemed like her car was going to come to a complete halt.

Audibly, Joan prayed, *"Oh, dear Lord, please help me."* She grabbed her voluminous, fluffy coat and flung it over the passenger seat, hoping to create the illusion of another person in the car. Her car would start to gain speed and then cut out. Joan silently prayed like never before as she approached the man looking into her car. *"Oh, Lord, please don't let my engine die right in front of him."* Joan drove like a statue staring straight ahead as she passed the man.

As Joan reached the top of the hill, she saw a single lone light in the distance below. It was a gas station in the middle of nowhere. The time was 10:00 p.m., and it was still open! Shaky and relieved, Joan pulled in and relayed her story and asked if the gas attendant could help fix her car. The kind older gentleman raised the hood, and in one instant, he spotted the problem. "Oh, little lady, your distributor cable needs reconnecting...you're lucky you made it over the hill...one wire is hanging on by a thread!"

When Joan heard those words, she knew God was with her. That night her faith grew, as well as her wisdom—She made a vow to take her dad's advice and stay on main roads!

Approximately one year later, now twenty years old, Joan was rushing around, tying up loose ends, and packing for her trip back to Los Angeles. The Colorado sun was beating down hot as she was in the kitchen cutting up food and making sandwiches with her shiny new butcher knife that she had bought the day before.

A knock outside of her screen door interrupted Joan's culinary plans. She laid her knife down, wiped her hands, and headed to the door.

Through the screen, she saw a guy dressed in khakis like a gasman.

"Can I help you," Joan said to the man behind the screen door. "Hi, ma'am, I'm with the Gas Company, and I'm checking the gas lines in this neighborhood. May I come in?"

Joan opened the door and as the man walked in, a strange intuition swept over her. Her mind scrolled back to the day before, when she shrugged off the feeling that someone had been following her while she was finishing her errands.

The way he looked at her sent a chill up her spine. Was this her imagination? "Where's the furnace", the man asked?"

Joan instinctively grabbed the butcher knife and turned to face him. One glance into his eyes, Joan knew she was staring at the face of evil..."*like he wanted to rape me.*"

Her body surged with an unknown supernatural courage and adrenaline. Joan held the butcher knife directly in front of her face, her body in a warrior like stance. With a sure-sounding conviction in her voice, Joan boomed, "Is that what you wanted?"

Startled by Joan's quick show of strength, the man stuttered, "Uh no, no...I think it's outside." He turned quickly for the door, and Joan watched as he ran hard down the street.

Heart pounding loudly and hands shaking, Joan quickly shut the door and locked it. She breathed a silent prayer thanking God for His intervention and filling her with an unknown courage and strength that she never knew she possessed.

I knew that God was very real to Joan. She said, "Life has a way of shaking you up, but I knew God was going to take care of me."

I wanted God to be my protector too. My eight-year-old mind and heart wanted the same peace and security that my cousin shared. I wanted to be sure that if I was in a car accident tonight that I would be in Heaven and with God for all eternity.

As Joan gave her audience an invitation to receive this free gift of life everlasting that Jesus offered, I remembered that Jesus said, "I am the Way, the Truth, and the Life, no one comes to God, except by me."

I did believe that He paid the price for my sin by dying on the cross so many years ago. *I wanted God for my life; I wanted to be sure that I would be with Him forever.*

My little heart was pounding as people were walking to the front of the church to ask Jesus to come into their hearts. I wanted to get out of my seat and walk forward too, but I held back, not knowing if this was what my daddy wanted, or if I was doing it in the way he wanted.

A battle raged as I stayed glued to my seat, but my heart and my soul surged forward into the Kingdom of Heaven while I prayed silently and fervently for Jesus to come into my heart. I was sincere, and I knew God heard me. I was elated that night...I was born again! It was a simple child's faith that led me into real life.

The truth that I whole-heartedly received that night has remained the anchor that has sustained me through every hardship. Admittedly, I see now that my knowledge and perception of God's character wasn't completely accurate. My eight-year-old mind was eager to enlist my Prince Charming to step in, love, and adore me. I was more than ready to receive the blessings and protection against anything and anyone who would hurt me. My life would be unbelievably great, and when I died, heaven would be the ultimate!

Boy, did I have a lot to learn. My walk with God has been an evolution of the heart as I learned to separate His truth from who God is and the God I thought He should be. The truth is that I'm sure I still have a lot to learn on this journey, but He remains my Prince, my Savior, my Father, my King, my Friend, and the One who has never left my side since that prayer so many years ago.

CHAPTER 7

ḶEMONS TO ḶEMONADE

"We toss the coin, but it is the Lord who controls its decision."

PROVERBS 16:33 (LIVING)

◇◇◇◇◇◇◇◇◇◇◇

A fter my prayer the night I heard my cousin, Joan, ask people to accept Jesus into their lives, my spirit felt light and free. Like the scene in Cinderella—it seemed as if the birds were singing a happy song that everything was going to be all right and help was on the way.

I was overwhelmed with a new sense of peace and security. God loved me, and I loved God. I had given my heart to the Lord, and He had given me eternal life. I was certain that along with the promise of heaven, He would protect me from harm and evil. My fears and anxiety slipped into the background as a new hope and expectation soared to the forefront of my thinking. I knew I was connected with the all-knowing, all-powerful Creator of the universe, and I felt safe. Some way, somehow God would be able to change and control my dad's angry outbursts so that we could be a happy family.

When nothing changed, I prayed harder and read my Bible more often. If I showed diligence and persevered in spiritual things, maybe

God would be pleased and answer my prayer. I was trying to be the best Christian I could be, but life remained as scary as ever. I assumed I must be doing something wrong...but I didn't know what.

Because I was desperate and God was my only hope, I continued begging and pleading for His help and protection; but it felt like He remained silent in this area of my life. I continued to be a good little girl for my daddy and God, but it never seemed to matter. My best was never good enough.

After a while, it appeared they both did whatever they wanted without any regard for me. I was angry, hurt, and terribly disillusioned by both; but at the time, I did not acknowledge such negative feelings toward God, even though He knew every thought I had.

With each disappointment and unanswered prayer, I buried my hurt and anger further and further inside my heart. I did not realize until much later in life that those were the beginnings of my rift with God. Only He knew that for a path of healing my heart and life were ever to begin, old wounds would need to be remembered and acknowledged as truth.

The daily pattern of my life was fear, anxiety, trying to avoid my dad's wrath by being good, pleading with God to intervene, and figuring out how to survive. Somewhere during this time period, a new element of pressure was added to the mix—sports.

Daddy led many teams, playing volleyball, basketball, and his favorite sport...softball. As we started getting older, he began pouring into his children the techniques and his passion for different sports.

It almost sounds ideal—a father spending his free time bonding with his children while playing sports. It coulda, shoulda, woulda been every child's dream, but each outing was filled with so much anxiety over not being able to meet his expectations and the consequences that followed if we didn't.

Some of my earliest sports memories centered mostly around softball and basketball, with the occasional side activities, like learning how to ride the giant old brown bicycle that Daddy brought home one day.

I was petrified to even hop up onto this beast of a bike. My feet barely reached the pedals, but Daddy reassured me that I would do fine as he hoisted me up onto the adult seat and launched me off down the street. One minute, he was with me and the next minute, I was sailing down the sidewalk on my own. With little instruction on braking and turning, my bicycle ride was short-lived as I crashed within yards of my starting point. I don't remember how many times I hopped up on that bike with my dad's no nonsense, "just do it" philosophy. It wasn't fun, and I have avoided bicycles ever since.

While living in Gardena, my dad started a weight training and fitness club in our garage for his buddies and any neighborhood boys who were interested in coming. They met at least once a week, practicing boxing, weight lifting, and over-all body conditioning. From my vantage point, it seemed like there was a lot of good times happening in the garage, but I would have loved to ask my eight year old brother, Marvin, his thoughts on the subject—was it fear or fun?

There is no denying that my dad was a born leader. He had great ideas, loved to teach, and had energy and enthusiasm that was truly infectious. It seems so sad that his own children couldn't have been the recipients of such talents, without all the convoluted emotions that went along with all the best parts of him. Along with learning to dribble basketballs and properly throw and catch softballs, Daddy was always coming up with different muscle strengthening drills that would make his children the best at any sport.

One day, Daddy came home with a nine pound, Everlast, medicine ball. Boxers used this sort of ball as part of their training in balance, coordination, and strength training. Daddy had Marvin, my little sister, Eileen (who was about five years old), and me stand an equal distance apart as he quickly snapped the medicine ball at each of us.

Our instructions were to reach out with two hands, catching and resisting the weight of the ball, so it wouldn't blast into our faces. If we could do this drill successfully, catching and passing a regulation basketball would be a piece of cake.

When it came to little Eileen's turn; She caught the weighted ball and held on for dear life, as both ball and Eileen were knocked three feet backward into the plate glass window of our back door.

Even though I was eight or nine, I have no memory of any details, or even the event, except for Eileen's recollection. She said, "I was rushed to a private doctor who stitched up the backside of my arm, near the elbow."

When I asked if Daddy was mad, Eileen said, "No---he seemed to be genuinely scared." Her answer made me feel happy because it was a normal parental reaction which seemed rare for my father whenever something didn't go as he had planned.

The potential for family closeness and fun was always there during sports, but the problem was the impending threat of his verbal and physical outbursts looming over us. It was the "not knowing" that kept us all on edge. As a child, this left me feeling off-balanced emotionally, always waiting on his unpredictability and imagining the worst possible scenarios.

I still find myself warring off old thought patterns from this de-structive, self-made thinking, where I envision the worst as a reality before anything had occurred. Little by little, I am asking and allow-ing God to do His transforming work in my life. I know that He has designed each of us to live one day at a time, enjoying life, and trusting Him as He walks with us each step of the way.

Life is unpredictable and always changing, but God's character remains solid and unchanging. The process of transformation has been slow but steady. As I hear His voice and His words in my head, I try to let them overtake and permeate my heart.

To jump ahead in the story, sports became the vehicle that propelled our family into the spotlight. In our souvenir booklet that was sold and autographed for thousands of fans over a span of two decades, there is a section entitled "A Dream Unfolds." This article details the beginnings of my twenty plus years as pitcher for The Queen and Her Court and helps answer the number one question I was always asked by fans and media alike——How did you get started?

Since the origins of my professional career in softball are outlined beautifully in the souvenir booklet, I won't repeat the exact details of that story here, but as promised, I will give you the emotions behind the facts and the reality behind all the dream-like words.

When I was ten years old, my dad signed me up to play softball in a little park league in Los Angeles, about ten minutes away from our home in Gardena. When the big try-out day came, I don't remember either of my parents being there, but Mom confirmed that she wasn't there. "Your dad must've taken you to try-outs," she recollected. This sounds logical, as he participated in everything that had to do with sports, but I don't recall being nervous or feeling pressure, so I assume that this was one of the few times he kept a low profile, remaining in the background.

My advance instructions from Daddy were to try out for shortstop and pitcher. I was sure shortstop was my destiny, as I had never really pitched before. For pitching tryouts, a row of girls lined up to pitch, and I noticed that I was the only one pitching with a windmill style motion, which means that I brought the ball up over my head and then around in a circular motion, releasing the ball by my leg, with a snap of the wrist.

At the end of tryouts, I was named the starting pitcher for the Red Devils. My dad was elated, and I felt happy that I could make Daddy so proud of me.

A monumental shift took place that day. Daddy continued to work on his pitching skills, but his pitching became more about being able to give me examples and help me with pitching visuals. His dream of pitching greatness shifted from him to me.

In the days ahead, my pitching improved by leaps and bounds. Did I improve so rapidly because it came naturally, or was it because of all the hours of practice and hard work? I think the answer is both. Even though I believe almost anyone (even those without natural ability) with the right instruction, determination, and hard work can reach high levels of athletic capability, a person will reach their sport's goals faster with some God-given natural skills.

Concerning pitching, it sure didn't hurt that I stretched up to 5'8" tall by the time I was eleven years old—only adding an inch in high school to become my current height of 5'9".

With Daddy's new focus on my pitching, our new regimen was practice, practice, practice. In fact, we practiced every day, rain or shine, for about five years straight.

At first when it rained, I would be happy, thinking we would take a break from pitching—no way...Daddy moved everything indoors, and I began to understand how nervous Mom used to be as I tried to keep balls from ricocheting all over the den.

We would eat and breathe softball. Many nights, our relaxation in front of the television became multi-tasking as we squeezed rubber balls to strengthen the wrist, or snapped balls up in front of our faces simulating the correct spins for each new pitch. In the beginning, we concentrated on speed, control, and placement. By the time I learned how to pitch, our garage door was riddled with so many dents and holes, Daddy had to replace it.

Because Daddy had so much knowledge of pitching, he began teaching me how to throw a rise ball and change-up almost imme-diately. Even though I needed to strengthen my "pitching muscles," I caught on to making the ball move from low to high right away. In the beginning years, having a pitch with such movement became my "ace in the hole" when I needed to strike out tougher batters. In recent correspondence with a gal named Glenda, who played centerfield on the Red Devils, she recalls, "You had it all, Rosie. You didn't walk too many and not many runs ever crossed the plate."

When I think back on my early days of pitching, part of me loved the new identity that was evolving from a shy little creature to superstar pitcher, who was loved and admired by all. It felt awesome to be good at something, and even better knowing it made Daddy happy. At times, the introvert in me longed to remain in the background and just blend in with everyone else, but that was not my destiny.

There is no doubt in my mind that I would have never achieved such a high level of success in pitching without my dad. He was incredibly talented in teaching and translating techniques in pitching, so I could understand and then perform the pitches he was describing. If a pitch didn't work, he would find a solution and come at it from a different angle and new understanding. Giving up was not in his vocabulary. Daddy gleaned knowledge from accomplished men pitchers, and then he would break down each bit of new information, so I could understand how to do it.

My childhood teammate, Glenda, remembers, "Your dad was a cool guy, and knew a lot about softball. I remember that he always stood behind the backstop, giving pointers and signals that he would share with each of us."

I chuckled, "Oh yes…so true." I didn't throw one pitch without getting a signal from Daddy first. I tried to get each signal without anyone noticing, but I know it must've frustrated our team coach at times when she was also trying to get my attention! It was a no-brainer for me as to who would receive my undivided attention. I had to go home with Daddy.

Our coach relented quickly to his authority over me, as success speaks volumes. The Red Devils finished the season with an undefeated record. Our team was named the all-star team of the league, and we went on to play a handful of games against girls four to eight years older than us. Glenda recalls that as all-stars we beat one of the teams 24-1, and her mom told her that people watching these games didn't believe that I was really ten years old.

The one vivid recollection that I have pitching at ten years old happened during one of our league games. I had finished my warm-ups to start a new inning and was finding my footing on the mound, getting ready to throw the first pitch. With bat in hand, a girl from the opposing team made her way to the batter's box. Moments before throwing the first pitch, the girl dropped her bat and broke down sobbing.

I was startled as coaches and parents from all directions poured onto the field to find out what had happened! I heard some saying, "Did she hit you? Where did she hit you?"

Finally, the hysterical little girl calmed down enough to say, "No, she didn't hit me, but she throws so fast I was afraid." A few more minutes elapsed as coaches tried to coax the little girl into the batter's box, but that was not about to happen. Someone else substituted for her, and she walked off the field.

I felt bad for her, but I remember thinking, *I must be pretty fast if she's afraid to even try to hit the pitch.* All in all, my summer adventure of pitching was a boost to my confidence, helping me to feel good about myself.

Sometime during my first softball season, our family sold the Gardena house and moved to the prestigious city of Rolling Hills Estates. Daddy always made things happen, and this move was a dream that he couldn't shake from his mind no matter how many people relayed their skepticism.

As the story goes, my parents sold the Gardena house for $32,000 and got a loan to buy an empty half-acre lot for $34,000 in Rolling Hills Estates. With five children and an unpredictable income, everyone thought Daddy was nuts. But nothing would deter him from his dream of having this little piece of heaven in this beautiful city on the hill, with spacious custom homes, white rail fences, and more horses per capita than any other city in California.

With a headstrong determination, Daddy proceeded full steam ahead. He got a loan for materials and enlisted every friend and family member to help build our home.

I remember going to construction sites with our whole family where we would break apart old used bricks, and carry stacks of them to our station wagon. If we did the work, we could have the bricks for free, saving money for our fireplace, steps, and other landscaping details in front of our new home.

Another big advantage was the fact that Daddy's brothers were very skilled in the construction field by this time, and before you knew it, we had a gorgeous custom home to live in.

By fall, we were settling into our new home, and I was starting fifth grade, attending a brand-new elementary school within walking distance from our house. Life was popping with newness and excitement, which seemed to affect Daddy's temperament in the best ways possible. I was improving steadily in my pitching, as Daddy and I worked toward the new season coming up.

Finally, sign-ups rolled around, and we were shocked to find out I was barred from the league. Many of the parents from the opposing teams got together during the interim and signed a petition that demanded I be eliminated from playing because I was too good, threatening that a majority of the girls would not sign up to play if the leadership allowed me to play.

Daddy fought them for a while, but they would not relent.

It made me sad, and I couldn't understand why I would be penalized for working hard and doing my best. This bump in the road was not going to stop my dad. He knew God had something better.

I remember how he shared Romans 8:28 with me, and I memorized that verse, "All things work together for good for those who love God and are called according to His purpose."

Little did I know that just a few short years down the road, this unfair event would be the catalyst that would catapult us into a family career that would last for a quarter of a century.

When I was unjustly banned from the girls softball league, my father used an expression, "When life gives you lemons, you can turn them into lemonade." It was the first time I ever heard him say this, and the idea of this positive outlook stuck with me.

Throughout the years, I must admit this expression has felt mixed to me. During the worst of days, it felt more like God turned my lemons into rotting lemons instead of lemonade. As life seemed to get harder and harder, it felt like Romans 8:28 got stuck in the mire of my doubt and unbelief.

It's as if Satan was whispering, *God surely doesn't work all things for your good, or your outcome would've turned out better.* Part of my healing was recognizing the subtle lies the evil one used to chip away my faith and hope in God.

By God's grace, I've learned that even if something that I expected to be good in my life turns sour; if unfair wrongs have been done to me; or if I have caused consequences upon myself because of my disobedient actions, God is still working behind the scenes accomplishing all His purposes for my life and the lives of loved ones around me. I learned that when I surrender all things to Him, things work out just as He has planned.

While things seemed like they were all working out in our new home in Rolling Hills Estates, life as I knew it was about to change in big ways. This was a sudden change of direction for our whole family. It surprised us all—but God wasn't surprised!

CHAPTER 8

HIS DREAM UNFOLDS

*"Trust in the Lord with all your heart, and lean not on
your own understanding; In all your ways acknowledge
Him, and He shall direct your paths."*

PROVERBS 3:5-6

◇◇◇◇◇◇◇◇◇◇◇◇◇

D addy sure had a way of making things happen; he was a mover
and a shaker. When he set his mind on goals, they came to
life. Over and over, I'd watch him get an idea, research it,
and if it got stuck in his brain, he'd persevere until his dream became a
reality. It was impressive. If he didn't know how to reach his goals, he
would find people who had accomplished what he wanted, pick their
brains of all their knowledge on the subject, and move forward in his
own success. The combination of my dad's fearlessness, relentless tenacity, and God's hand of blessing on his dreams were an unstoppable force.

Changes were invading every area of life as our family made the
transition from Gardena to Rolling Hills Estates. Unfortunately, change
never has been my "cup of tea," even if it was the best thing for me. Only
until I took a real hard look back at my childhood did I understand the
"whys" behind my resistance to change.

Knowing my surroundings seemed to create more of a safeness with predictable outcome when it came to interactions with Daddy. I learned at a very early age that controlling as much of my little world as I could, helped me prevent chaos outwardly, as well as inwardly.

For a season, control proved itself to be a good friend that helped me make it through each day. As was the case with so many areas of my life, God, in His mercy, had to break the patterns of control that were deeply ingrained in my psyche, and re-train my brain to release the control and learn to trust Him instead.

I've discovered God speaks softly and re-trains His children in very gentle ways, if we let Him. Unfortunately, my fear and resistance required His heavenly sledge hammer a number of times throughout the many stages of my healing process.

Moving was exciting and scary at the same time. Without any additional income, it seemed like we moved about a hundred notches up the ladder of worldly success. One day we were in a small three-bedroom, one bath home, and the next day, we were in a mansion that sat on a half-acre of land with bedrooms three times the size of our Gardena home. It felt like we were really living in grand style; it was a little slice of heaven up on a hill where the streets were lined with lush trees, white rail fences, and horse trails for miles. A new house, new school, new financial status, and a lot of new bills and stresses arrived overnight.

It's strange the things I remember about our big move. Included in our new home was an intercom system which was super high-tech back in the sixties. In each bedroom was an intercom with buttons that enabled us to talk to each other from room to room. I thought this technology was amazing until I heard my dad's booming voice over the intercom and realized that he now had the capability to locate and then call us to wherever he was in the house.

Early on, we were all trained to push the appropriate button in return and respond immediately with, *"Coming, Daddy,"* and proceed to run to him as fast as we could.

One day, my dad was sitting at the desk where the intercom controls were located, as I stood about six feet away in the kitchen. I discovered something that sent shivers up my spine. Out of nowhere, I heard my brother, Marvin's voice. He was talking to someone, and every word he spoke was coming over the intercom loud and clear. Daddy was listening intently. It clicked in my brain, *Oh my gosh, Daddy can hear everything we say if he wants, any time of the day or night.* I casually went about my kitchen duties, but silently prayed Marvin wouldn't say something that would get him in trouble.

Shortly after this incident, I alerted my siblings to my new discovery. After that, we had whole conversations whispering quietly in each other's ears, or mouthing silent words as far away from that intercom as we could get! It felt like we were living like hard-core secret agents, but it wasn't fun. It was survival. No matter what, I trained myself to only speak appropriate words that would be pleasing to Daddy...just in case he was listening!

When September rolled around, I started the fifth grade at Rancho Vista Elementary School, which was about fifteen minutes walking distance from our new home.

Up until this point in my life, I would describe myself as an average student, respectful, super shy, very attentive, speaking as little as possible, and always observing others and my surroundings with an eagle eye.

With the new school year, something else began to emerge—a new identity of sorts. I was the new girl who could rival the boys in any sport. I could run, throw, and catch as well as, or better than the top jocks in my class. With this newfound attention as an athlete, I was secretly hoping the boys would think I was cute too.

I was boy-crazy; but, only in my fantasies. If one of my fantasy boyfriends would have ever spoken to me, my heart would have jumped out of my chest, with little or no words coming out of my mouth. Nevertheless, picturing a boy as my future husband made school a fun place to be, no matter if we talked or not.

Besides physical education, I loved reading. Our teacher would pick some type of adventure book and read a chapter to the class a couple times a week until we completed the book. I was thoroughly captivated by the images of the heroic characters of each book, as they forged fearlessly with unstoppable courage through the jungle, or escaped danger paddling a canoe down the Amazon River.

One day, during our special reading time, I felt an uncomfortable pressure of my bladder coming on. Since I was trained never to interrupt adults, I silently prayed that I could hold on until our reading time was over. I wanted to interrupt the teacher, but he kept reading, and it was ingrained in me not to disrespect elders. My breathing quickened as I began to tighten muscles and rock the lower half of my body. The situation was becoming unbearable. My thoughts turned to panic, hoping to avoid the impending disaster that was about to happen.

Suddenly, my teacher paused from his reading and glanced up for just a split second. I threw my hand up to the sky, and with a restrained calmness in the sound of my voice, I asked permission to use the restroom. Permission granted.

I got up from my desk as nonchalantly as possible and headed out the door. Five feet from the classroom door, the floodgates started opening. By the time I reached the restroom, the damage was done. I contemplated my next move, wishing I could disappear like the invisible man and reappear in a change of sweet-smelling school clothes.

Knowing that I had to decide what to do pretty quickly, or the teacher would wonder why I was taking so long, I opted for removing and throwing away my soaked underwear. Fortunately, I was wearing a skirt that day, instead of long pants, or hiding the evidence would have been completely impossible.

I went back to class, and quietly slipped into my seat using every precaution to keep my skirt down, hoping no body parts would be exposed, and hoping the pungent smell wouldn't rise to the surface of everyone's noses.

The rest of that day I watched closely to see if anyone glanced my way or suspected my humiliating secret. I didn't tell anyone this story for years as it seemed to define the wimpy, little girl who would let things like that happen without having the courage to stand up for herself, even if it seemed in opposition to adult authority.

As I began making more healthy choices to face my fears and confront wrongdoings head-on, this story became a great source of limitless hours of laughter. I still have etched in my memory the unsuspecting classmate who rounded a corner, slipping in my pool of urine and exclaiming, "Ouew! Where did this water come from?" My lips were sealed!

After school let out, my daily routine was to walk home, change clothes, and almost immediately begin softball practice. I spent countless hours pitching in our driveway. If Daddy wanted to include fielding and batting practice, Marv, Eileen, and I headed back to Rancho Vista in our softball-filled station wagon and worked hard honing our skills on the little school baseball diamond that was little more than a grass field with a small backstop.

Every time we practiced at the school or a nearby park, I always hoped people would be close by watching. I thought that maybe this would help keep Daddy's outbursts in check. During our practice sessions, before we started touring, I don't remember receiving punishment for my pitching, but batting was another story. If Daddy became exasperated with our lack of performance while batting, he'd start a count of whips with his belt that we'd receive after practice, when we got home. Now that's what I call pressure!

One practice, he was so mad that he started the belt count with a new standard. Hitting the ball was not good enough. We had to hit the ball perfectly in the center. My heart dropped every time the ball popped up or hit the ground, instead of a line drive. Each of our belt totals were sky high. Driving home that night was like heading to the guillotine...certain pain and torture. I cannot adequately describe the scared feeling of doom in the pit of my stomach before our trips to his bedroom, but I can give you the sure-fire rule that Eileen and I adhered to before we received our punishment.

When Daddy asked who wanted to go first, Eileen and I readily responded simultaneously with, *"I do, Daddy."*

It's not that we had all this courage. It's just that experience told us: *"Above all, you never wanted to go after Marvin."*

Eileen and I always bent over, gripped the bedspread, holding on for dear life, and kept as still as possible. In addition, our responses afterward were always filled with deeply heartfelt apologies for our poor performances, and sincere promises that we would do better next time.

You might be thinking, if Marvin had the most lashes coming, it would be better to go last. Maybe our dad would be worn down and tired by the time he got to Eileen and me?

Not a chance in a million years! Marvin had spunk...maybe even a little defiance. He was constantly moving, flinching, and turning different directions, which worked Daddy into a hot lather of determination to show him who was boss. With Marvin, the audible counting always ceased, and it turned into a beating that seemed endless. On a number of occasions, Marvin's male instincts to defend himself resulted in a natural reflex, blocking Daddy's blow. When this happened, we could see that Daddy was visibly stunned for a moment, like the quiet before a brooding storm. Seconds later, it was war, as all hell broke out against my precious brother, Marvin, with me and Eileen shaking and watching in horror.

No...we definitely did not want to follow Marvin!

To help with our batting skills, Daddy bought a pitching machine. The first one he purchased was probably designed specifically for baseball, as it had a mechanical arm that retrieved our softballs from a bin, flinging them toward the batter, like an overhand throw. Later, we used a more advanced pitching machine that had two spinning tires that could be adjusted to throw risers, drop balls, and fastballs over 100 mph.

Along with the hours we spent using this first machine, comes the one practice session that will be forever etched in our memory. Daddy was teaching us how to bunt, so we were all close to him listening intently, with one person at home plate, trying to lay down a bunt. We weren't catching on fast enough, and Daddy was losing his patience. His voice was getting louder, and the words were getting more degrading as his intensity started to escalate. He jerked the bat out of the hands of whoever was at the plate, and said, *"I'll show you how it's done."*

Daddy put down a bunt and turned to us, yelling and screaming. Once he started ranting, it seemed like he'd never stop. That is…until everyone including Daddy, forgot that the pitching machine was still throwing balls automatically instead of manually.

A ball rocketed forward from the mechanical arm, blasting him in the head…surprising everyone, but most of all, Daddy. He was shaken for a moment, returning to his angry ranting at us with a new vigor that had no end in sight. Just as his words were gaining the momentum of a locomotive…WHACK…another blow to his head. He forgot to move away from home plate.

Everyone watching was frozen in fear. We knew where the blame would fall. There would be consequences for "our stupidity," but an amazing thing happened. Daddy was genuinely dazed and dumbfounded, as he stepped slowly away from the plate. He was speechless. Believe me, so were we. To our surprise, practice was over without another word.

Sometime during the fifth grade, Daddy came up with another idea. I'm not exactly sure of the thought process behind his idea, but Mom gave me the details leading up to it.

After we moved, we stopped attending church in Gardena, where Daddy had been so instrumental in heading up many of their sport's teams. With that part of his life gone, he was restless and bored. Not involved with any teams, Daddy decided to get boys and girls together and start his own teams.

He printed an exciting flyer, inviting boys and girls (the ages of his own children) to join "The Rolling Hills Kids Klub." We passed out flyers to everyone in our school, and kids were taking them home to their parents and bringing back signed permission slips to join our RHKK.

It seemed Daddy's new venture was catching on like wildfire. If one person joined, they would tell all their friends about the fun they were having and others would want to join too. We started with just a handful of kids and grew to over one hundred in the span of three years. Our club was the hottest thing on the hill; it was more popular than the Girl Scouts in our area.

Besides entering us into sports tournaments, we had really fun activities like trips to the mountains, talent shows, swim parties, sleepovers at our house, BBQ's, pancake breakfasts that started at 4:00 a.m. with a secret "kidnapping" of each kid in their pajamas (the parents were notified in advance), and wild and crazy games and competitions with lots of rewards and prizes for winning.

Everyone loved "Mr. Beaird," and I loved having more people around. During this time period, there was a lot more light-heartedness and laughter. Overnight, it seemed like I was respected for my athletic ability, well liked, and over-the-top popular.

Our Kids Klub girls' softball team won every tournament that we entered; and after two years, parks refused to let us enter. When that happened, Daddy set up his own tournament, putting up one hundred dollars of his own money (this was a lot of money in the 60's), as well as trophies for the team that won. His tournaments were always a success, with teams sending in their entry fees from everywhere, hoping to win the prize money. After all was said and done, we still won, so he didn't have to give away one single penny.

During the week, Daddy would run practice for whatever seasonal sport was going on at the time. There were so many kids that the focus was off of us and onto them. He designated Marvin, Eileen, and me to lead small groups in certain drills, while he worked with the other kids. Daddy gave one hundred percent of his knowledge, time, and enthusiasm into improving each person's talent.

When it came to sports, I was changing from an ultra-shy, mousey girl to a fierce competitive force to be reckoned with. Still, I looked on with envy, wishing Daddy's interaction with me and my siblings could be given with the same patience and light-hearted, encouraging tone as everyone else.

When choosing teams in school or at our Kid's Klub, I was the girl who was always picked first. That really boosted my self-esteem. At the same time, I couldn't help feeling bad for the kids who were chosen last. Being so popular did backfire on me once…in a big way.

Our Kid's Klub was having a swim party at someone else's home. As I was playing ping-pong, others were splashing in the pool. I began to hear rumblings of kids shouting to start relay races in the pool.

I knew where this was going, so I disappeared as fast as I could into the house, heading for the nearest bathroom. My plan was to hide out until the races were over. I couldn't swim, and I was deathly afraid of the water. So far, I had disguised my deficiency by participating in other activities.

Within minutes, I could hear people calling my name, and soon a knock came on the bathroom door, "Rosie, your dad wants you out by the pool."

My heart sunk. As I was making my way to the pool, I tried to quietly clue the others into the fact that I couldn't swim; but sure enough, team captains were named, and I was the first person chosen.

The scariest part involved diving into the pool, not to mention actually swimming in a race. Daddy knew I couldn't swim, so I was hoping that he'd get someone to replace me. I was scared to death and humiliated that I couldn't swim. His solution was to have me swim my leg of the relay starting from the deep end and swimming toward the shallow end, where the next swimmer would take over.

His last-minute instructions were to put my hands together above my head and dive as far as I could into the middle of the pool. He said if I dove far enough, I would be in shallow water soon, and I could run in the water even if I couldn't swim!

There was no way out of this; I was petrified with fear! Ready, set, go! I took a giant leap into the unknown abyss, followed by a loud belly flop, arms flailing, and gulps of water penetrating my mouth and nose. I made it to the side of the pool, pulling myself along the edge until I touched the bottom of the pool. My legs moved in slow motion against the water, as I attempted to run to the other side as fast as I could. This was a frightening, embarrassing, and deeply humiliating experience on the inside, but outwardly I remained smiling, confident, and laughing—revealing no sign of fear, pouting, or anger because Daddy forced me to participate. I knew better. Daddy would have reacted to that kind of behavior by setting up more relay races, until I repented of my poor attitude and changed the look on my face.

When the others started shouting, "Let's race again," I was long gone, disappearing inside the house, crying in the bathroom, and waiting for the idea to cool down. I managed to avoid any more water trauma for the next four years. On tour, there were plenty of swimming pools where Daddy wanted me to come out and swim, but I told him that I wouldn't have time to fix my hair before the game, or swimming might make me too tired to pitch. Those excuses usually worked.

The problem was resolved my freshman year at high school, when physical education included a semester of swimming. The prestigious surroundings in the Rolling Hills and Palos Verdes area guaranteed many homes with private pools in the backyard, or family memberships to an elite country club nearby, where all my classmates attended private swim lessons each summer.

When swimming at school started, it seemed like I was the only one who sheepishly raised my hand to admit I couldn't swim. Nevertheless, I still have fond memories of my soft-spoken and very patient instructor teaching me the fundamentals of freestyle, backstroke, breaststroke, and sidestroke. I'm sure she could see I was very tentative, but I managed to try everything she taught me, finally learning how to swim.

To this day, I love swimming laps very slowly for exercise. Over the years, I would swim laps after each game on tour, in cold (mostly un-heated) pools, and then soak in a hot-as-I-could-stand-it bath or Jacuzzi. From night to night, this cold-hot treatment seemed to help my sore pitching muscles more than anything else.

After being barred from the girl's park league, Daddy found an ASA (American Softball Association) women's softball team that I joined. I felt like a loner on this team because the ladies were much older; I was only eleven, plus Daddy discouraged interaction, keeping me separate. Regardless of the age difference, I became the number one pitcher, and it was exciting when our team won the league and went to the play-offs.

Daddy would have my sister, Eileen, who was too young to play, warm me up instead of the team's catcher. I know this must have ruf-fled feathers. The whole season I could feel the tension between my dad and the coach. Daddy wanted complete say-so of everything I did as pitcher, but that wasn't going to fly with this coach. They had many heated discussions because Daddy gave me every signal and coached me from the sidelines.

If my catcher gave me a signal that was different from my dad's, I always threw the pitch Daddy signaled. There was a big-time power struggle with me in the middle. Neither person was going to give an inch.

I do not remember the particulars, but as I was warming up to start our first game in the play-offs, the coach and my dad had a big argument.

Daddy motioned for me to come off the ball field, and I came run-ning. We packed up my softball gear and left. Not too much was said, and I certainly didn't question his actions or complain...so that was that!

Later, Daddy found out that our team lost, which seemed satisfying to him. I felt neutral, as I was quickly learning that my feelings never mattered anyway. The way things were going so far, it seemed like my pitching career was going to be short-lived, but nothing was going to deter Daddy. He got on the phone and set up more practice games with me pitching with our Kid's Klub against anybody and everybody that he could find. He didn't care who our opponents were…he just wanted matches.

It felt like no one could defeat us. It was at one of those practice games, someone jokingly said to my dad that we could probably win with only a pitcher and a catcher. Daddy agreed—and that idea stuck in his brain.

After thinking it through, Daddy decided to put this plan into action, adding a first baseman and a shortstop. Even though he believed I didn't need any fielders, because I was striking out almost everyone, we realized that it was necessary to have at least four players. When it was our turn to bat, if the bases got loaded, there needed to be a fourth person at the plate, batting.

This new four-person team format worked like a charm. Without really trying to, we created quite a buzz, attracting crowds of onlookers…that is, until about the third or fourth inning with scores like 20-0. It was especially disappointing to Daddy, seeing the excitement of our spectators turn to boredom, and gradually exiting the bleachers.

During this time period, Daddy had heard of two teams that were currently touring professionally. When they came to our area, he took us to see them play. I don't remember many details, but after we saw the King and His Court, a four member men's fast-pitch softball team, headed up by world renowned pitcher, Eddie Feigner; Daddy waited patiently to talk with Eddie after the game. Daddy was telling him all about me, and I shyly shook hands with Eddie as I was introduced.

Later, I found out that Eddie generously invited us to his place to see me pitch, with a special invite to go water skiing on his boat at Lake

Elsinore. I was nervous at the prospects of doing either of these things in front of this man whom my dad seemed to place in such high esteem. I was glad when we didn't end up going skiing because I couldn't water ski or swim.

However, I did throw a few pitches in Eddie's front yard. From Daddy's reaction on the car ride home, I don't think it yielded the results he was hoping for.

A short time later, we saw the California Cuties, headed up by Trino Palacios. Daddy and Trino talked for a long time after the game, and Daddy seemed hopeful, brimming with excitement about the possibilities of turning his favorite sport of softball into a money-maker. Trino had given him the name of a few booking agents that might be willing to schedule games for us across the United States.

In addition, Daddy contacted all our relatives in Utah, Texas, and Nebraska, asking them to try and book games for a summer tour. My Aunt Opal and Uncle Aubry ran with their new mandates and booked quite a few games.

On our end, there was so much to learn and so little time. I began to work feverishly, learning how to pitch softballs for strikes with a blindfold, from second base, from a kneeling position, behind my back and between my legs. Daddy knew that winning 20 to zero wasn't going to keep fans interested, so we needed other tricks to keep the fans excited.

My dad was a ball of fire promoting his new team, "The Queen and Her Maids." In later years, we changed the name, "Maids" to "Court," as we replaced girls on our team with guys, who wouldn't have appreciated being called maids!

Throughout the years, I have always been amazed to watch my dad in action, getting people to say yes, paying money to watch a team they had never seen or heard of before.

Daddy was a promoter extraordinaire and a master salesman. Especially in the beginning, he sold the "Rosie" whom I would eventually become, which made me feel like we were pulling a fast one on people. Once I acquired the talent that he was promoting, he was on to something bigger and better. This always left me feeling "not quite good enough" and insufficient on the inside.

A perfect example of this was when Daddy booked us to do an exhibition game at my middle school. To get the gig, he said I was going to do all these amazing things, like throwing the ball behind my back, which I had never done before. Even though this pitch soon became one of my most deceptive and effective pitches, in the beginning, I could not, for the life of me, throw it for a strike. The pitch always went five feet to the right of my catcher.

A couple of days before our performance, panic started to set in because I knew I couldn't do it and would be humiliated in front of my peers. So we came up with a plan to get us by. Right before I threw the ball behind my back, Eileen would slide smoothly to the right so it would look like I pitched it perfectly where she was standing. I only threw one pitch like that to fulfill our obligation of doing what my dad said I could do. Our plan worked; everyone seemed impressed.

Our four-member softball team was moving full steam ahead. We had our first tour booked with games. There was nothing and no one to get in the way of what I thought was going to be that "once in a lifetime" summer of traveling outside my home state of California, playing softball.

Little did I know that my life's path was being etched in stone, and I didn't have a clue to all the twists and turns that were ahead of me!

CHAPTER 9

ḤITTING THE ROAD

"Be strong and of good courage, do not fear nor be afraid
of them; for the Lord your God, He is the One who goes
with you. He will not leave you nor forsake you."

DEUTERONOMY 31:6

◇◇◇◇◇◇◇◇◇◇◇◇◇

In 1965, the Vietnam War was in full bloom; *The Sound of Music* was a hit on the big screen; The Beatles played to thousands of screaming fans at Shea Stadium, and The Queen and Her Maids began to play.

I'm sure there must have been a mile long list of details that my parents needed to complete before we left for our very first summer tour. My day was just beginning the moment the bell rang, signaling that school was out. There was a new intensity and urgency to not only hone our athletic abilities, but also develop new showmanship skills and routines that we would perform before the actual game even started.

Daddy spent hours on the phone putting a summer's worth of games together consecutively, which would also work geographically. This was no easy feat, especially since no one had ever heard of us.

The next big task was deciding who would be on our team. We placed an advertisement in the newspaper announcing "try-outs," and we selected two girls. One of the girl's fathers was a successful realtor and ended up donating a station wagon, which he leased to us for the summer. In exchange, we lettered it with red, white, and blue stars and stripes, and an acknowledgment of his realty company. I'm not sure if it helped his business much, as we were going out of state, but Daddy talked him into it, and getting our mode of transportation was just one more huge detail off the list.

Before we put the ad in the paper for players, it seemed like we were having a hard time coming up with the right combination for the strongest team possible. With only four players, we spent hours simulating different plays to figure out how each person could manage a couple of positions, covering the entire softball field.

I still remember the day Daddy called a family meeting for a big announcement. He had found the perfect addition to our team. He had a mischievous twinkle in his eye and a wide grin as he began describing our new teammate. When he said that we already knew this person, I thought, *something's up*, but I couldn't quite figure out what. After his prolonged description and build up, he made us play "twenty questions." This was so frustrating…especially since he was trying to sound serious, but laughing at the same time.

Finally, we gave up and begged him to tell us. He relented and gave us her first name…Lotta. We moaned. Daddy got us all excited for nothing. Then came the last name…Chatter…So her full name was Lotta Chatter.

I was disappointed at his hoax and wanted to end this silly game. Then Daddy announced we were going to meet Lotta Chatter right now.

The mystery ended…our very own brother, Marvin, was going to don a cute little blond wig and play the part of a girl on the Queen and Her Maids. We were dumbfounded, but Marvin had an especially stunned look on his face.

Daddy spent the next twenty minutes excitedly detailing the character of Lotta Chatter. We all agreed with our dad...no one would think of disagreeing. Our brother would be better, faster, and stronger than any twelve-year old girl we could find. He worked out with us every day, so he knew all the routines, and besides that, Marvin was family!

As Daddy continued to describe the comical role that Lotta Chatter would play, I wasn't sure what to think, but I knew that this new idea was one that Daddy had brainstormed for countless hours, and it was not going to be up for discussion. I mostly felt sorry for Marvin.

As it turned out, in the seven years that Marvin played as Lotta Chatter, he despised everything about it—Marvin hated it!

In retrospect, was my dad's idea of Lotta Chatter a good one? A resounding YES! It just wasn't something my brother Marvin should have been forced to do. It was like forcing a square peg into a round hole, with Daddy pushing and Marvin resisting the entire seven years. What an explosive combustion this created for our entire family.

Years later, my baby brother, Norman, claimed the part, taking it to a whole new level of creativity. It was like he was born for this role to make people laugh! Besides entertaining thousands of fans over the years with all his spur-of-the-moment antics, he could have me in stitches at the drop of a hat, on any given night.

There was almost always a troublemaker or heckler in every crowd. It was excruciating to watch Marvin, quiet but witty, trying to shut down each loud mouth in his soft spoken, but defensive manner. Somehow his mannerisms only made matters worse. On more than one occasion, it resulted in a physical fight between the two, behind the bleachers, following the ball game.

I empathized with my brother. Marvin took everything people said so personally. His self-esteem was so damaged that I'm sure he felt like this was just one more attack on his character. In many ways, we were very much alike, only I had the ability to fake it better.

In contrast, because their personalities were so different, Norm would respond to the same type of heckler with loud, put-him-in-his-place humor, drawing the attention of the entire crowd. Either the heckler would shut up or both would continue the jovial bantering until the end of the game. Either way, the loud mouth was comical putty in Norman's hands. After the game, the heckler and all his friends would storm the ball field thanking my brother for such a fun night, hoping for his autograph.

I chuckle thinking back about some of the funny things that we incorporated into our pre-game show. I suppose we got away with some of those cheesy routines because of our ages...9 to 12 years old, with my baby sister, Karen, who was six years old, joining us in some of the pre-game routines. When we were young, people didn't think "cheesy," they thought, cute!

Right after Daddy introduced us, we'd run onto the field, starting at first base, following each other around the bases. When we reached home plate, we continued on to the pitcher's mound where we formed a circle and proceeded to do a little clap routine in perfect unison, ending with our hands together and then raised to the sky, accompanied by a loud cheer. This little routine managed to stay in our pregame show a couple of seasons until we got the talent to replace it with more skilled and technical routines.

In our first brochure, (I use that word loosely...it was really an 81/2 by 11 piece of paper, colorfully designed and folded over in three sections), there was a picture of me holding up money. In the caption below, I challenged anyone to get a hit off me for five dollars. This was definitely something that no other traveling team was doing, and it created tons of excitement for the spectators everywhere we traveled.

Before each game, Daddy would choose four volunteers—a man, woman, boy, and girl. When he made this announcement, audiences were thrilled, as hands shot up all over the ballpark. People cheered loudly as their friends stepped up to the plate.

I remained smiling and carefree outwardly, but inwardly, my determined game face was on. It would be unacceptable to give away any of our hard-earned money. I tried not to take anyone for granted, but usually the only volunteers I had to worry about were the men.

All they had to do was hit the ball so that it stayed fair between first base and third base, with no bunting. In other words, with no one fielding their balls, the participants didn't really have to get a legitimate hit...the ball just had to stay between the two white lines. This was such a crowd-pleaser that we kept it in our routine for about seven years, increasing the reward to ten dollars for a hit.

The first season I gave up a couple of five-dollar bills, which was well worth the positive publicity that it stirred up in the softball world. Nevertheless, following the loss of our first five-dollar bill, we had a strategy talk afterwards, coming up with a plan that helped us get the money back.

Daddy would congratulate the guy, build him up as invincible to the listening crowd, and then offer him double or nothing to try it again! By this time, the audience was worked up into a roaring frenzy. It would have been shamefully impossible for any guy not to try it again! You can bet your bottom dollar that whatever pitch I had thrown previously, he would never see again! This was a win-win for us. Most every time I got the money back and the few times I didn't, it created so much excitement the people loved us and wanted us to come back the next year!

Another routine we included when we were young was meant to have the feel of a knife thrower hoping to hit his target. I am not sure that the people appreciated or respected the difficulty of this stunt, but we all knew if I messed up, someone could be seriously hurt.

It went like this. Two of my teammates would be on either side of home plate about ten feet away. I would throw a blazing fast ball over the eighteen-inch home plate, and each player would take a giant step towards home plate to build suspense. After approximately three pitches, their toes would be touching both sides of the plate, and I would fire the last pitch accurately down between them. From night to night, with all kinds of weather conditions, field conditions, and human conditions, I had to be perfect. This feat made me incredibly nervous, but I couldn't even think any kind of negative thoughts, or I would tighten up and hit one of the players. It was hard to be me, but I definitely did not want to be whoever got the task of putting their toes on the plate. Let's put it this way, who can be perfect? My teammates knew I was "almost" flawless; but it was inevitable, each season I miss-fired at least a couple of times. It was nerve-racking to know when that time would be.

To this day, my sister Karen recalls that she dreaded each night on tour because of that one single routine. She had good reason to say that because my worst blunder in those seven years involved her.

With the finale one pitch away, and twenty toes touching home plate, I fired the last pitch. The moment I released the ball, I knew it was big trouble as the pitch whizzed through the air, smacking poor Karen in the mouth. The audience was hushed and every eye zeroed in on Karen. She tried not to show any reaction to the disastrous pitch, standing as still as a statue, with streams of the telltale blood dripping down her face.

I couldn't believe she didn't cry. Plan "B" was now in effect. Our instructions were to end on a good note, throwing another pitch successfully down the middle and running off the field with the applause of the audience. I was incredibly apprehensive and Karen seemed to be in a state of shock, as she averted her eyes from me, looking straight forward at the teammate across from her. The fact that she refused to look at me made me twice as nervous. If the ball came at her again, she'd never see it coming to move out of the way. My brain was now on high alert.

With a constricted wrist, tight arm, and psyched out mind, I let go of that speeding bullet and SMACK...I hit Karen in the leg!

There would be no saving this act. It was a disaster! People came running onto the field from everywhere to see if she was okay, and even though she was in great pain, Karen knew what actions were required.

She dismissed the injury quickly, and retreated to the dugout in true professional form. I couldn't believe how bravely she had reacted.

The following day, at our team meeting, there was no mention of her bravery. Instead, Karen was chastised and scolded for not getting out the way of my pitch. Daddy proceeded to give a demonstration on the art of moving ever so subtly and slightly out of the way of a speeding bullet, without alerting the attention of the audience! Outwardly, we all parroted, *"Yes, Daddy,"* but inwardly our thoughts were unanimous, *"Impossible!"*

In the early years, when we made an appearance at high school assemblies, and private company events, Daddy would call for volunteers to stand on each side of home plate to get a little audience participation, since we weren't able to play a game because it was indoors.

I was presented with a most daunting task, when we performed for all the high-ranking councilmen in our area. Daddy chose two men, one being the mayor. A small area in the dining room was cleared to pitch. The room was dark, and the floor was slick, as they approached the portable home plate. Both men were laughing and completely relaxed, as if they had already consumed one drink too many. As their toes touched home plate, their confidence in me oozed, while their beer bellies hung over the plate, eliminating an extra four inches. If they could've only seen the bloody night with my sister Karen, they would've run for the hills! I fired...success! Daddy was beaming, and everyone applauded! I was extremely relieved! Although I never hit anyone apart from my own teammates, I was glad when we discontinued almost all indoor pitching events. As my youth disappeared, so did my naiveté and confidence when it came to pitching indoors. The reality of the potentially dangerous consequences became paramount in my brain, screaming "red alert," and in turn affected my pitching abilities.

After a lot of arduous work, we had put together a pre-game show that we hoped the audiences would appreciate for their hard-earned $2.00 adult and $1.00 for children tickets.

The price of admission seems laughable now, but when you consider that gas was 31 cents a gallon, a loaf of bread was 21 cents, and you could buy a candy bar for a nickel, those prices to see us perform were a good amount of money.

Behind the scenes, Mom, who was an excellent seamstress, bought red, white, and blue striped cotton material to sew all our shorts and even stylish matching headbands to keep the hair out of our eyes. For our tops, she bought about a dozen white cotton short-sleeve blouses and sewed appliqued red and blue stars on each of them. It was a far cry from the easy fit and breathable material that sponsors lavished on us in the years to come, but for the first tour, those uniforms did the trick.

When the dust settled, we left California with ten people in our nine-passenger station wagon, followed by a homemade equipment trailer that Daddy built from scratch. Unfortunately, every time it rained, all our gloves and cleats were soaked, adding double the weight until they completely dried.

At the last minute, a ten-year old girl from our Kids Klub was added to the seven family members and two girls whom we chose from our try-outs. It seemed like our motto was "the more the merrier." We were like squished sardines in that station wagon, but we were little kids, and it was a new adventure. Within a week or so, Daddy saw the light and sent our little Kids Klub friend home on a bus, which created a little more room.

It would be amazing if I could "click" an archive section on my computer and pull up any of the events and games of my choice that we played in the span of twenty years. There have been so many cities, ball parks, and hotels that most have become a distant blur. However, I do have some vivid memories of the very first game that we played out of state.

It seemed unbelievable, as we drove up to what seemed to be a covered minor league stadium in the city of Brenham, Texas, located between Austin and Houston. This was the first time I had ever played under the lights, and it was exhilarating! Throughout the years, night games became my favorite. Everything is more charged up and exciting. It always felt like my pitches were faster and moved better when the sun went down.

We played a women's team and won easily, but the clear detail that has remained with me all these years occurred after the game ended. I accompanied Daddy to settle up the finances with our sponsor, as Daddy made it my job to record all the details of each game in a little black book…along with names, addresses, and any other pertinent information that would help us book future games.

That night, I found out that we were contracted to receive a flat guarantee of $350. After we got paid, I couldn't believe we earned that much money for playing a ball game. Daddy was on cloud nine!

Even though we walked back to join up with everyone else in the car, it felt like we skipped back because of the lilt in our steps. I could almost hear the calculator going off in my dad's brain. If the tour continued like this night, all money worries would be over by the end of summer.

The next day we traveled about two hours to Georgetown and had a pretty decent crowd, but the terms of payment were different. We were to receive a percentage of 50/50, which ended up $298 for us.

It's so weird that I remember the exact figure, but my memories almost always are closely connected to the temperature reading of my dad's perspective on each situation. He was a little disappointed that our share of money was less than the night before; but by the time we reached the car, his spirits were lifted, and we certainly agreed that almost $300 for a day's work was fabulous!

That is where the memory of cities and financial details end. We continued our Texas games and each night's pay went down, down, down. Daddy's dream of averaging at least $300 a night flew out the door, which cast a foreboding spirit of negativity on all our daily activities.

Little did we know that by the time our first tour concluded, we would encounter many cheating sponsors and bookers who lied through their teeth with financial promises that turned out to be flat zeros.

Those first few tours were important learning experiences, and eventually Daddy keyed in on all the loopholes, shoring up our contracts, so we wouldn't be burned.

That first year we agreed to play any women's teams, little league, and pony league age boys, but that didn't happen. We ended up cutting our teeth on about thirty men's teams.

If we found out ahead of time that a men's team was scheduled to play us, Daddy would consent to play, and try to persuade them to combine their team with women, which didn't always happen. I struck out a lot of men that summer, which really helped me grow as a pitcher, but it helped to have women sprinkled in the line-up. If necessary, Daddy would signal me to walk a guy to get to the next female batter…a sure out.

By far, the most interesting dynamic to witness was when we actually played little league teams our own age. The term "little league parents" came to life as moms and dads literally crumbled with bad sportsmanship as their little boys struck out time after time, dejectedly walking back to their dugouts. I personally got tired of parents and their boys spouting off with such poor attitudes because they couldn't win. We would hear jibes from adults in the audiences, saying, "This isn't fair" and "We could win if both teams played baseball."

Now is the time I'm wishing I could pull up a video archive of our second tour. We found a girl who was a hard-core tomboy and wasn't the least bit intimidated by the opposite sex. She could throw a baseball overhand like a rocket, and we were just waiting for some sniveling boy team to yell that it wasn't fair.

I loved the shock on their faces when we accepted their baseball challenge. I switched to the first base position and watched as our overhand rocket thrower mowed through their line-up. After a couple innings of this, everyone in the opposing dugout, as well as the stands, simmered down with their attitudes and became content for me to come back in as pitcher and throw an inning blindfolded, or from a kneeling pad or from second base.

Life on the road presented many new challenges, but some of those obstacles didn't seem as difficult because we were so young. It was more like a journey of excitement and newness.

Over the years, we stayed in some of the highest quality accommodations and ate at some of the finest restaurants around the world, but nothing can replace the fun we had trying to save money by eating free hot dogs, sodas, candy, and popcorn after most games.

In the beginning, our contract asked the sponsors to provide some form of lodging...hotels, motels, or homes. Many generous families invited us into their homes, but there were nights where all pre-planning fell short, and we had to fend for ourselves.

Some warm nights, after the crowds had all gone home and the ballpark lights were off, we'd pull out our sleeping bags and find a nice spot on the bleachers to fall asleep under the beautiful, starry sky. It's certainly hard to believe I was ever so young that I could pitch a ballgame, sleep on a wooden bleacher, and wake up the next morning without any sore muscles, ready to pitch the next night. I wouldn't remove those times from my memory bank for anything.

We were certainly creative on that first tour, sleeping on Salvation Army cots, and lots of park and recreation or YMCA floors. Some mornings, we would wake up and see lots of faces peering through the windows watching us sleep, but that seemed exciting too, especially if the faces were admiring, cute boys!

The most memorable place we stayed came about because we had three days with no games, and therefore, no lodging, as we were passing through West Virginia. Daddy found a telephone booth and started flipping through the phone book, as we waited in the car. Finally, he hopped back into the front seat and announced that he got us a three-day stay at the orphanage in town, in exchange for a ballgame and performance for the kids.

Everyone seemed to enjoy the ballgame, and I felt good inside to be able to bring some fun and entertainment to all these children with no parents. During our entire stay, the kids and staff lavished such kindness and generosity to us, inviting us to eat every meal with them. The last night together, they had a banquet, where some of the children performed. When they asked if we'd like to participate, Daddy quickly volunteered Eileen and me to sing a duet.

My heart sank. Now the night would be nerve-racking for me. Getting up in front of people was so difficult, even when I knew what I was doing. It was much more difficult with no plan, and in the spur of the moment.

With a few minutes to come up with a song, Eileen and I decided on a Grammy winning novelty song that came out in 1963 and continued to be popular in 1965 as a television commercial for a board game. It was a humorous parody about complaints from camp, with a catchy little tune, that everyone was singing. Without much time or thought, we surged full steam ahead into our A cappella duet. The song was "Hello Muddah, Hello Faddah by Alan Sherman.

We looked out to a sea of smiling faces and everything seemed great until we came to the chorus. As Eileen and I belted out, *"Take me home, Oh Muddah, Faddah, take me home I hate Granada"*, we sensed the temperature of the room change from hilarity to somberness, with smiling faces fading to blank stares. There was no stopping that stupid, insensitive song…we had to finish what we started! We were in a room filled with orphans, listening to three choruses of begging parents to take them home, with words like…*please don't make me stay, I promise to not to make noise, and let me come home if you miss me.* Eileen and I wanted to curl up in a little ball and disappear.

As we concluded, there was a spattering of polite, reserved clapping, but we felt like we had just administered a dagger to each of their hearts.

It took days to get over our huge blunder. To this day, part of me still cringes just thinking about it.

About one month into our tour, the little lefty whose dad leased the car for us, slid into second base and broke her leg. We had no choice but to send her on the next flight home.

That was tough on all of us, as our strongest line-up included her, along with Eileen, Marvin (as Lotta), and me. In addition to cutting our strength as a team, I felt scared and more vulnerable around Daddy, hoping he wouldn't zero in on everything I was doing wrong. Having more people around was definitely a plus to keep the blame off of me.

The real gut-wrencher happened weeks later when Daddy let us know that Mom would be going back home too, along with my baby brother Norman, who was about three years old.

I was petrified with fear and felt a sense of desperation in my heart for her not to leave. My insides were screaming, *"Please don't leave,"* but I knew Mom had no say so over Daddy, so I kept silent.

Leading up to her departure, I cried and prayed for God to intervene, but there seemed to be silence on His end also. As the days got closer to their departure, I was sick to my stomach, but I forced myself to block out any painful emotions. These were some of the beginnings of becoming the "professional emotion-stuffer" that would rule my behavior for years to come.

Tears spilled over my face as we gave hugs and waved our goodbyes, but the most difficult thing was getting back into that station wagon feeling unprotected and forcing myself to cease the tears and put on the cheery, smiling face for my dad. I willed my head to bring reality to the forefront of my brain, and control my responses. I thought, *Daddy will get angry if I don't stop crying. He won't admit to spanking me for being sad and crying, but he will turn this into something else that I did wrong, and then I will get punished for ruining his day.* No matter what, I knew I had to fake it if I didn't want trouble…I put on the smile!

Each day was filled with new things, both good and bad! There wasn't any part of me that thought we were going to ever do another tour like this again, but I should've seen the signs. Daddy was trying everything he could to gain more popularity and recognition for our team—many of his ideas were successful.

In addition to playing the ball games, he attempted some last-minute advertising to get the biggest crowds possible to attend our games. Every ticket was another dollar in his pocket.

To alert as many people as we could of our arrival to play that night, we hooked up our public address system and drove down all the main streets announcing that The Queen and Her Maids were in town.

Each of us would take turns holding the two speakers out each window as our vehicle rolled slowly through the streets with Daddy announcing a la Barnum & Bailey style, *"Come one, come all, to see the famous four-member team from California play at such and such park, at such and such time."*

Even though we were young, this was embarrassing! As we held those screeching speakers out the windows, our heads were ducked down as low as possible, hoping no one would catch a glimpse of our faces. At that moment, none of us felt like famous celebrities; it was very humbling! Luckily, we discontinued that form of advertising after our first tour.

Thinking back, I have to admire my dad's creativity and tenacity to try everything he could think of to help us move forward toward success. Besides playing the ballgames and collecting every name and address of any possible future prospects, Daddy contacted every radio and television station as we passed through each city, hoping to get more publicity and notoriety.

When I saw the movie *Coal Miner's Daughter* with Sissy Spacek portraying the legendary country singer, Loretta Lynn, and Tommy Lee Jones playing her husband, Doolittle, it was very reminiscent of Daddy and me doing hundreds of media interviews, in hopes of connecting with the right people and making it big!

At first, Daddy did most of the talking, but inevitably, the interviewers would turn the questions to me. So he spent hours teaching me how to respond to their questions until my answers were perfect.

At first, I was very intimidated by all the media, with their big microphones and high-powered television cameras pointed at me, but after years of being the one who handled most of the talking, it became second nature to me…even enjoyable.

That first year, I dreaded each interview because afterward we would go over everything I did wrong, so I could improve. I was always afraid I was going to say the wrong thing, making Daddy upset. With time and practice, I learned that Daddy would be satisfied if I mentioned a handful of the pertinent buzzwords of information. It's like when a movie star goes on television to promote their latest work. The publicist's goal is to get the name and particulars out to the public, so they will go see the movie or event.

Another thing that made interviewing less stressful is when I discovered that ninety percent of media personnel asked the same twenty questions over and over, so I memorized the response Daddy wanted and learned how to deliver the answer without sounding like a parrot.

My favorite and most prestigious interview happened about ten years into my career on The Tonight Show, starring the famous Johnny Carson. He was a master of wit and truly made each of his guests feel completely at ease, including my sister, Eileen and me. He was hilarious with all his antics and expressions, as he went down for the count swinging, adding to my list of strike out statistics. On the show that night, I also struck out the then, current homerun hitter for the Los Angeles Dodgers, Jimmy Wynn.

The night was a complete success, and like most anything we accomplish in life, that achievement really began with a lot of hours and hard work, years earlier.

As summer ended, The Queen and Her Maids headed back to California after logging thousands of miles across the United States, and even a few games in Eastern Canada.

I couldn't wait to return home after being on the road for so long. I wasn't sure what my future would hold, but I knew that my life had changed forever.

With the first day of school just weeks away, I would finally have something exciting to write in my "What I did over the summer" essay!

CHAPTER 10

HIGHER LEARNING

"Teach us to number our days, that we may gain a heart of wisdom."

PSALM 90:12

◇◇◇◇◇◇◇◇◇◇◇

Once softball entered our life, my school days seemed like a blur; a necessary government requirement. For me, life was scripted early on, and the scenes didn't include things like dances, homecomings, boyfriends, after-school activities, or a graduation ceremony. I was long gone on our summer tour when my high school diploma came in the mail.

Homeschooling wasn't as popular when I was growing up, or I'm sure my dad would have hopped on that idea. Twenty-four/seven at home with Daddy...*Now, that's a scary thought!*

I knew my future was etched in stone when Daddy sent a signed note to our high school counselors stating that he wanted Marvin and me to be exempted from taking any SAT tests. College was not in the picture, and this was certainly not a topic for discussion.

I knew my life was not the "norm" as I sat in a separate classroom with a couple other high school students while the rest of my classmates completed the SAT tests. When teachers and kids asked why I wasn't participating, I repeated a rehearsed, acceptable answer, "My career is in professional sports, so I don't need college."

Truth be told, Daddy never asked my opinion on the subject. I kept my mouth shut, and did what was expected as deep seeds of resentment, bitterness, and frustration were forming below the surface. Would I ever have any say or control over my own life? I was starting to feel trapped!

Within the first month of returning home from our first tour, plans for a second tour began. Letters requesting our team came pouring into our mailbox.

I felt different as I entered my last year of middle school. After spending the summer winning ball games, striking out hundreds of batters, receiving applause each night, and even signing countless autographs, I felt pretty good about myself. I was still reeling in the afterglow of this new identity where people lavished me with compliments that made me feel like I was talented, beautiful, and really loved. Then I entered the eighth grade, and my bubble burst as I discovered I wasn't really all that special.

Didn't my classmates get the memo? I was no longer the quiet, mousy, unconfident girl…I was a unique individual…a celebrity.

Something new did happen that school year. As the Queen and Her Maids shot full steam ahead, the Kids Klub came to a grinding halt because there was no longer enough time to do both. With the ending of our Klub, came the termination of all the friendships that I thought were solid. I was sincerely shocked to have girls, whom I thought were my close friends, walk right by me in the school corridors without so much as a glance or hello. *Wasn't I the same girl that everyone chose to be with, just three months earlier?* It was a very hurtful realization.

While I was gone on tour, everyone moved on to priorities beyond sports. The wow factor included make-up, style, fashionable clothes, music, and most of all…BOYS. Since I had nothing to do with this new guide of "being cool," I was out!

In the mid-sixties, the media redefined beauty, and I didn't come close to this new image. In 1966, an uber-skinny, seventeen-year-old Brit named Twiggy, with her big blue eyes encircled by long black painted lashes, angelic face, and mod, angular hairstyle, became the World's first supermodel.

A year earlier, a sleek and slender Cher took the world by storm releasing the hit, "I Got You Babe." Guys and girls everywhere were trying to emulate the wild and wacky bell bottoms and funky vests Sonny and Cher wore, and girls were using flat irons to duplicate Cher's satiny, long, straight, black hair with long thick black bangs.

Years later, I bought my very first pair of red tie-dyed bell-bottom pants. By then, they were extinct from the fashion scene, but I didn't care. I had dreamed so long about "feeling groovy" with a pair of bell bottoms that I wore them anyway.

There was one girl from our Kid's Klub who seemed to have achieved a status above the rest. She had the hairstyle that I desperately wanted. Picture Marlo Thomas in the 1966 television sitcom, "That Girl." Her clothes were out-of-this-world adorable, and her stylish straight hairdo with perfect bangs and a little flip up at the ends was my dream. If I could achieve such a look, maybe I could feel beautiful?

I began dialogues with Daddy, only in my mind, trying to convince him that such a look would be right for me. As usual, I would give up the idea because I was sure he would veto it. If I didn't ask, there would be no rejection, and hope of my changed look would remain alive and well in my fantasy world…Weird thinking, right? These are the thoughts and actions that exist when a person is totally under the strict and complete control of another.

I couldn't quite work up the courage for the new hairdo talk, so I began a new, but deceitful, daily regimen in hopes of becoming more beautiful. Each day I left the house with no make-up, then I made a pit stop to the restroom before my first class where I applied a little make-up for the day (If you can imagine, white lipstick was the rage in the sixties.). Of course, I removed any trace of the make-up right before my ride home. I hated sneaking around, but it didn't seem like there was another choice at the time.

As meticulous as I was, the inevitable happened. One day, I forgot to remove the make-up. When I hopped into the car, I recognized my mistake the moment I saw my dad's face. Of course, he wanted to know *what was that crap all over my face?*

My heart was racing as I covered with an innocent little lie, blaming a girl from school who wanted to experiment with her make-up on my face. After a sufficient speech from Daddy, with me outwardly agreeing with all his key points about the unnecessary need for make-up, the subject was dropped. *I wish I could have told him how I really felt, but after all was said and done, avoiding conflict and lying felt like two new friends who worked well for me.*

One day during a lunch break, I popped into the girl's restroom before my next class. Three girls were huddled around another girl I knew from one of my classes. She was hysterically crying, and everyone was trying to console her. Everything seemed kind of hush-hush, but eventually one of the girls showed me a note that was given to the crying girl with the number 69. She said that some guy was spreading rumors that she did something with another guy. The eighth grade was the first time that I had ever heard the F-word. I had no idea what they were talking about, but I knew it must be terribly offensive, so with the appropriate look of horror on my face, I said, *"I am so sorry."* I made a mental note to figure out what they were talking about.

Cussing wasn't allowed in our family. If I was really angry at my brother, I did call him a "butt," and afterwards, I usually felt extremely guilty. I have never heard my mother curse and can only remember hearing Daddy use the F-word once in the middle of the night.

That fateful night occurred when Eileen and I shared a large bedroom right next to my parent's room. I woke from a deep sleep to

Daddy's booming voice, shouting and screaming at Mom. The cussing wasn't the scariest sound coming from their room. I knew that Mom was getting beaten bloody.

It seemed like I should do something, but did nothing! I knew if I secretly called the police, they would come and Daddy would talk his way out of anything he was being accused of. He would know that one of us made the call, and it would be all over for me! So, Eileen and I just nervously shook and cried anguished tears in the dark, waiting for the beating in the other room to be over. In our typical family fashion, no one said a word about it the next day. We finally saw our Mom emerge from the bedroom later in the afternoon, with a full leg cast.

Twenty plus years later, we asked about that horrific night, and Mom said that our dad flew into a rage because she wasn't interested in his sexual advances. After the damage was done, she drove herself to the hospital where she made up some flimsy excuse, which no one believed. They proceeded to tell her that her leg was broken.

The unmistakable, unspoken message that washed over our brains was…*if you stand up to Daddy, he will win. He is invincible, and there is no one who can stop him.*

The unsolvable question for me was where was God in the midst of all our pain and suffering? I had lots of questions and no answers. It didn't feel wise to stand up and speak honestly to Daddy or God, so I buried my thoughts. After all, I didn't want to make either of them mad at me!

As I have learned, being an encouraging parent and pushing your children to accomplish their best involves walking a fine line. Unfortunately, during my growing up years, I felt like my dad didn't find that balance. He pushed all of his children so hard to be their best, that it seemed to backfire, resulting in never feeling worthy or good enough to merit his love.

At the beginning of my freshman year in high school, Daddy wrote in the front of my new binder:

Be the task, great or small,
Do it well, or not at all!

His handwritten words were very special to me, and I believe this saying was meant as inspiration and encouragement for me to do my best in every class. Sadly, because his actions were so harsh, my interpretation seemed to contradict those written words. I desperately wanted to please my dad, earning his approval and love. Unfortunately, I could never seem to live up to his expectations, so those meaningful words got twisted in my brain.

Years later, I realized that the dialogue sounding off in my brain went like this: *Rosie, no matter what you do in life, great or small, achieve PERFECTION, or don't even try at all.*

That interpretation was absurd, leaving me paralyzed with fear. As a result, I was afraid to step out of the box and attempt anything new or different because I knew I could never be perfect. Now I understand that failure is going to happen if I try new things, but that doesn't mean I shouldn't try. Failing is a part of anything that is a worthwhile accomplishment in this life. In fact, failure is probably a sure thing, especially in the beginning of any endeavor, but that doesn't mean it is bad! It's strange, the narratives that dictate how we live our lives. The good news is that with God's help, we can change our behavior and live life to the fullest, if we are willing to take a good look at how our life stories and faulty belief systems have taken us down a destructive path, contrary to the truth God meant for us to embrace.

No matter how bad I wanted it, I never felt like I was entering the "cool chick zone" with guys at school. I always wished I could capture their admiration and attention just like I was able to do on tour, under the bright stadium lights. I bemoaned the fact that I was so shy. While I chastised myself for not being a better conversationalist, realistically, I knew Daddy would shut down any kind of a relationship with the opposite sex, if it ever started.

My confidence hit new lows with an incident that occurred while walking home from school. A boy, in a carload of testosterone, yelled out as they zoomed by, *"Hey, girl, why are you so flat?"*

I didn't flinch, or even glance in his direction, but continued walking straight forward like a walking statue, waiting for their car to pass. I thought, *surely, he didn't direct his rude comment to me.* Silently, I whispered a prayer, *"Please let there be a girl walking behind me."* When the car was no longer in sight, I slowly rotated my head 180 degrees to discover that I was the only person on the dirt path for as far as I could see. *What a bummer!* That was not exactly the desired response from boys I was hoping for, and yet it could be another explanation for not getting the desired attention that I yearned for from the opposite sex. It was a sad, long walk home.

This called for desperate measures. I had to get some courage and make some changes. The first thing on my list was asking Daddy if I could cut my hair and have bangs. My little sister, Karen, took scissors to the front of her hair, so my mom had to cut bangs to even things out. I was so envious. She didn't really get into much trouble that I can remember. I wished I could do something like that, but I just knew it wouldn't be the same outcome for me. Daddy would say I was older and should have asked.

I gave myself a one-week deadline to work up the nerve to ask him. One week turned into two weeks, then three, then a month. I tried talking to myself in every manner I could think of, but at the end of each night, I would chicken out!

I was disgusted with myself. I hated myself for being such a wimp. I prayed. I searched for openings to approach him with this subject. I tried to find him in the perfect mood, which never happened.

This whole story sounds ridiculous even as I'm writing it, but it became so monumental that each day drained me of strength and left me with a feeling of defeat and disdain for my lack of courage. Finally, the end of another week rolled around, and I had had enough. I couldn't live one more day without getting this over with, even if he said no. I had to ask. Once again, I couldn't spit the words out. My parents were heading to bed for the night. Their door closed!

I was pacing in my room, talking to myself. After another hour had past, I tip-toed up to his closed door. *Now is the time, Rosie. Just knock... march in...and ask.* I willed my knuckles to knock. Daddy seemed startled to see me as it was now about 10:30 p.m.

The calm speech I had conjured up for months came out in crying and hysteria, as I pleaded for bangs. Out of all the ways I could've approached my dad, this was undoubtedly, the worst scenario possible. I saw his facial expression change, thinking, *what have I done?* Fire started to ignite in his eyes. It felt like I was seconds away from getting the beating of my life.

He said, "I ought to get my belt out and let you have it for coming in here acting like that." Here I was shaking in my paper-thin pajamas, with no padding to cushion the impending blows, wishing I could hit a rewind button on this night.

It seemed I was doomed...then out of the blue, things took a surprising turn.

Daddy shouted out, "Jeri, go get some scissors, take her out of here and cut some bangs. You better not ever do something like this again... you understand?"

Boy, did I ever understand!! I was shaking so badly; I couldn't even enjoy the fact that my dream of having bangs was coming true.

That episode was never talked about again. However, the next morning, I smiled into the mirror, and saw VICTORY! Now I could be "That Girl!" World...Look out...here I come!

CHAPTER 11

NEW SEASONS

"To everything there is a season, a time for every purpose under heaven."

ECCLESIASTES 3:1

◇◇◇◇◇◇◇◇◇◇◇◇

As a teenager, I'm glad I didn't know ahead of time that my future would include almost a quarter of a century performing as a professional athlete with The Queen and Her Court, and being the only one of my brothers and sister to play every season. I know the idea of this would have been shocking to me, but with the great advantage of being older and looking back, I can see God's sovereign hand and purpose over the events in my life, both good and bad.

As we prepared for our second tour, I worked very hard on honing my pitching skills, developing more strength and speed, as well as more movement, with variations of the riser, drop balls, change-ups, and a knuckleball.

Each year for Daddy's birthday, I would vow to work diligently to perfect a new pitch as my present to him. That usually brought a smile to his face. The last and most difficult pitch that I mastered and gifted him with was a flat curve ball.

Some of my wrist strengthening drills involved pitching from a farther distance than the women's regulation mound, which was forty feet away. The farther away from home plate, the better my curveball worked. As I moved up to the correct distance, it seemed impossible to get that twelve-inch softball to curve any substantial amount.

I didn't give up though, and after a few birthdays rolled by, I was able to make good on his birthday promise. It was so satisfying to work so hard, and then be able to strike out batters with this new pitch added to my repertoire. Since I was right-handed, I mostly used the curve ball on right hand batters; they'd swing and it would curve just out of their reach. Whether entirely good or bad or somewhere in between, the pressure to please my dad pushed me to put in the time to develop this pitch.

To make anything, like a business, succeed at a high level, there needs to be a person behind the scenes pushing and promoting day and night. That person was my dad. He would eat, sleep, and breathe The Queen and Her Court with every person he came in contact with. He took on the roles of owner, manager, promoter, and coach... accomplishing incredible things in a short amount of time.

Before our second tour, Daddy booked us on our first television show, "Truth or Consequences," hosted by a young Bob Barker, who is better know for the twenty-five years that he emceed on "The Price is Right."

By 1966, "Truth or Consequences," left NBC and became very successful in syndication. This turn of events worked out well for us, as our episode was picked up all across the United States and Canada, replaying our performance many times for years after, in re-runs.

We were amazed by the number of people who came to our ball games over the next five years, asking if my sister, Eileen and I, were the same girls whom they saw on that show.

The premise of the show was to ask contestants silly, trick questions that they invariably failed to answer, resulting in a consequence, which usually meant that they had to participate in an embarrassing stunt. Our episode brought about one of my all-time favorite reactions!

Eileen and I were asked to come down to the show on the same day that the Southern California little league champions were to be in attendance. These boys were riding high as Bob Barker acknowledged all their great accomplishments, and then singled out the two best players on the team, stating that it might be fun to have a contest of boys against girls.

Unbeknown to the boys, it appeared that Eileen and I were randomly chosen from opposite sides of the studio audience. Bob proposed that the girls would be pitcher and catcher; and if the boys could get a hit, they would both win a prize. The boys responded enthusiastically, indicating that they were certain their prize was already in the bag.

Bob suggested that perhaps we'd like to warm up first, as these boys were very skilled batters. As rehearsed, I acted as if I hardly knew what I was doing. While warming up in our most girly fashion, Bob was getting feedback from the boys. They were beaming with confidence, as hitting one of my soft little ding-drop pitches would be no problem at all. In fact, they proudly stated that there was no girl alive who could ever come out on top in this type of a contest!

If you could have seen, up close and personal, what Eileen and I (and thousands of television viewers) saw in those next few following minutes…it was classic!

Their self-assured expressions turned to disoriented shock, as I threw my first blazing strike from between my legs. The little leaguer stood there bewildered, confused, and disoriented, as his only exclamation to Bob Barker was that this contest was definitely not fair as he was certain that somehow Bob had given me a "trick arm"—the audience roared with laughter!

That comment didn't make sense to me, but at the moment, it was the only thing that his poor brain could compute! Our first national television experience was a definite hit for us!

The next five seasons were packed with so many new and life-changing events that it would be impossible for me to recount them all, so I'll highlight a few of the happenings that impacted me the most.

In the softball world, The Queen and Her Court, were exploding with more and more success and popularity as each season passed. With the opening of one media door, ten more open doors would follow as a result; but I will always have a deep-felt sense of gratitude to those daring pioneers who believed in us and gave us a chance, before we had become an established brand.

One of those doors that opened early on, paving the way to other opportunities seemed like a dream, even as it was happening. In 1965, big news in the sports world came as Houston built the world's first multi-purpose, covered sports stadium, nick-named the "eighth wonder of the world."

Daddy got it in his head that this was his next goal. He was going to get us booked into the newly built, thirty-five-million-dollar, Houston Astrodome!

It was the middle of the summer on our 1966 tour that Daddy excitedly told us after hours of cold-calling, he finally got a phone number of someone who could okay an exhibition and get us in the Astrodome.

I couldn't even imagine what my dad would have said, or how he could possibly talk this person into giving us a chance to perform in such a prestigious and talked-about facility as the Astrodome. He had nerves of steel and such a persuasive way with words that I thought, *Well, if anyone could accomplish this, he could.*

We were waiting anxiously as Daddy finished his call, and walked out to give us the result of his conversation. Sadly, the answer was *"probably a no."* It just seemed too risky for the guy to book us considering the fact that he'd never heard of us. Beside that, the booking would be too last minute.

The guy's answer seemed pretty final for all of us, but not for Daddy. His reaction reminds me of the hilarious scene in the movie, *Dumb and Dumber*, where Jim Carey is trying to assess his chances of getting the girl of his dreams. Carey says, "What are my chances? She replies, "Not good." Carey says, "Not good...like one out of a hundred?" She responds, "I'd say more like one out a million."

Carey's face clouds over in contemplation...then brightens and beams, as he shouts, *"So you're telling me there's a chance."*

Somewhere in that "no" conversation with the public relations man from the Astrodome, Daddy heard hope, and a slight flicker of a chance to change his mind from a "no" to a "yes." Daddy called back the next day, and I'm not sure what all was said; but we were headed to Houston's famous Astrodome. We were elated, jubilant, and screaming as we jumped up and down!

A couple weeks later, we were filled with awe as we walked onto the AstroTurf ball field and viewed the giant two-million-dollar scoreboard, surrounded by the orange and red stadium seating that was radiant in spectacular technicolor.

We were scheduled to put on our pre-game show, followed by a game against the local sportscasters and media all-stars.

I tried not to feel intimidated by everything I saw, but did make note that I had to run to the restroom a half a dozen times during our warm-ups. Despite the fact that I was extremely nervous, I regained my focus, as I remembered that the awesome dome and my opponents didn't matter. Impressing Daddy and doing everything he instructed was my supreme goal for the night.

Even though I felt like I didn't pitch as well as normal because I had to put away my steel spikes, pitching in tennis shoes, so I wouldn't ruin their AstroTurf; the night was a success and definitely helped us skyrocket to a new level of popularity.

Once Daddy got his foot in the door of one major league stadium, we ended up playing in many more stadiums, belonging to teams like the Anaheim Angels, Philadelphia Phillies, Atlanta Braves, Texas Rangers, and Chicago White Sox.

Along the way, I faced many baseball players, including Hall of Famers, Willie Mays, Carl Yaztremski, Johnny Bench, and Dave Concepcion—the last two being part of the Cincinnati Reds "Big Red Machine" World Champion winners in 1975-76.

Reporters always asked me if it was harder to pitch to major league baseball players or fast pitch softball players. I discovered that it was easier to strike out baseball players because they weren't use to the closer softball pitching distance and rise balls. This very valuable pitching strategy was cemented into my brain after I made the mistake of throwing something different, other than a rise ball, to Johnny Bench on *The Mike Douglas Show*. Big blunder...his ball almost took my head off on National television!

A much better television outing happened in 1970, when my dad and I were flown to New York City to appear on *The Dick Cavett Show*, where I struck out three out of four of the 1969 "Miracle Mets," following their incredible World Series upset over the Baltimore Orioles.

The show was aired live, Eastern-Standard Time, so we alerted all our family and friends to watch the recording on the west coast three hours later.

Instead of seeing me pitching on *The Dick Cavett Show*, our friends viewed what everyone on the West Coast saw that night...a pre-empted live broadcast of the unexpected, scary happenings of Apollo 13, which was America's third moon landing mission. We couldn't believe it! What were the chances of that happening the same time our appearance occurred?

Years later, in 1995, a big smile came over my face as I saw the film reenactment of Apollo 13, starring Tom Hanks. To my surprise, inserted into the movie was the actual footage of Dick Cavett's live opening monologue, and the preempted footage of the problems happening on Apollo 13.

I wanted to shout out loud to the moviegoers, *Hey, everyone, that was the show that I was on. You just didn't get to see it!*

At eighteen years old, my world was softball, so I never fully comprehended what happened the night our television spot was preempted, until the movie came out. As a teenager, I was annoyed that our show wasn't shown and that we'd miss a big opportunity for more national exposure. Years later, as my world expanded beyond softball, it was shocking to view the scary space account of Apollo 13 on the big screen...a story that almost ended the lives of our astronauts.

Just like getting us booked on *The Dick Cavett show*, my dad was always thinking outside the box when it came to publicity and promoting The Queen and Her Court. Shortly after our Dick Cavett escapade, Daddy made arrangements for me to be on *The Dating Game* with show host Jim Lange. This was so out of my comfort zone, especially since I had never even gone out on a date. I was given pre-arranged questions to ask the three different guys who were sitting a few feet away behind a partition. I hardly ever talked to boys, so these questions seemed over-the-top and very embarrassing for me. They had sports and sexual overtones, like "What base would each guy try to get to on our date." The questions seemed like I was an experienced dater, which was so ironic since I had never even kissed a guy at almost eighteen years old.

I cringed every time I rehearsed the lines, but I willed myself not to feel awkward, as my real objective and instructions were to say as much about our team as possible. If I could mention "The Queen and Her Court" on national television, Daddy would deem me a success and mission accomplished!

I was extra nervous because this whole thing was unfamiliar territory, but Daddy had an additional plan, which added to my stress. He would be in the audience, along with my brothers, sisters, and some teammates, to view the show. To ensure that I picked the most upstanding guy on the dating panel, he had a member of our group give a loud whistle—once, twice, or three times to indicate whether I should pick guy number one, two, or three.

When it came time to choose, the audience was clapping so loudly that it was really hard to distinguish how many whistles I heard…so I picked bachelor number two and hoped for the best. As it turned out, there was a pair of athletic, 6' 8" twin brothers, as number two and three. I chose one of them.

A few days after the show, Daddy called The Dating Game, and informed them I would not be able to go on the date to San Francisco because of my busy softball schedule.

The person in charge told my dad that we had signed a contract obligating us to fulfill our agreement, which included going on the date. So I went, and that was my first official, but not real date—not exactly what I had dreamed of having for a first date.

The cameras filmed segments of our date that seemed pretty staged, and I was relieved that a very talkative chaperone went along with us. My "show date" seemed like a very nice guy. Unfortunately, the whole experience felt awkward because I knew my dad's expectations were for me to keep everything professional and generic. In addition, I was simply inexperienced and shy.

No matter what media opportunities came our way, Daddy saw to it that we rehearsed and performed to the very best of our ability, so we could advance the popularity of The Queen and Her Court. My favorite case in point was when Daddy and his second wife, Carol (Yes, after years of neglect and abuse, Mom filed for a divorce), my sister, Eileen, my baby brother, Norm, and I tried out for the game show *Family Feud*, hosted by Richard Dawson in the late 70's. The moment Daddy got the call that we were chosen to compete against another family, he bought the two editions of the home game that were available at the time, setting up mandatory practice nights each week at his house in Rolling Hills.

We treated these practice sessions with serious diligence, memorizing every possible answer in the Family Feud home game. We even pre-designated Carol and me to compete in the lightning round for

$10,000, should we actually beat the other family. Hours were spent listening to a category, with me shouting out the surveyed number one answers, while Carol followed up with the number two answers.

The night our show was taped, Eileen, Norm, and I wore our Queen and Her court uniforms with our team name plastered on the front of our shirts. Also, Daddy had us sign a team picture that he presented to Richard Dawson on air to get as much exposure as possible.

I can't stop the huge smile that involuntarily spreads across my face every time I watch the recorded videotape of my dad executing his planned presentation to Richard Dawson. It was not very discreet but definitely well thought out and genius!

Playing the actual game on television was incredibly exciting and got the adrenaline pumping. When our family actually ended up on top with enough points to beat the opposing family, it seemed surreal. During the commercial break, I was being checked for sound and told where to stand. Carol headed to the sound-proof room, so she couldn't hear my answers in the lightning round. As I felt the pressure mounting, I tried to remember to breathe and stay calm, so I could think clearly.

Back from commercial, cameras were rolling...5-4-3-2-1. Next thing I knew, Richard Dawson was putting twenty seconds on the time clock and asking me questions at an unbelievably rapid pace.

I yelled out the first thing that came to my brain, racking up over half of the points that we needed to win the big money...the hardest part was still to come.

Carol was whisked out, replacing me on center stage, and given the same questions.

She remained cool as a cucumber while giving her answers. After she finished, I felt like her answers put us over the top, and I was right!

It was like a dream when we won $10,000 and about twenty of our friends and family came running from their studio seats, joining us on stage, and congratulating us with hugs and cheers, with cameras still rolling.

I felt exhilarated for many weeks following that show. After reviewing every single question and answer that was asked on the show, we discovered that three out of five of the questions in our lightning round given to Carol and me were identical to the ones we had practiced at home. As it turned out, between the two of us, we gave every number one answer for the highest number of points given in the survey! All our hard work really paid off!

I could see that the same diligence we poured into our Family Feud appearance was creating a high demand for The Queen and Her Court in all sorts of new ventures. One of my favorite media experiences, which really took me out of my comfort zone and stretched my acting skills, was a national RC Cola commercial. Through the magic of modern technology it can still be seen on YouTube by searching "RC Cola Midnight Softball." The "Me and My RC" commercial was accompanied by a catchy little jingle and a cute story line of "girls vs guys" on the ballfield with me as the pitcher, my sister Eileen as the catcher, and even my little sister Karen as a teammate in the background. We filmed for three nights from dusk to dawn producing a one-minute commercial. Pitching was the easy part—coming up with the "perfect take" to make the final cut was a little more challenging. After a pitch, I would run to the dug-out, pull a bottle of RC Cola out of an ice chest and take a big gulp, while making sure the label was facing toward the camera. I cannot watch this part of the commercial without remembering the dozens of takes each scene required before producing perfection. Two times I missed my mouth because I was so worried about the label facing the correct way. The director yelled, "CUT" as the cola dripped down the side of my cheek! When the dust settled, the commercial turned out better than I could have imagined!

During this season of growth and expansion for The Queen and Her Court, my childhood was characterized with the highest of highs and the lowest of lows. Everything felt new and groundbreaking, with Daddy at the helm pushing us to levels of excellence that I would have never thought possible. Failure was not in his vocabulary. Success was to be attained at any cost, but I don't think he ever fully realized the extent of the price he paid with his family over the course of his life, to achieve this desired success.

I thought, if only every new venture could have been accomplished with the flawless precision as our night on Family Feud, then maybe Daddy would have lightened up. This would have helped me not to feel so conflicted every time I thought of my relationship with him, my growing up years, and life in general.

Unfortunately, for every perfectly executed happening on our road to success, there were a hundred events that brought stress, anxiety, fear, and severe consequences of emotional and physical pain.

Only time and God's tender mercies have helped to make sense of the haunting memories that plagued my heart and soul. Even thoughts of the harshest realities in my childhood seem like a lifetime ago, and I no longer feel I have to suppress each memory to subdue the pain and confusion I used to feel. After years of reflection, I'm convinced that a good portion of my healing took place as each family member broke "the silence" and started bringing the dark things to light with each other. I have noted that those of us who subscribed to this therapy started moving forward in positive ways, and those family members who didn't, remained stuck. Recently, Eileen recalled a three-week time period during one of our earlier tours where, just like clockwork, every other day following our ball games, we all got a beating for our insufficient softball performance.

I acknowledged her memory as fact, and exclaimed, "It was craziness…I thought we were jinxed! I even have a distinct image of the ballpark and pitching mound in my brain where the three-week spell was finally broken in the city of Kingston, Ontario, Canada. I wonder how many of Daddy's leather belts disintegrated into pieces over our butts on those earlier tours?"

I continued, "How about Holland, Michigan—that was way worse!"

Eileen shook her head up and down in acknowledgment.

The night started off very promising, with a large crowd and a local organization who expressed an excitement about having us return the following year, even before our game started. Daddy was all smiles!

Going into the last inning, we had the game all wrapped up with a win, but somehow, we misinterpreted what Daddy told us to do, and did something entirely different. This opened the door for our opponents to take the lead. In the short amount of time remaining, we were unable to turn the score around and we lost.

Following this disastrous and unexpected conclusion, you could feel tension in the air. We knew our dad was fuming, and we were certain the worst part of the night was yet to come. I planted a smile on my face but felt sick to my stomach, as the other team presented each one of us with a pair of Dutch wooden shoes as a token of appreciation for coming to their city of Holland. They also offered an invitation to join them for a special dinner.

Eileen and I usually didn't eat following ballgames, so we asked to be driven back to our motel as Daddy and the others went to dinner. When we got to our room, Eileen and I were a ball of nerves, asking each other over and over, "Do you think Daddy will give it to us tonight?"

In an effort to calm our anxious minds, we made a plan to put our swimsuits on and head down to the pool. After a few laps in the chilly water, we huddled in the corner of the unlit pool, shaking and shivering, awaiting our fate, like criminals doomed to the electric chair. We were hoping that if we were out of sight when he returned, perhaps we would be out of his mind.

With each passing minute, we desperately prayed that somehow God would calm our dad down before he returned, and this horrible night would be over. After a couple hours passed, we felt a glimmer of hope and started discussing the possibility of quietly heading back to our rooms.

Suddenly, we were startled back to reality with the sound of our dad's booming voice echoing from the second story balcony, "Eileen, come up here."

She replied, "Coming, Daddy."

Our eyes locked for a brief moment as I tried to bolster her courage, whispering, "Maybe he just wants to talk to you."

Who was I kidding? Our hearts sank to the depths as Eileen obeyed. My mind was whirling...*my name wasn't called...am I in the clear? Should I go up, too?* For a brief moment, I thought about running and hiding somewhere...anywhere. If I did that, how would I survive? I'm sure that Daddy would find me. He wouldn't stop until he found me. There were so many games left to pitch this season. Finally, I decided I had no other choice but to go back to my room and wait for my punishment too.

Nothing can describe the horror of hearing my dear fourteen-year-old sister's cries, as she endured her beating through the paper-thin walls of our motel. My mind was racing. *Surely, the other motel guests would hear the disturbing sounds coming from Daddy's room and call the front desk, or maybe the police.*

My roommate, Debby, informed me that my dad had already dealt with my brother, Marvin, so I knew, when the sickening sounds died down, I would be next.

Then came the knock on our door, and Daddy stormed in. His words were loud and scary as he moved briskly toward me. Instead of instructing me to get in his room, he kept fuming and screaming in my face.

With my sincerest apology, I promised him that he would not see any mistakes like tonight again. I guaranteed he would see a difference in my whole performance for the rest of the season! Unbelievably, I sensed Daddy's temper was defusing, and he was calming down.

When he left my room, I thought I was going to collapse, knowing the enormous beating I had just escaped. Simultaneously, I felt relieved and guilty that Marvin and Eileen got the punishment, and I didn't.

The only explanation for such a turn of events was that I was his pitcher, and any injuries and bruises might result in consequences hindering my ability to perform to his highest standards.

The next day, Daddy took Eileen to the local emergency medical center, where she was diagnosed with a broken eardrum. Upon hearing that, it seemed to me that Daddy treated Eileen nicer for a few days, acting like the abusive husband who showers his battered wife with presents as penance, following her beating.

I was silently seething with anger because of his despicable behavior toward my sister, whose character was nothing but kind, caring, gentle, and generous from early on. Daddy even dubbed Eileen with the most enviable nickname in our family, "Sweet Leenie," making me more infuriated by his actions and lack of self-control toward her, or any of us, for that matter. He beat "Sweet Leenie" knowing that she didn't have an intentional, rebellious bone in her body.

What could our dad possibly be thinking? Certainly, nothing rational! His behavior was craziness, and it felt like no one could stop this merry-go-round of insanity.

On a number of occasions, I was certain that other people witnessed the secret abuse, and I hoped they would confront Daddy, so he would change. That hope died, when I recalled the incident in Michigan where my brother, Marvin, was getting a physical beating that ended in broken ribs. We could hear the terrible pounding and punching sounds as clear as a bell from our room next door; the walls were practically shaking.

Suddenly, through the mayhem, there was a knocking on Daddy's hotel room door. We plastered our ears against our own door to hear the voice of a cousin, by marriage, who happened to be staying at our same hotel. There was an eerie silence as our relative said, "Umm…Royal, is everything okay in there?"

I thought, *Obviously, he heard what we heard, and he knows Marvin is getting beaten. Finally, someone will call my dad on the carpet and bring the truth to light. Maybe all the relatives will find out what's been going on, and then they will make him stop this abuse.*

There was a long pause, and Daddy finally said, "Give me a minute, Roger, and I'll be right out." I don't know what else was said between them, but life stayed the same...our family secret remained concealed.

It was like Daddy had a mystical power and charm over people. He was unstoppable. Whatever he worked and prayed for, he obtained it—no matter how he treated his family. It was confusing, and it seemed like the sort of behavior that God shouldn't allow, especially since Daddy professed to be a Christian man.

An equally confusing issue was God's silence and seeming neutrality on the subject of my prayers...my asking Him to stop the abuse. I begged God to intervene, but nothing changed. It seemed like even God couldn't or wouldn't step in and save us. These conclusions distanced me from the God I believed in. From everything I read in the Bible, it seemed that God was powerful enough to do anything; so I was left with the reality that He deliberately wasn't intervening for me.

Like with my earthly father, perhaps, I was displeasing and not good enough for my heavenly father; or maybe, He didn't love me as much as I thought He did. I wanted to trust God, but I certainly didn't understand His seeming aloofness toward my desperate pleas. Underlying seeds of doubt concerning His goodness, love, and protection for me were forming as a false assessment of God's character. I was desperate to escape my frightening life, and enter into a new season, but I wasn't sure what my exodus would look like. Somewhere along the road of survival, I was certain of one thing—If change were to ever happen for me, I would have to come up with a plan, apart from God, to seize complete control of my life.

CHAPTER 12

LOOKING FOR LOVE

"Keep your heart with all diligence, for out of it spring the issues of life."

PROVERBS 4:23

◇◇◇◇◇◇◇◇◇◇◇◇◇

It was apparent to me that I was never going to have a boyfriend if I didn't somehow pump up the volume, so guys would notice me. I commanded everyone's attention when I was on the pitching mound, but becoming the "extrovert Rosie" at home was quite a different story. This action catapulted me way out of my comfort zone.

During my senior year in high school, I did have fun flirting a little more, and one guy in particular was reciprocating. Unfortunately, that all ended quite abruptly when he made the fatal mistake of obtaining my phone number and actually calling our house. I suspected that he was going to ask me to the prom. When Daddy received the call, and questioned me about my male schoolmate, wanting details, I feigned ignorance as to who this guy could possibly be.

In the days following, I felt bad as I intentionally cooled the laughter and flirting between me and the boy. I started becoming scarce around school, completely unavailable.

After that episode, I realized that with Daddy, any hint of a relationship with a boy was impossible, so I kept to myself most of the time, with any infatuations remaining only in my dreams.

No other possible relationships were on the horizon until Daddy struck up a deal with the director of our local YMCA. He bargained for free memberships in exchange for some advertising in our next souvenir booklet.

Following our practices, at least a couple nights a week, we'd all head to the YMCA with Daddy. At that time of night, it seemed like Eileen and I were the only two girls there, with rooms of guys working out all over the place—that was just fine with us! Most of the time, Daddy had his own workout regimen, so we perused the area looking for cute boys.

One night, we spotted two good-looking guys shooting basketball. We giggled, as Eileen chose the brunette, and I chose the blond-haired guy, as our secret boyfriends. What fun we had spotting their whereabouts each visit and showing off all our sports skills in basketball, billiards, and especially ping-pong, while trying to remain aloof and nonchalant.

Over time, we began conversing, laughing, and joking, as we shot a game of pool. Eileen found out that her guy had a girlfriend, but it seemed my fella, Rick, was available…so I continued my cat and mouse flirting. I loved the excitement, believing nothing would ever materialize and feeling safe that Daddy would never even know.

I was shocked out of my socks the night Rick proposed the idea of the two of us going out on an actual date.

All my cool facade came tumbling down as I fumbled for just the right words, finally letting him know that my dad was super strict, and I didn't want to ask him, because the answer would probably be "no."

How uncool was that! The last few months of portraying the part of a sophisticated and mature senior in high school flew right out the window in one breath. Much to my surprise, Rick insisted that I should at least ask. Somehow, he made me feel courageous enough to give it a try, so we agreed that I would ask my dad and let him know the outcome next time we saw each other.

After coming together a number of times over the course of a week, I felt humiliated to acknowledge that I chickened out, and didn't ask. By the completion of seven days, I was resigned to the fact that our relationship had to end because I was such a "wimp." I fell into my patterned mode of operation, making myself scarce at the YMCA to avoid the inevitable embarrassment. To my surprise, Rick hunted me down, angrily stating, "If you won't ask your dad, then I will."

I knew he meant it, giving me a deadline to complete the task, before he was going to step in and do the asking himself. *What did I get myself into?* Asking Daddy if I could date was quite nerve-racking, because it was unknown territory; on the other hand, I was elated that my handsome suitor wanted to go out with me enough to step up to the plate on my behalf.

The following evening, with a couple more years under my belt since the "bangs" episode and a little more maturity, I popped the question. I think my request took Daddy a little by surprise. After a brief contemplation, he started asking me all the pertinent details of what my date would entail. You could have knocked me out of my chair! I would never have guessed that my wish to date would be up for consideration or discussion.

With his mental calculator, he assessed an hour for dinner, one hour for playing billiards, and thirty minutes travel time. After estimating my planned date of no more than two and a half hours, he said, "Well, I suppose that would be okay...as long as you're back by 10:00 p.m."

Inside, I cringed just a little as I felt a bit embarrassed to tell my twenty-one-year-old date that I had to be back so early; but, overall, nothing could dampen this monumental moment for me...I was flying high!

When the big night arrived, Rick extended a brief, but gentlemanly greeting to my dad at the door, and we departed for our timed date. Rick took me to a popular Mexican restaurant about ten minutes away in Rolling Hills. Somewhere between being seated at our table and taking our last bite of food, we vetoed the allotted one-hour billiards time. After all, we had been playing pool together for the last three months at the YMCA. I didn't want this night to feel like the same old thing...not for my special first date. Instead, we opted for a drive to a beautiful location on the cliffs of Palos Verdes, overlooking the majestic Pacific Ocean.

I felt comfortable and relatively relaxed as his car rounded each new turn. Upon reaching our romantic destination, my stomach tightened briefly as I recalled my recent conversation a few days earlier with Debby, my friend and the shortstop on our team. I was wondering aloud if she thought I would receive my first long-awaited kiss. Debby responded with a resounding *"yes,"* and she continued by giving me a play by play of the happenings that would proceed the kiss. We laughed hilariously, as it seemed she was reading from some kind of dating handbook.

Debby declared, "First, he will yawn and stretch both arms up. As they come down, the right arm will go around your shoulder. The next time you lock eyes, he will go in for the kiss."

I doubled over in laughter, but sobered up fast as she continued to describe the type of kiss I was going to receive...a French kiss.

Stop the presses. *"Be serious, Debby! Yuk! How gross! No way that will happen!"*

I was jolted back to the present as Rick's car came to a halt. We continued making light conversation, as we gazed out over the picturesque crashing waves before us...and then he yawned!

It was like Steven Spielberg was directing our beautiful scene from a pre-written script...and ACTION! Every last detail happened just as Debby predicted. Much to my surprise, my first kiss was an overwhelming delight, with two thumbs up.

Over the next few months, Rick and I saw each other two or three times a week, but Daddy would only be aware of maybe two more dates. Even though he consented to those dates, it was clear that he wasn't so keen on me getting serious about some guy. So, I opted to stay on Daddy's good list while continuing to see Rick behind his back.

I felt guilty that I had to be so secretive and deceitful, but I felt like I was put in between a rock and a hard place. We would go out when my dad was gone and be back before he got home, without him ever knowing.

We did have one close call that almost gave my poor mom an ulcer. Rick parked his car out of sight at the end of our street, and I snuck out of the house, meeting him. We strolled hand in hand along the horse trails and then up a grassy hill that overlooked the hustle and bustle below. Even though I fondly named our spot, "make-out hill," we did have many wonderful conversations, as we sat side by side on the soft grass.

I knew this night was getting later than I should be gone. Our tour was approaching fast, and I wanted to spend every second I could with Rick, so I temporarily dismissed my usual sense of urgency and caution.

Upon arriving home, I was shocked to see Mom frantically waving and beckoning me to enter our house through the sliding glass door of her bedroom, instructing me to quietly retreat to my bed as fast as I could.

I complied, without a word.

The next day, I found out that Daddy came home early and asked, "Where's Rosie?"

Mom quickly covered for me, and replied that I had gone to bed early, praying that my dad wouldn't decide to check in on me.

I felt really awful that I caused Mom to lie and feel so much stress. I vowed not to put her in that position again.

With promises that Rick would write, we left in June for our summer tour. I really hoped our relationship would continue when I returned, but that wasn't realistic.

I received one very generic letter from Rick, and I sent him one back…that was that!

I was really sad that his letter didn't reflect any of the sentiments that I received in person, but I was relieved at the same time, as Daddy opened and read all our mail before it was given to us. I can't remember, but maybe I even cautioned Rick that this would happen. Regardless, it was emotionally difficult moving on from my first crush and getting back into the rigors of tour life.

The fast pace of traveling, promotion, and playing ball games every night of the week helped divert my gloomy heart those first few weeks, but at night, I would return to thoughts of Rick.

One night, following our game, the sponsor requested that we join him at his restaurant in town. Daddy accepted, and we all accompanied him. I was exhausted but put on my professional, smiling face, as I was seated at the same table with my dad and our sponsor.

His café was active and alive with energy, as it seemed like everyone from the little town crowded into seats for a 10:00 p.m. meal to get an up close look at The Queen and Her Court.

Daddy was busy talking with the adults while I silently ate. I was tired and bored to be at the adult business table. The one thing I loved was the music playing in the background. I knew Daddy hated all the current rock and roll music, forbidding us to listen to any of it, but he couldn't control this environment, as teenagers were putting their coins in the jukebox, playing records that boomed all my favorite songs.

My mood started changing as my toes tapped the rhythm of each song underneath our table. Another coin dropped…*Ah, The Doors…one of my favorites.* I silently sang along. *Hello, I love you, won't you tell me your name. Hello, I love you, let me jump in your game.*

Strangely, I sensed eyes on me, and I glanced up over my dad's shoulder. A cute young guy was singing and enjoying the song as much as me. *No, wait…he's not singing with me, he's singing to me. Maybe I'm imagining this.*

I nonchalantly scanned in his direction again, discovering that his eyes remained intently focused on me. With each "I love you" that Jim Morrison belted aloud, my secret admirer visibly and passionately pronounced each word to me. I was admittedly flattered and amused...I wanted to break out into laughter, but remained coy, sneaking a quick peek, and looking away without cracking a smile.

I was so thankful that Daddy's back was facing my singing minstrel as he mouthed each chorus and verse for me to see. He knew that he had my attention.

As the song ended, I panicked a little, hoping he wouldn't march over to our table and profess his undying love in person, saying something stupid in front of my dad. Shortly after my serenade, Daddy said goodbyes at our table.

As we headed to the exit, I locked eyes with my singing Romeo and acknowledged his grand efforts to win my heart with a queenly smile and a nod of affirmation. After all, it was the least I could do, considering the fact that he took my mind off of Rick and etched a side splitting and lasting memory that has survived for decades.

Daily, our team experienced unexpected happenings and humorous events of everyday life that kept us laughing and sane, as we traveled from town to town each summer.

Early on, Daddy discovered that Canada was a hotbed of fast pitch softball fanatics, who were chomping at the bit to have The Queen and Her Court come to their town.

Many summers, we would start our tour driving in our maxi van up the West Coast, playing games in Oregon, Washington, and then crossing the Canadian border into British Columbia before traveling east through each province, until we reached Ontario or even Quebec. Because we were so well received, we stayed in Canada a month or two before we would head south, dipping back into the United States.

Canadians were zealous about hockey in the winter and fast pitch softball in the summer, so when The Queen and Her Court came to a Canadian town, everyone and his dog showed up to cheer on their local sports team.

Over the span of my career, it felt like we played in every nook and cranny of North America. Some towns were so small, they were hard to locate on a map. We marveled at the unusual sounding names of many of the towns, like Salmon Arm, Red Deer, Medicine Hat, Swift Current, Moose Jaw—and those were the more populated cities.

At first, upon entering the smaller boroughs, viewing their population sign of a few hundred, we would be disappointed. We figured, even if every single person showed up at our game, there wouldn't be much of a crowd. Soon, we discovered people would come from miles around to see the big event. The bleacher seating would fill up fast, with hundreds of fans overflowing down the first and third base lines…five and six rows deep of people, encircling us, sitting in folding chairs or on the grass, against the outfield fence.

It was thrilling beyond belief! I was amazed that people paid to see us play when they didn't even get a seat and were so far away.

Daddy spent hours teaching us how to exaggerate our movements, and project our voices during our pre-game show…as if we were performing on a stage for that one person who was the farthest distance away.

Besides the huge crowds, our Canadian tours were characterized by welcoming receptions, admiring fans, main streets with one hotel atop easy access pubs on the ground level, hardly any American fast-food chains, and extremely tough competition.

Before each game, Daddy would try to discover the caliber of our competition, when he talked to the sponsor.

We did the same, as we perused the main street, trying to get the low-down from the locals. You would be surprised by all the information we could uncover about each player, as beaming hometown folks would well up with pride, divulging statistics about their homerun hitter or fastest base stealer. We were all ears!

It was a fun game for us. Early on, we discovered that their rating system was very different from the United States. A "B" rated Canadian team was equivalent to an "A" team back in the states.

Every little Canadian town had a team of that higher caliber, so we couldn't make mistakes. They all wanted the bragging rights of saying they beat The Queen and Her Court.

Out of over one hundred games per season, we lost only a handful. Our best year, we were defeated only once, and the worst was around twelve losses, which is still a great percentage in the world of sports... but not for us!

If I had a bad game, I always loved the fact that the next night we would play miles away against different opponents, and I could find redemption within twenty-four hours. The only exception was the incredible phenomenon we experienced while traveling across Canada.

If a guy got a hit, or homerun, or God forbid we lost—somehow, it seemed like every detail of our game reached the next town before we did! Someone always knew someone else miles away, and they were passing on as many details about us as we were trying to obtain about them. This did create an increased amount of pressure, but fortunately, The Queen and Her Court almost always came out on top.

My teammates would delight in ribbing me after a well-fought win, with the next day's sports headlines reading, "Queen Defeats Local Heroes," giving me most of the recognition. In the press, I tried to dissuade reporters by letting them know that on my best nights, I could only tie a ball game...it was my teammate's great hitting that produced the win. Even though that was the truth, it was hardly ever written up that way.

By the same token, the times we were defeated, I received all the credit too, with headings twice as big as normal blasted across the newsprint... "Queen Dethroned" or "Queen Falls Hard."

Sports fans want and crave, loving, cheering, and idolizing their champions, and I was driven to give them my very best...to be what they wanted. Over the years, I felt their love and adoration become a huge part of my identity; but there was always an underlying sense that this great love and admiration that I received was very conditional, and would disappear in the blink of an eye, if my performance level dropped.

Perfection was my internal mantra, and failure was to be avoided at all cost. Flawlessness seemed to be the requirement, by both Daddy and my fans, to prevent ruining the devotion I had labored so hard to obtain. If I won one hundred games and lost one, the question was always, *"What happened to you?"* I remained smiling, but my mind would scream, *Are you nuts? I just said I won one hundred games!*

I know that it was just curiosity, but for the girl whose identity was immersed in precision and excellence, it was a stark reminder that no matter how hard I tried, I was still a failure.

This kind of thinking was cemented into my brain one night after I threw a perfect game, which means the opponents score zero and no players even reach first base. A perfect game wasn't really our goal, because it could be potentially boring for the fans and lessen future attendance. Very often, I would purposely throw slower, straighter pitches the opponents could hit, or Eileen would whisper in the batter's ear that a change-up was coming, so the batter could hit the ball. We did this to keep the audience's enthusiasm high. However, somehow, this particular game concluded otherwise, and I remember feeling very happy and accomplished with my perfect game.

While mingling with the crowd following the game, a guy came up for an autograph, wanting to know what went wrong tonight?

I thought, *Am I being punked?* I honestly thought he was joking, but he was dead serious. He wanted to know why one of the opposing batters got five consecutive foul tips before I struck him out!

My "perfect game" bubble burst wide open as I answered his ridiculousness with a sarcastic tone, *"Just trying to create a little excitement for my fans."*

At that moment, I wrestled with the dilemma at hand. No matter how hard I tried, I would never be good enough to please everyone. Deeply ingrained in my psyche was the nagging reality that my fans, as well as my dad, would reject me if I didn't perform up to their high standards of absolute perfection. Unfortunately, that same line of thinking was projected onto the image I formed of my heavenly Father.

Keeping up this high standard of flawlessness was exhausting, physically and mentally, but I was relentless to find the love and acceptance I so desired…so I stayed on this anxiety-filled merry-go-round, while God looked on…waiting patiently for me to come to the end of myself, so He could show me the truth. Until then, I continued my quest for love by saying, doing, and being the best I could be on and off the softball diamond.

I've heard it said, if you've been unsuccessful in finding love; try changing the places you go, people you see, hobbies, activities, and lifestyles. Replace your patterns with new ones.

At eighteen years old, my life and career seemed etched in stone. I anticipated no new changes on the horizon, personally or professionally, but God had a different plan that summer.

Every once in a while, my sister, Eileen, and I will recount the incredible details of this event and know now, as we did then, that as strange as it seemed, we saw the hand of God moving on our behalf. While this new occurrence didn't happen to my siblings and me, it did alter and affect our future lives in dramatic ways.

Up to this point, even though my parents did not have anything that even resembled a marriage from my vantage point, it was expected that we look like a harmonious, loving, and perfect family to outsiders. Without going into a lot of details, let's just say that Daddy moved on romantically with other women while Mom was required to remain the faithful picture of happiness. We all saw things going on that were unacceptable, but nobody would dare question any of Daddy's actions.

The few times that Mom questioned his actions, he twisted scripture references to justify his behavior. Somehow Daddy turned the tables, so that everything was always her fault. An undeniable fact remained: Divorce would never be an option. While I had great expectations to escape this bizarre lifestyle, it seemed Mom was destined to remain in despair and stuck for life.

Our family narratives became a confusing dichotomy that eroded my faith in God as well as my warped view of marriage and family. Because God allowed Daddy's actions to continue unchecked, I deduced…maybe, his justifications to Mom were correct. My finite mind could only presume that God's hand of blessing and approval was on my dad. The only other feasible option was that God was not as strong or powerful as the Bible claimed…unable to bring Daddy to his senses. It would have felt sacrilegious to admit such incorrect thinking, so we all fell in line with the "craziness" and joined him in prayer to find a happy relationship, outside his marriage. One thing, for sure…when Daddy was happy, we all could be happy.

Fast forward to the summer of 1969. With the exception of our games each night, Daddy's restlessness was palpable. His unhappiness made life on the road very pressure-filled, with constant tension, and apprehension.

One day, he came to all of us kids and confided that he would be fasting before the Lord, in prayer for seven days, asking that the Lord would give him an answer for direction in his life, following the fast. I wasn't sure what to pray for, but we all joined him, petitioning God to answer.

Daddy prayed with great faith and expectation; but to tell you the truth, I just couldn't picture "an answer" from God just supernaturally flying in from nowhere. At the end of his fast, there wasn't even a mail stop scheduled where we would receive unexpected or exciting news that would cheer him up.

About four days into Daddy's prayer vigil, I made a collect call back home to Mom in California, just to touch base and talk. In her voice was a sense of urgency. She wanted to let me know that she had secretly met with a lawyer and was sending divorce papers to our dad via her brother, who lived in the Pittsburgh area. He would deliver the papers to our sponsor when we played that scheduled game.

It may seem odd to some that my mom would start divorce proceedings while we were halfway across the United States, but we both knew that this would be the only possible way to make it happen. I was glad that she let us know in advance, so it wouldn't be a surprise; but I dreaded his reaction and the aftermath of having to be around Daddy after he discovered what Mom had done.

Following our conversation, I told Eileen about Mom's plan. We grabbed a schedule of our future games to see when we played around Pittsburgh. It was three days away.

"Oh my gosh!" It was like a light bulb went off in our brains simultaneously. The divorce papers were arriving Sunday, in Pittsburgh, on the seventh day of Daddy's prayer vigil! We couldn't believe it! We knew we were witnessing the supernatural, perfectly orchestrated hand of God, but our stress mounted as we weren't sure how Daddy would view this turn of events.

When Sunday came, we had an afternoon game against a championship men's team in the Pittsburgh area. As we drove to our game, Daddy seemed discouraged and sullen, as the seventh day had arrived with no apparent sign or answer from God.

Anxiety pulsed through my veins, as I anticipated the secret coming of those divorce papers.

After viewing our opponents, my previous anxiety disappeared and was replaced with the realization that I'd better put all my energies and focus into the game at hand. The opposing team looked "first rate!"

I saw our sponsor pass a manila envelope to Daddy sometime during our pre-game show, but didn't pay attention to see if he even opened it.

Everything was going from bad to worse. The crowd was small and there was no fence, which meant everyone was getting in for free.

Daddy would be boiling over that! On top of that, we lost the game…a sure formula for a meeting with the wrath of Royal and his leather belt.

Following the game, we met with fans and proceeded to pack all our equipment as usual, awaiting our doom…like so many times before. As we hopped into the van, Daddy was already seated in the driver's seat—waiting—with an unrecognizable expression on his face.

Eileen and I are unanimous in remembering this day so long ago. We beheld the Spirit of God moving, as we witnessed a miracle right before our eyes.

Daddy was visibly shaken and silent. Instead of the normal, expected tongue lashing, heading back to our motel, he quietly said that he needed time alone and asked if we would like to go to the movies.

Was I hearing correctly? Did Daddy just say, "go to the movies?" It was like the parting of the Red Sea…a miracle! We couldn't believe what we were hearing. Instead of receiving the predictable, harsh punishment for losing the game, he gave us money and dropped us off at the theater where we watched *A Man Called Horse*, starring Richard Harris.

I don't ever remember discussing the outcome of our game that afternoon, and for the next week, Daddy even seemed like a kinder, gentler man. Because of the remarkable timing of those transpiring events, when we returned home that summer, Daddy allowed the divorce to be settled without a fight.

However, even though the judge approved finalized divorce papers, dictating a specific alimony, child custody, and financial distribution, with our parents signing publicly in unified solidarity; behind the scenes, everything was disregarded. Mom submissively yielded to every verbal mandate that Daddy implemented, overruling everything the judge had set up.

The custody outcome went like this: Eileen, Marvin, and I lived with Daddy in Rolling Hills, and Karen and Norman stayed with Mom. On weekends, the three older siblings headed to Mom's house and vice versa.

The Bible says that God hates divorce and the reason He is so adamant about the subject is because it is so detrimental to the men, women, and children whom He loves so much. I agree, having seen, counseled, and read about the immense hurt and damage divorce has done to countless couples and children.

In our case, I couldn't pretend to feel something I didn't. It felt like God was giving us a reprieve. This divorce was a long time coming, with Mom being biblically justified many times over, and I think God allowed it to end.

I was happy for Mom and for the two days each week that I could live in relaxation and free expression. It felt like some of the oddities and dysfunctions flew out the window. I could be normal for a few days each week. We were celebrating different scenery, new life, and freedom. Hope was in the air!

CHAPTER 13

HOOKED ON A FEELING

"I can do anything I want to if Christ has not said no, but some of these things aren't good for me. Even if I am allowed to do them, I'll refuse to if I think they might get such a grip on me that I can't easily stop when I want to. For instance, take the matter of eating. God has given us an appetite for food and stomachs to digest it. But that doesn't mean we should eat more than we need. Don't think of eating as important, because someday God will do away with both stomachs and food."

I CORINTHIANS 6:12-13A (TLB)

E ven though I felt an undeniable dread in the pit of my stomach, I didn't anticipate what my life would look like after the divorce of my parents. I hadn't considered daily life following our summer tour which was also the summer after I graduated high school.

With Mom, Karen, and Norman gone, and Eileen and Marvin at school for most of the day, I felt isolated and alone. At eighteen years old, it seemed life should be filled with friends sharing exciting exploits and new adventures together; instead, it became me falling into Daddy's winter rhythm during the week with hopes of some invigorating scenery on the weekend.

It's not like I wanted to experience life as portrayed in a "Girls Gone Wild" video—I just needed to figure out who I was apart from my dad and softball. My desire to grow up and be independent seemed reasonable to me, but probably felt threatening to Daddy and the future of The Queen and Her Court.

I thought it might be fun to get a job during the winter and share an apartment with my friend and shortstop, Debby. When I casually mentioned these thoughts as a possibility to Daddy, he proceeded to expound on why this was a bad idea. Even though he didn't exactly say "No," I instinctively knew if I brought that subject up again, I would hear the word "No" along with an even lengthier speech. I was disheartened and crushed in my spirit.

It was during this time period that a new way of coping with my disappointments and pain intensified. I needed something to soothe the pain and create patterns of comfort and relief. Food became my drug of choice. I was caught in the "momentum of addiction." My addiction to food became my survival mechanism, helping me to mask and manage some feelings like fear, sadness, loneliness, anger, guilt, and shame. It wasn't until years later, as I starting fitting the missing pieces of my developmental years into the puzzle, that I was able to identify some of these underlying feelings that were the catalyst to my over-eating.

As with any addiction, what seemed like a quick and easy fix in the beginning, soon spiraled into an out-of-control lifestyle that felt like the never ceasing "monkey on my back." On the surface, it appeared as if I just needed to have some good old fashion self-control, which led to more guilt and shame, and kept me in the grips of the addiction cycle.

From early on, I always felt I was fat. It was revealing and almost shocking to me as I looked back at childhood pictures to discover that I wasn't fat at all. *Why did I think that? How did I become obsessed with my weight and food?*

Because I was an athlete and constantly exercising, most onlookers would never have suspected that I anguished over food for about a ten-year period, which helped to keep my craziness hidden as the perpetual "grand secret."

Our summer tours were a reprieve for my obsessive thoughts of calories and food intake as each day was filled with a fast pace of new people, places, and tough ball games to win. Our rigorous schedule enabled me to lose fifteen to twenty pounds at the drop of a hat. Of course, when our tours ended, the winter blues hit me with a vengeance, and I fell into my same destructive thought patterns, obsessions, and compulsions with food that took over my being from morning until night.

While living with Daddy, I welcomed our weekly Tuesday and Thursday excursions to the "All you can eat" smorgasbord restaurant just down the hill from our house. I would have enjoyed anything that got me out of monotonous office work. I tried to make our lunches last as long as I could.

After the divorce, Eileen and I accompanied Daddy to the grocery store each week. These trips were quite the extravaganza. I know we must have purchased some kind of nutritious food, but for the life of me, I can't think what that would have been. Both of us remember stocking our cart with ice cream and cookies…all of our favorite treats from Sara Lee.

All food events made for a more relaxed and fun atmosphere around our house. It seemed as if I was following all of Daddy's cues and patterns, which left me feeling anxious in later years, fearing that I was destined to be just like him.

He didn't drink, smoke, or do drugs, and neither did I. That was a good thing! Food was a different story. It seemed like he was not as depressed when we were eating…it was how we all coped.

During my bleakest overeating days, I polished off boxes of cookies and quarts of ice cream that always felt fabulous going down, but it was depressing minutes after the last bite. It was my philosophy, as with most seasoned over-eaters, to polish off every forbidden trigger food in one sitting, so I could start fresh and be perfect the next day. Even better yet I had a laughable mantra that was, *I'll start my diet on Monday.* How many cakes and pans of brownies did I have to re-bake the next day, re-cutting a few pieces out of the pan, so no one would know I ate the whole previous pan myself?

There was one specific time that gorging myself worked in my favor. On one of our shopping trips, we bought a twelve-pack box of chocolate covered Ding-Dongs. With our laundry room door tightly closed, I started un-wrapping the aluminum foil encasing each chocolate covered delight, and I began devouring them as fast as I could. The first three were awesome going down; and it would have been nice if I could have stopped at that point, but it seemed like a ravenous mad woman over-took my body, as I crammed all twelve down my throat.

I thought my private chocolate eating party sounded like fun, but as I neared the end of my gorging extravaganza, self-contempt and ut-ter disgust exploded in every fiber of my body and brain. As I secretly stuffed my face, I was acutely aware, like never before, that I had a severe problem. I was so out of control and felt powerless to do anything about it. This was an important acknowledgment, and one of the first times, but not the last, that I recognized that I had a problem and needed help. After the episode, mental clarity wasn't the only outcome. My stomach hurt so bad that I uncharacteristically made a beeline to the bathroom and threw it all up. Just the thought of that horrendous experience kept me from eating another Ding-Dong for over thirty years.

It seemed like food was my enemy. I felt like a hopeless mess and somehow wished there was a way I could just turn my brain to an "off" button. *Was I always going to be consumed with thoughts of calories and food?*

At the time, I didn't fully realize that my problem was not spe-cifically what I was eating, but *what was eating me* on the inside. The weight I would always gain back during the non-touring months didn't seem to affect my pitching too much, but I definitely felt self-conscious playing those first few weeks on tour with thousands of eyes on me in our team uniform, with the tight polyester knit shorts. I would try not to think about it but always wondered what was going on in the minds of onlookers in the audience.

Eileen and I commemorated the year we were the heaviest with a picture we took of ourselves on an all-paid, very lavish pre-season trip to Hawaii. We were flown in with a group of Hollywood celebrities that included Leslie Nielsen, (best known for his comedic roles in *The Naked Gun* movies, Harvey Korman, (ten-year comedic side-kick on *The Carol Burnett Show*), and Peter Marshall (fifteen-year game show host of *Hollywood Squares*).

The Hollywood celebrities were to take on Hawaiian celebrities in a benefit softball game to be played at the Honolulu Stadium in Oahu. We were their secret weapons—pitcher and catcher—to ensure that the Hollywood celebrities would come out on top as the victors!

During our week stay, Eileen and I played tennis with Kevin Dobson, (television actor best know for his roles on *Knot's Landing* and *Kojak*) and Stacey Keach, (stage and television actor); we toured the coast with Anson Williams, best known as Potsie, from *Happy Days*, and soaked up some sun by the pool, or at the beach with many of the others from our group.

Even though I felt a genuine camaraderie from everyone, Eileen and I couldn't help but feel self-conscious around the wives and girlfriends, with their size zero bodies and extravagant, one-of-a-kind outfits that they wore each day.

One day, as we leisurely lounged with our group, a beach vendor popped over to our cabana with an armful of beautifully crafted knit bikinis, searching for interested buyers.

All the ladies swarmed like bees, examining her wares. I thought it would be fun to at least take a look, even though I knew those teeny-tiny bikinis wouldn't come close to fitting my buns. At that same moment, our sponsor, who took a real liking to Eileen and me, very good-humoredly said something like, *"I don't think there's anything your size in that box."* I smiled and gave a little chuckle at his friendly remark, pretending his comment didn't faze me, and trying to move on to a different subject as fast as I could, so embarrassment would end.

Nightly, we were picked up in limousines and taken to fabulous restaurants. The gals in our group were always dressed to the nines, which was kind of intimidating. It was like we were witnessing a fashion show of beauties, with an endless array of spectacular outfits for every new occasion.

One evening, it seemed like all the ladies got together and decided it was going to be formal attire night, as they made their regal entrances in long, flowing gowns. Eileen and I showed up in nice slacks and really felt like geeks! *Talk about feeling like the "odd persons out!"*

When we got back to our hotel room, we re-enacted every awkward detail, laughing our heads off, and thanking God we had each other, dressing similarly.

The next morning, we decided to go shopping for dresses, vowing to spend whatever dollar amount was needed, in preparation for our group's next meeting. We desperately wanted to fit in with everyone else. It wasn't easy, but we managed to find two floor-length dresses in our sizes that made us feel elegant.

As planned, everyone received instructions to meet in the lobby, where we would be escorted to Don Ho's restaurant and treated to one of his live performances.

As Eileen and I stepped out of the elevator, we couldn't believe our eyes! Once again, there seemed to have been an impromptu meeting, where the other gals all voted this night to be "casual dress attire only night." We shook our heads in embarrassment and laughed! From that night on, we made sure we asked what everyone was wearing before we headed to the other functions!

When the day of the big game arrived, we slid right back into our comfort zones as we walked onto the ball field, leading the Hollywood

Stars to their first victory in five years. Being a size zero and wearing beautiful outfits didn't matter so much as we transformed from "fish out of water" to the heroines of the team. The last inning was completed in high style, as I finished the game by having all my celebrity teammates sit down in the infield, while I proceeded to strike out the last three batters with only ten pitches.

Trips like this one to Hawaii and other winter tours to South and Central America helped keep life exciting…a diversion from the inner turmoil and outer chaos that seemed to be swirling all around me.

It was hard being around and observing my vivacious dad ride high during the touring summer months and repeatedly sink into the depressing doldrums when winter arrived. His mood would swing from high to low like a pendulum, year after year, following our tours.

Even though I was aware of his change in personality, I guess I was unaware of the full extent of his melancholy, because I had always been in school. Now that I was home all day, it hit me like a ton of bricks square in the face.

Although it is a little vague now, Daddy and I had certain routines that we adhered to Monday through Friday. Two or three days a week, he paid me an hourly wage to work in the office with him…answering letters, organizing, and brain-storming for future events and games.

Our day would start when he woke. I never knew exactly what time that would be which left me feeling a little off balance. If Daddy woke up early, he would come marching into my room with a smile on his face, clapping his hands, and loudly singing a little song that he made up…sung to the tune of "The Farmer in the Dell" repeating the lines, *"It's time to get up, it's time to get up"*…over and over.

Of course, I responded with a reciprocal smile, and got up immediately; but inwardly, his early morning wake-up call felt invasive, and I commenced my day, feeling angry and in a foul mood.

In my teens, I remember feeling justified when I read a little verse from Proverbs 27:14, "If you shout a pleasant greeting to a friend too early in the morning, he will count it as a curse!" I always wanted to show that verse to my dad, but I'm sure it would not have been received very well. Rather than hearing my heart, I can only imagine I would have received a long speech, peppered with countless verses pointing to my rebellious, unpleasant nature, along with continued wake-up songs. This would happen until he noticed a change of attitude on my part.

Because I hated being taken by surprise or caught off guard, I developed a new strategy, which involved developing a keen listening ear while I slept. This allowed me to hear the slightest movement from another room and be awake before Daddy opened my door. Consequently, to this day, I am a super light sleeper.

Normally, my family matched our schedules, timetables, and moods to our dad's plans and disposition, regulating the temperature of the room to match his feelings.

Nevertheless, kids will be kids. I chuckle remembering the night Daddy was taking a hot bath to relax while Marvin, Eileen, and I were playing a board game at the dining room table. Forgetting that he was just a room away, we were extra carefree…laughing over the silliest things.

Daddy yelled, *"Quiet down!"*

We heard his message loud and clear but by that time, we were clearly out of control with our giggles. Every glance into each other's eyes, and each silently mouthed word sent us into irrepressible fits of laughter, followed by extreme efforts to quiet down. In our best attempts to stop, we placed our hands squarely over our mouths to subdue any escaping audible sounds.

Within minutes, Daddy's voice boomed loudly, *"If you're going to laugh, then laugh…but stop the snickering."*

The recollection of my brother Marvin attempting to turn his snickering into an acceptable forced laughter will be forever etched in my memory bank. Unable to cease laughing, Eileen and I fled from Marvin's presence and out of each other's sight, into separate rooms to prevent unwanted consequences.

Unrestrained laughter was like a medicine. It felt good to laugh. Life seemed so serious, and, most of the time, I felt like my train had jumped the tracks. I was desperately trying to get back on track and maintain control…before anyone noticed.

Fear of Daddy always helped me to conceal any angry or disrespectful words to him, but it was getting harder and harder to contain my true feelings of wanting to be independent.

The Bible says, "out of the mouth, the heart speaks." My heart and brain were definitely dialoguing constant messages that wouldn't be acceptable to Daddy, so I raged on the inside. I felt guilty because I knew God was hearing all my real thoughts. Even though I disciplined myself to keep silent, it seemed like Daddy must've sensed my restlessness for change because he started tightening the screws on everything I did—my attitude, my performance, my appearance—*nothing about me was good enough!*

After a while, his unrelenting monologues sounded like the same broken records that went on and on and on…computing as blah, blah, blah to me.

I wanted to scream at the top of my lungs, *Shut up, stop talking, and listen to me!* But…I didn't.

There were a few isolated times that my siblings and I succeeded in jolting our dad into speechlessness, but those incidents happened in very unconventional ways…like the time Daddy was talking with Eileen.

It was a couple of weeks before her wedding, and like most brides, she cut way back on her eating to look fabulous in her gown. Eileen was feeling a little weak as Daddy stood non-stop talking to her in the hot sun. She knew something was wrong, seeing black spots. Eileen began desperately looking for an opportunity to interject a word into his conversation; to let him know that she was starting to feel dizzy.

Minutes passed. Interrupting became futile. It was impossible to get a word in edgewise. Her last thoughts before she passed out and dropped to the ground were, *"If I faint, he'll have to stop talking."* He stopped!

While I achieved the same outcome as Eileen, and did feel victorious over my dad; I also felt ashamed of myself for the way I stunned him into silence. We were on the ball field. It was one of those practices where I was like a locomotive, going in the wrong direction, heading for disaster. Daddy was on me like "stink on a skunk". It seemed as if I couldn't do anything right. Every derogatory word was flung in my direction. Tension was mounting as he continued his disparaging one-on-one speech. I was trying to give him the appropriate lip service, so he would stop, and we could continue our practice…but Daddy was relentless, pin-pointing my lackluster softball performance with my stinky attitude.

I think he nailed it…he was right, but since I couldn't share what I was really feeling, his diagnosis became a moot point. Things got worse when he began predicting my failure and comparing me to one of his sisters whom he deemed fat, loud, irritating, and rebellious. This analogy was one that I had heard countless times before, but now it was grating on my nerves, with a new intensity. As I kept an attentive, responding face, I was desperate to stop this conversation.

Daddy said, *"You know who I'm talking about, right?"*

Of course, I knew who he was talking about, but for some reason, I feigned naivety.

He continued, *"Do you know what 'BJ' stands for?"*

Sure…I knew that these two letters represented the initials of my dear aunt's name, but with the most sincere, realistic, soft-spoken innocence that I could muster up, my reply was a disgusting sexual connotation, using those same initials.

We were both stunned! I had never spoken those words out loud and wasn't even sure where I had heard them. All I knew was that I had better keep that same steeled look of innocence on my countenance, or I'd be feeling the back of his hand across my face, for my snotty sarcasm.

My heart was beating wildly as I prayed that he didn't realize I was being purposely rude and crude. The expression on his face was pure surprise and shock that abruptly ended all talk, as he muttered some-thing inaudible and gave orders to continue practice.

Not a word about that day was ever mentioned again. In retrospect, I believe, somehow, both our missions were accomplished. He stopped ranting, and I had a better attitude for the next couple of hours, as I felt so grateful to God that I came out of that little episode without any bodily harm!

It was clear that I had a lot to learn about how to deal with people, conflict, and life in general. My coping skills certainly left a lot to be desired. I knew food wasn't the answer, but I had no idea how to find that happy, balanced life that I desired. There were lots of questions with no clear answers, so I continued moving forward the best way I knew how.

The Momentum of Addiction
The Last Addiction—Why Self-Help Is Not Enough
By: Sharon A. Hersh, MA, LPC
(Printed with permission from the author.)

Addiction is in motion when a person, place, substance, activity, or ideology becomes what you think about when you wake up in the morning, what you plan for, what you hide from others, what you spend money on, what causes guilt and/or shame, what you spend time trying to mitigate, and what you determine to eradicate, only to find yourself in the cycle again. Your addiction becomes the momentum of your life. It is the most significant relationship in your life.

When people believe that they are powerless to alter their worlds, they will be at risk for an addiction. The paradox is that the addiction ensures their ineffectiveness.

Addiction goes deeper than obsession and compulsion. It is worship. It is giving my heart and soul over to something that I believe will ease my pain and provide an outlet for my fury at being out of control in a world that hurts me, scares me, or leaves me alone.

Addiction creates a way of life—a way of being in this life—that is fueled by a deep, deep need to worship something or someone. The addict bows at the altar of a central activity that takes away stress, pain, and loneliness for a while and gives him or her a sense of control. All addictions include a re-creation of a more palatable world. In addition, we believe that our chosen idol creates a world that is better. All of us long to recreate. The soul longs for rest—relaxing, letting down, having someone else do the work. Like a magic carpet, our addictions allow us to dissociate from reality and connect to a god that seems to work much better than any god we may have learned about in Sunday school.

CHAPTER 14

THE GREAT ESCAPE

*"Therefore a man shall leave his father and mother and be
joined to his wife, and they shall become one flesh."*

GENESIS 2:24

◇◇◇◇◇◇◇◇◇◇◇◇

E
very August, I always loved when all the television networks
would start airing little trailers for the upcoming new fall season of shows. For me, this signaled that our summer tour was
ending, and I would be home in weeks. In the same way leaving home
in June was exciting as I started gathering clothes to pack one month
ahead of time; returning home was equally over-the-top exhilarating
for each one of us...except Daddy. The anticipation was electric as we
secretly started our countdown of days remaining.

Each year, we witnessed a visible change of despondency wash over
our dad's countenance as the weeks on tour became days, so we kept
the glee out of our voices and off of our faces, but inwardly, we felt like
children waiting for Christmas morning.

Upon returning, I always looked forward to seeing Mom again, but
I was especially eager to try the new church that she and my step-dad
had started attending. At our last mail stop, her letter informed me

of their decision to change churches. From what she observed, there seemed to be a number of cute guys floating around. *Hallelujah! That sure grabbed my attention…I was all ears!*

Putting all my super sleuth skills to work, it didn't take long to determine if there were any possibilities for me in the "guy" department.

From our pew, Mom pointed out the core families of the church, many who were related to each other. Right away, I spotted three handsome brothers in one of those prominent families. The youngest was my age and had long, flowing brown hair, reminiscent of the sixties and seventies. He seemed to be available. My subtle chase was on!

From the beginning, I thought Bruce Black was just what the doctor had ordered. He was carefree and full of spunk and adventure, attributes I so desperately craved. He had an independent, "devil may care" attitude that was completely foreign but certainly enviable to me. This initial assessment of his character was spot on.

Early on in our relationship, my eyes bulged open when I saw a stack of crumpled, unpaid parking tickets overflow as he opened his dresser drawer. I expressed genuine shock, worrying that this would cause big trouble with his parents and eventually, the police…but he laughed it off as no big deal.

It wasn't long before that very scenario happened, making my words prophetic. Bruce was pulled over with a warrant for his arrest, taken to the police station and put in jail…all as a result of those unpaid parking tickets. Bruce was bailed out immediately, and the incident became just another humorous tale of invincibility.

I loved that Bruce was so entertaining and full of life. He was always joking, and creating an air of lightheartedness that was very alien to me. On our first date, we grabbed a bite to eat, followed by a short drive to an industrial section of buildings, where he pulled out a set of keys and gave me the private, grand tour of the family-owned business. That night, my thoughts loosely etched a future where Bruce's family business spelled "job security" representing his potential to always take care of me.

We went to church together, played sports together, and I absolutely adored his family.

In addition to everything else, Bruce played guitar in a Christian band with some of his best buddies from church. I loved hearing him sing and play, particularly when I was privately serenaded with songs that he wrote...especially for me. *Life could not get any better. Everything about our relationship felt like forever love.*

At nineteen years old, I was on top of the world. That winter, the tide of my life seemed to be changing for both me and my dad. My relationship with Bruce seemed to be flying under the radar, as Daddy was focused on his own new romance with Carol, whom he also met at his church.

I was happy for him as he described his angel with the beautiful smile and hair flowing down to the middle of her back. Coming from a background of oddities, I paused, only briefly, with reservations about their relationship, when I learned that Carol was so much younger than my dad—she was three years younger than me. But if Daddy was happy, my chances for happiness would probably increase too.

I was head-over-heels in love with Bruce. There was never a fight, harsh word, or conflict. I wish I would have known that such smooth sailing in our relationship was a definite "red flag"—an indication of two perfectly honed "avoiders" coming together with intentions of avoiding conflict at all costs.

Instead, I was sure Bruce was sent by God to be my knight in shining armor...saving this damsel in distress. I wanted to love and be loved, and I desperately needed to be independent from Daddy. The puzzle pieces seemed to be fitting together perfectly.

As I reflect, years later, I would have to be honest and say that, in addition to being extremely naïve, I did move forward, forcefully jamming some of those pieces of the puzzle together, sensing a warning in my spirit that this relationship definitely wasn't as flawless as it appeared.

One of those Spirit warnings took place on a fun trip to hear Bruce's band perform some songs at a banquet for a local Christian church. I was so proud to be sitting in the audience, watching "my guy" use his talents to glorify God. With a couple songs remaining, Bruce took the microphone and announced he'd be singing one of his favorite songs. I couldn't wait!

He began his rendition of "Imagine" by John Lennon. *"Imagine there's no heaven, it's easy if you try. No hell below us, above us only sky..."*

I knew Bruce idolized the Beatles...more specifically emulating John Lennon. He imitated the way Lennon talked, sang, and played his guitar...*but that was all for fun, right? Now I wasn't so sure.*

I cringed, as the words that poured out of Bruce's mouth seemed sacrilegious. I barely wanted to look around the room, wondering if people were thinking what I was thinking. Although Lennon's words were poetically euphoric to the ear, hoping for a future peace among mankind, the lyrics definitely didn't match up with the teachings of Jesus. I couldn't understand why in the world he would be singing this song at a banquet, filled with people who probably desired to have a closer walk with God?

The 1970s media seemed to be constantly highlighting Lennon's anti-God philosophies and headlining his quotes, where he was always blaspheming God, and bragging that the Beatles were more popular than Jesus.

It just felt completely wrong and even though I wasn't the one singing, somehow, I was embarrassed and ashamed before God, wanting to sink down in my chair as the song seemed never-ending.

When the concert concluded, I slipped away to the restroom to hide for a while, waiting for the room to clear and to rethink our relationship. I felt confused. After being restricted from listening to all the current music for so long, I loved the fun and freedom of joining Bruce in Beatlemania, but I certainly didn't want to worship or elevate the lads from Liverpool higher than God.

As I silently debated whether Bruce and I were on the same page spiritually, a group of exuberant teenage girls bolted into the bathroom, primping and giggling in front of the mirror.

My ears perked up, overhearing their plans to try and catch the eye of a certain cute guy in the band. *Wait a minute…they were talking about Bruce!*

All internal warnings came to an abrupt halt as my competitive juices kicked in high gear. I thought, *We'll just see who gets the guy…you girls don't have a chance!*

Burying all concerns, I made my way back to Bruce, smugly claiming him as we walked arm in arm back to the car. *Maybe I was overreacting. After all, we both were Christians, right?* I didn't want to upset the apple cart, so I did what came naturally—I pushed my feelings down and pretended it didn't happen!

The second Spirit prompting took place on a trip to the mountains with Bruce's family. As his parents could sense that our relationship might be heading toward a permanent union, Bruce's dad took us aside for a heart-to-heart talk. He shocked me with a question that went something like this. "Would it be a problem for you to quit touring with The Queen and Her Court if you and Bruce wanted to start a family or if traveling was causing problems for your marriage?"

I quickly replied, "It wouldn't be a problem, if that is what we both decided."

That question haunted me for weeks. I felt like a liar. Who was I kidding? Of course, there would be a BIG problem if I told Daddy I was quitting The Queen and Her Court…all hell would break loose!

Later, I shared my concerns with Bruce, and he assured me that he would never ask me to give up my career, which helped push down the concerns of such a possible dilemma ever causing problems in our future.

If only I knew then, what I know now...courtship problems don't disappear when couples marry, they amplify one hundred percent!!

In all honesty, God's audible voice booming from heaven probably would not have deterred me from my idealistic views of love and the plans I determined to set in motion. Marriage seemed to be the answer to all my hopes and dreams of living an independent life...bursting with love, happiness, and fulfillment. I had set a course, and it was full speed ahead.

During Bruce and my courtship, it seemed that our "love bubble" held strong even when we were separated by extra months away from each other due to winter tours to countries in South and Central America.

While I felt a mixture of excitement and sadness at the prospect of being gone so long, Daddy and Carol had married already, so he was beyond thrilled to open up this new avenue of travel, exposure, and income, with his new bride by his side.

As it turned out, our tours to these Spanish speaking countries were exhilarating, educational, exhausting, and the closest experience we would encounter to feeling like Hollywood's elite, with paparazzi appearing out of nowhere just to take our pictures.

Our ball games were preceded by lots of media and press conferences. Every time our small plane landed in a new country, there were sport's reporters waiting at each airport to ask lots of questions in Spanish, while an interpreter gave them our answers. Meanwhile photographers snapped hundreds of pictures as we flashed our pearly whites.

After repeating this scenario a couple of times, the turbulent, bumpy flights caused our stomachs to do cartwheels, but we remained the consummate professionals as we continued the press tour with barf bags in hand, always disembarking the plane with waves and smiles.

I was genuinely astounded as "La Reina y Su Corte" caught on like wildfire. The Latin Americans were amazed that we could take on the best nine men in their cities with our four, and still come out on top with the victory.

Generally, our opponents handled their loss gracefully, extending us respect and good sportsmanship following each game. But occasionally, we would encounter a few unusual outbursts.

One of our all-time, top five most bizarre reactions happened in Honduras, Central America, with an opposing pitcher in the very first inning of the ball game. After each of our four batters had gotten hits off him in succession, the poor guy stood stunned on the pitcher's mound. Without saying a word, he threw down his glove, ran out into centerfield. We thought he was going to trade positions, but he hopped the fence, and we never saw him again! Now it was our turn to be stunned!

As we compiled victory after victory, the media coverage continued at a break-neck speed, reporting the details of each night's events. It seemed surreal to see our faces on every magazine cover, headlining the front of all the sport's pages for weeks.

Everyone sought for our attention, and we were lavished with gifts and accolades everywhere we went. These tours weren't like anything I'd ever experienced before. I felt an indescribable exhilaration as the Latin American fans put us on a pedestal so high that I thought I'd never come down.

As the media started plastering our pictures everywhere, we couldn't venture outside our hotel rooms without creating quite a stir. This accelerated instant celebrity status seemed mostly like fun and games to us, as fans and photographers waited hours to get autographs and pictures.

The first time a photographer snapped our pictures relaxing poolside, it seemed humorous, but soon felt invasive, as the media started requesting Eileen, Debby, and me to pose in our bikinis.

One poolside photo shoot ended up being a favorite memory for the ages, as Debby and I conspired to suck in our stomachs on the count of three to appear super skinny, but I guess we failed to tell Eileen, who never let us forget the fact that she looked ten pounds heavier when our photo was splashed across the front of the sport's page the following day!

As word of our appearances spread, the crowds got bigger and bigger, with fans storming the ball field, not only for autographs, but touching and fondling our bodies...That was shocking!

At first, we tried greeting the crowd while standing back-to-back with each other...like frightened rabbits fending off a pack of wolves. Soon, we discovered that wouldn't work, so bodyguards were assigned to each of us. After the last out of the ball game, we were escorted at top speed to a secluded area where we waited at least an hour for the crowds to disperse.

One night there was a miscommunication following our game. The sponsor assigned a bodyguard to me, who, I found out later, was a well-known champion boxer in his country.

Wanting to do his best to protect me, he grabbed my arm, and loudly commanded people in Spanish to clear a path for me.

Somehow Daddy didn't realize who he was, thinking my bodyguard was a random fan manhandling me. Daddy grabbed a bat, preparing to attack this boxer who was standing his ground, ready for a fight.

Through the chaos and deafening sounds of the crowd forming around me, I repeatedly screamed to Daddy, *"He's my bodyguard."*

Turning to the boxer, I shouted, *"Mi papa, mi papa."*

Finally, they both comprehended what I was saying and relaxed. Unable to speak to each other because of the language barrier, both men gave the other a nod of apology, as the boxer resumed his task of getting me to a safe place.

That night, it seemed we waited an extra length of time before being escorted to the vehicle designated to drive us back to our hotel. Surprisingly, there were still hundreds of fans waiting for us. Once we got in the car, I relaxed, smiling and waving as we slowly departed... that is, until kids started hopping on the car and running alongside, covering every space of window with their faces looking in at us; until it was so dark inside the vehicle that we could barely see each other. For a moment, I thought, *Either the kids will rock our vehicle so hard it will tip, or they will get run over.* Fortunately, no one got hurt, and it turned out to be just an exciting night to remember.

While it's certainly true that we received celebrity status with everyone rolling out the red carpet everywhere we went, the flip side of the coin was days filled with exhausting, pressure-filled, hard work.

In those rare quiet moments of each day, the two prevalent thoughts running through my brain were, *I really miss Bruce, and I hope I can perform well enough to please Daddy.*

If we had any spare time in the day, Daddy would schedule private practice sessions, which were actually more stressful and exhausting than the games themselves.

Finally, we managed to get an afternoon off, which turned into our "big blunder" in Venezuela...one that Eileen and I will never forget. We desperately wanted to catch some rays and get a little tan before we returned home to California. There was about an hour and a half down time, so we got permission to go to the pool that was at the top of the skyscraper hotel where we were staying.

Before we left, Daddy gave us a big speech filled with lots of do's and don'ts. He was concerned that the sun would zap our energy and wear us out before the game. We assured him that we wouldn't let that happen, promising to play at our tip-top performing status.

After all the hassle of getting Daddy's consent, we were so disappointed to discover no sun, only a dreary cloud cover. Nevertheless, the weather was warm and being outdoors felt better than being in our room, so we each grabbed a lounge chair and before long, we were out like a light.

When we woke from our little catnap, Eileen and I were horrified to discover every part of our bodies (*luckily, we wore visors*) from the neck down, was lobster red.

We spent the next three days doing the best we could to cover up the fact that we were in horrible pain. We spent hours taking cold baths and applying soothing lotions to our agonizing sunburns.

Our laughter, at the sight of each other lying nude on the cool sheets of our beds turned to moans and groans as we had to put on bras and underwear. Every article of clothing felt like a sharp knife to our sensitive skin, but there was no way our dad could ever find out about our unfortunate mishap.

Every pitch, every catch, every movement was excruciatingly painful, but it was "mind over matter" because the show had to go on. You can bet we never made that mistake again!

As an adult, I fully understand that there must be hours of relentless effort for those who want to make it to the top; but as teenagers, my siblings and I referred to our foreign tours as "*Boot Camp.*" If we could make it through this, our summer tour would seem like a breeze.

After being gone a couple of months in a foreign land where we witnessed, firsthand, the distinction of an upper elite class of people living in a country with the poorest of poor people and seemingly no middle class, we felt like kissing the ground as our plane touched down in the United States. We were proud and honored to be Americans and live in such a nation of opportunity for all.

Above all, I couldn't wait to see Bruce again, and resume the relationship we had started months earlier. Without skipping a beat, we fell right back into our easy rhythm and all seemed right in my world again.

Even the harshest, most derogatory words and rants from Daddy, at our practices preceding our summer tour, rolled right off me, like water off a duck's back. My escape was a stone's throw away...I was going to become Mrs. Bruce Black.

Unlike my brother-in-law, Gregg, who requested a private meeting with my dad, asking permission to marry my sister, Eileen, as we all tried to listen to their conversation from the adjoining motel room,

Bruce and I shared our decision to get engaged and marry following our summer tour.

Following our last game of the season, I had a little over two months to plan our special day, which landed on November 17th.

I wasn't the girl with lists of details and requirements that had to be in place before I married. In fact, I didn't have the slightest idea how to plan a wedding; but fortunately, my soon-to-be mother-in-law very graciously came to my rescue, helping with a lot of the pertinent details.

I'm always amazed by the brain's capacity to remember, as well as forget, the events of our lives. If you showed me a picture or described the happenings surrounding everything from my bridal shower to the wedding day, it would probably jog my memory, but for the life of me I can't even remember what my wedding dress even looked like. There are only two things that stand out when I think of that day so long ago. The first was standing in a reception line, following the ceremony with Daddy and Carol on one side of me, and Bruce on the other side next to his parents as we greeted all our guests entering the fellowship hall of our church. I know I received certain instructions before our wedding as to the positioning of each person in that line from Daddy, who made sure my mom and step-dad weren't close to him.

Mom never complained and never allowed me to feel like there was any kind of tug-o-war for attention. Even though it must have hurt her feelings, she was always gracious, understanding, and never heaped any guilt on me.

Over the years, I did feel ashamed that I couldn't speak up when I felt something wasn't right, but the guilt was nothing compared to the anxiety and uncomfortable tension I experienced as I introduced my dad and Carol as *"Daddy and little Mama"* to each guest...per my dad's pre-instructions.

Carol looked more like my sister, so I didn't know what the heck people were thinking, as I repeated this over and over. I cringed with embarrassment and hoped no one would ask what I meant. Finally, I breathed a sigh of relief as the last person passed out their congratulations, and we all sat down.

As the night was winding down, I was so exhausted. I couldn't wait to escape and be alone with Bruce. His parents had given us enough money to honeymoon in Hawaii, but since I had been there a couple times, we decided to save some money and drive up the coast of California, stopping off at popular spots along the way until we reached San Francisco.

I was feeling like royalty as I spotted the limousine that Bruce arranged to drive us to our first night's stay at a luxury hotel nearby.

No specifics come to mind, but by the time we reached our hotel, Bruce and I began our first night as man and wife with the very first explosive and intense argument of our relationship...it seemed unreal!

We eventually patched things up, but a few nights later, we quarreled again. I locked myself in the bathroom to try and make sense of things and only came back out when my non-violent husband threatened to kick the door down.

This was not what I had envisioned in my "happily ever after" dreams, but expectations still ran high. It was just a bit of a rocky start and I hoped life was not throwing me from the frying pan into the fire.

CHAPTER 15

BROKEN DREAMS

"For I know the plans I have for you, says the Lord. They are plans
for good and not for evil, to give you a future and a hope."

JEREMIAH 29:11

◇◇◇◇◇◇◇◇◇◇◇◇◇

N othing could have dampened my spirits as I moved my
meager belongings from my childhood home in Rolling
Hills Estates to the tiny second story apartment located
on a bustling, heavily trafficked boulevard in a not-so-great section of
Long Beach.

I bounded up two flights of stairs like a gazelle, over and over, with
a lilt in my step. I had an optimistic enthusiasm as I hung up my clothes
and arranged wedding gifts in drawers and cupboards of our kitchen
that didn't allow for more than a capacity of two people at a time...that
is, if you didn't want someone's elbow in your side.

Admittedly, every room of our one-bedroom apartment was min-
iature, and a radical down-size, compared to my dad's house...but, at
that time, it didn't matter that the walls were paper-thin, there was no
laundry room, and our view was nothing but concrete and cars from
every window.

In reality, everything about that first apartment was dreary, but what it represented was so much more than what I could see with my physical eye. It seemed like it was the first step to my glorious future. I was filled with an indescribable euphoria that made me feel like I was the Mel Gibson character, William Wallace, in the scene from *Braveheart*, as he rode his horse back and forth, laden with blue war paint, and defiantly bolstering his men to have courage to fight for what they believed in. Lifting his voice above the cheering crowds, with sword raised high to the heavens, he shouted, *"They'll never take our freedom."*

Freedom—it felt good and settled comfortably in my soul. I was an independent woman. I wasn't completely sure what that would look like, but I had a husband who promised to faithfully love, cherish, and take care of me until the day I died. On top of all that, my favorite fast-food restaurant, Taco Bell, was right across the street. It seemed like that was going to be a hard combination to beat!

My four months of settling into married life and uninterrupted "playing house" flew by. Before I knew it, spring training, in preparation for our next tour, was upon me; but during that short period of time on my own, I felt like I gained a new adult-like strength and maturity that would be with me when Daddy and I connected again.

Daddy suggested a walk as he talked non-stop about upcoming plans for The Queen and Her Court. I was quietly listening; mindlessly inserting what I deemed as appropriate responses to his narratives.

Thinking back, the only thing I can possibly remember is perhaps, I drifted off into other thoughts and didn't respond with as much enthusiasm as Daddy wanted. At least, that was the only thing I could deduce when I was caught off guard…WHAM…a solid slap across my face materialized out of nowhere.

Shocked, beyond belief, I began apologizing repeatedly as fast and sincere-sounding as possible…for what…I wasn't sure. I spent the next hour trying to soothe and diffuse the volatile situation I was in, assuring Daddy that he could count on me to be a better person.

The ride home that day was depressing. My dad's subliminal message to me was loud and clear. Married or not, he was in control and running the show. He let me know with an iron fist that I'd better be on board, or there would be consequences.

It was a hard pill to swallow, realizing nothing had changed. As always, I knew I had to do what I was told. By the time I got home, I renewed my determination to make all the pieces of my life work...*I just had to be a little sharper, more perfect, and never...ever, let my guard down again in Daddy's presence.* I would lower my expectations and reframe our relationship, with the emphasis on employer to employee instead of father to daughter. At least, I figured I could find solace, comfort, and love to muster up the strength I needed to please my dad by returning home each day and falling into the loving arms of Bruce...*Right?*

That day transported me from my temporary respite back to reality. Admittedly, it stunned me for a moment, but it was the life I knew for twenty years, so it felt relatively normal, and the adjustment didn't seem out of the ordinary. What I didn't anticipate was the extra pressure of adding a husband to this dysfunctional mix, as well as all the shocking and idealized misconceptions of being married to a guy who I thought I knew completely, but didn't really know at all.

Looking back, I married the man that I hoped Bruce would become instead of who he really was. I was a scared and hurting young girl, hoping for a savior...perhaps a god to miraculously rescue me from my woes...an impossible task, especially for a guy who was also searching for his identity and self-worth, and probably hoping that marriage would provide the missing piece of the puzzle for him too. I had put all my hopes and dreams for happiness in Bruce's basket; I never anticipated that in the next four and a half years, that basket would be crushed beyond repair.

I am so thankful that the passing of decades, in addition to God's magnificent healing of my heart, has turned even the most painful memories into stories I can retell in the light of humor and grace.

Our first couple of years were filled with the normal ups and downs of two very different human beings coming together, trying to figure out how to find harmony in a cohesive way, and attempting to handle the summer months apart the best way we knew how. Shortly into our marriage, the inevitable happened with my brother, Marvin, quitting the team and departing in the worst possible way…he just disappeared without any explanation to Daddy.

To those of us who lived life alongside Marvin, we understood and were even a little envious. No explanation was needed. Unfortunately, when he left, it was a bummer for those who remained, having to listen to all the negative rants from Daddy meant for Marvin's ears, but certainly voiced as warnings for us.

I also felt sad and very concerned for my brother's well-being as he had mountains of suppressed anger and was void of direction or a vocation, and he was starting his destructive spiral down with bad choices and drugs that would dominate most of the rest of his life.

To my utter surprise, Bruce let me know that he thought it would be fun to take over Marvin's role, so we presented the possibilities to my dad, who moved into the idea cautiously; but soon Bruce won him over with his athletic talent and quirky sense of humor that was sure to be very entertaining for our audiences.

I was elated! This new turn of events was more than I could have ever hoped for. If this plan worked, each summer, we would never have to be apart again.

Even though I did think that this was an answer to my prayers, I soon discovered that daily life on the road, with both my dad and my husband present, added enormous amounts of pressure to my plate, as I was constantly trying to show my undivided allegiance to both of them, striving for perfection for Daddy, on and off the ball field. In addition, I was attempting to rein in Bruce's unpredictable, and sometimes irreverent, behavior. It became unbearably difficult as Daddy demanded complete control of everything and everyone around him, while my free-spirited husband wasn't about to be molded into any kind of suffocating box.

As much as I begged, coerced, charmed, and manipulated, Bruce could not, and would not, change for anyone...not even me. So the hope of my husband playing with me for many years ended after one season.

Deep down, how could I blame him? The relationship that I had with my dad was not normal. Even though I loved pitching and many aspects of touring, I would have quit too, if I thought that was a viable choice.

Nevertheless, Bruce's decision not to play another season knocked the wind out of me. I found myself wishing he had never toured at all. All the possibilities of what could have been left me feeling more alone and angry, reasoning that things could have been different if the two men in my life would have gotten their acts together...for my sake.

It felt like my knight in shining armor was heading for the hills, leaving his damsel in distress to face the fiery dragon alone. I was in a catch twenty-two, and there were no good answers looming on my horizon. So I sucked up the heaviness and disappointment, trying to suppress emotions and the feeling of being unloved. I was determined to move forward, making the best of the cards that I was dealt.

With this new realization that Bruce would not be there to protect me, my idealized love bubble was smashed to smithereens. I felt scared and alone. After that tour, it seemed like some of the main things that appealed to me in our dating relationship didn't translate into the nitty gritty of marriage and real life...where real bills demanded payment, problems had to be solved, and heartfelt emotions needed to be addressed with one another. Of course, that would require some kind of honest communication between us.

If I brought up a problem or was baring my soul in any way, Bruce would laugh it off and dismiss me as easy as throwing another parking ticket into the drawer. I tried every method, both good and bad, that I could think of to break through his nonchalant, "devil may care" exterior. I was trying to reach his heart.

I longed to be loved and known by Bruce. I was sure that if I tried hard enough and prayed diligently, God would surely bless our marriage.

As days passed, it made me sad to realize that even though Bruce and I went to church every week, we didn't connect on any kind of spiritual level. In fact, I was deeply concerned whether Bruce had made a real commitment to Christ at all. When I asked about his relationship with God, our conversations always ended with his same mindless, superficial responses.

I wanted to scream, (*I'm sure I did scream, at times.*) *"Just be real with me…you can trust me…I just want to know you."*

I was so disillusioned with marriage, love, God, and life in general. With the exception of the wonderful family that I married into, everything about my relationship with Bruce was the opposite of what I had imagined. My sadness was diverted many times by my in-laws, who provided temporary reprieves from the realities of my marriage… including a three-week European vacation with Bruce's parents, two brothers, and their wives.

In hope of the deep soul connection that I desired, my efforts to keep communicating started turning into more fights, with a flood of tears and pleading from me. When that didn't work, our interaction resorted to lots of sarcasm and hurtful words flying around.

It was during this time period of my life that I became proficient in all cuss words, great and small. Unfortunately, my attempt to shock Bruce into being real with me resulted in a bad habit that added heaps of guilt and shame to my already disgusting view of myself.

For a while, my newfound vocabulary served as an effective way to release some of my anger on and off the ball field. Somehow, it gave me a false sense of strength, as I portrayed the "tough girl" who could endure anything life could dish out.

Of course, with the exception of Bruce, I muttered these coarse words in my mind or under my breath, so my dad wouldn't hear.

Years later, I began to slowly change. I finally allowed the Holy Spirit to start His healing work on the inside; but before that happened, there was an incident that did put a pause on my ugly behavior.

After years of communicating back and forth, Daddy finally landed a long sought-after tour to Japan, with a promotional ploy of offering $10,000 to any team that could beat The Queen and Her Court. With this came the task of convincing sponsors that it would not destroy the traditional Japanese men's honor if they were to lose to women.

We ended up winning four straight games, all nationally televised in their entirety on Prime Time Network television, with an audience of thirty million viewing each of the four telecasts.

Each night was electric and the pressure was intense to look sensational, as we played opponents composed of Japan's major league all-stars in the beautiful Tokyo Giants Stadium.

The crowd was buzzing. Two marching bands were playing so loudly on the first and third base side that it was hard to think straight, and reporters were flitting all over the ball field acquiring as many interviews as they could before the game started.

We were all feeling the surging intensity in our veins to perform at our best. I knew what I had to do, and I was praying I could live up to everyone's expectations. I set a course in my brain to give one hundred percent, and nobody had to light a fire under me. I was dialed in to impressing everyone with brilliance.

I can't recall what or how my dad's pre-game pep talk was delivered to ensure perfection from me, but evidently it rubbed me the wrong way...my blood was boiling!

Standing on the pitcher's mound, in between pitches, I turned my body toward centerfield, so Daddy and the crowd couldn't see, and I silently mouthed a string of vile words before turning around to position my feet back on the pitching mound. I continued this pattern for several innings, in an attempt to release tension and get my emotions under control. Finally, we scored a few runs at bat, and I breathed a sigh of relief, as I took my place on the pitching mound in a much calmer state of mind.

Now in a more relaxed posture, and in an effort to soak up more of this grand experience in my memory bank, I gazed slowly toward the outfield; intentionally trying to let every detail of this magnificent occasion and milestone saturate my brain.

I gazed toward centerfield, zeroing in on a diminutive red light coming from one of the many high-powered television cameras that was filming our game. My heart almost stopped as I realized this camera alone could probably see my tiniest facial blemish like it was under a microscope. My stomach tightened. I knew I was in big trouble if Daddy saw the replay and read my lips.

The Bible says, "Out of the mouth, the heart speaks," and now the true ugly condition of my heart would be on display for all to see. God and I both knew who I was becoming, but it felt like neither of us could turn things around.

I threw up all kinds of prayers, promising God I would change, if He would help me out of this jam. Later that night, we all met in my dad's room to watch a recorded tape of the telecast. I held my breath, barely wanting to look at the television, and trying to divert Daddy's attention with chatter during the times I thought the cameras were filming close-ups of me. To my relief, the editing was favorable, and I vowed to never do that again.

I knew I desperately needed to change. It was exhausting, trying to keep my true feelings muted as my life seemed to be sliding down a deep dark hole at full throttle. I couldn't find the brakes to slow the inevitable collision from happening.

My personal life was in a slow decline with intermittent distractions, like buying our first home. Daddy masterfully negotiated the whole deal for us, persuading the seller to knock off thousands of dollars, by offering him cash and convincing him to bypass all real estate agents, eliminating enormous dollar amounts in fees.

In addition, Bruce and I wouldn't have to pay monthly house payments, because I set up an agreement with my dad to pay down our loan at the end of each touring season, with part of my salary.

With financial burdens and stress eliminated each month, you would think that two people could be happy with more time spent on pleasing each other…but the downward spiral continued, with arguments increasing.

Bruce and I would rise up in our own way during each fight. I used deadly sarcasm, pushing for some kind of emotional connection, other than casual indifference. If I pushed Bruce to the brink, he would retaliate with a fist through the closest wall or door or break something I cared about to shut me up.

At first, I thought this might lead to an explosion, but it would be worth it, if it led to finding an emotional crack that I could penetrate. Instead, the results usually caused me to be scared, along with financial consequences, like not getting our deposit back, due to structural damages, when we vacated our apartment to move into our new home.

There was only one time that I can remember ever breaking through to any kind of real emotion from Bruce during one of our impromptu verbal bouts. Words were flying back and forth, and Bruce began picking up my things, threatening to smash them to pieces.

I was furious because I felt so completely helpless; he always used this tactic that abruptly ended our arguments, on his terms. I thought, *Two can play that game* as I quickly scanned the room and headed for Bruce's prized possessions. He had designated an entire wall, in our tiny apartment, to proudly mount and individually display every cherished Beatle album in existence.

In a split second, I grabbed his albums out of their holders, removed their jackets and started rapid-firing them across the room as I yelled; *"If we're going to throw things, let's throw your things…this is really fun."*

Truth be told...while it appeared that I was bent on destroying all Bruce's treasured LPs, I intentionally flung each record with great precision, and my purposeful pitcher's control, like a rock skimming over the surface of water preventing any damage. Inside I knew that it would affect our budget as he would surely replace the broken records with new ones.

The real fun was seeing that he finally understood how I felt for once as I witnessed genuine panic and distress wash over his face. He blurted out heartfelt pleas and the sincerest apologies.

I stopped. I finally had his attention. For the next few minutes, I felt Bruce heard my heart as we talked and picked up all his albums, returning them to his Beatle's shrine...but I could be wrong. Perhaps he just realized you don't push your wife to her wits end when she's standing next to your cherished belongings...especially if her profession involves firing a softball like a rocket!

Ultimately, I discontinued intentionally pushing his buttons when I recognized that the physicality had possibilities of turning toward me instead of inanimate objects. This was not an option for me, as it represented more of my scary childhood that I was running from.

The few times it seemed like our fights were starting to turn physical, I put up my fists, with all the false bravado that I could muster, standing my ground as I screamed, *"Come on, Big Man...Hit a girl...You can't hurt me any worse than my dad."* Talk like this seemed to stun Bruce into retreating, so that nothing really happened, but I would have turned tail and ran as fast as I could if I thought that I was in any real danger.

The real danger had nothing to do with what the physical eye could see, but the slow decline in my spirit, and the heavy feelings of discouragement and depression that were finding a permanent residence in my heart. The unending pain of rejection was swallowing me up, and I was rapidly losing hope that I would ever find love...so I retreated. I did what I had to do, on and off the softball diamond. I was always smiling on the outside, numb on the inside. I was the *"great pretender,"* trying to fool everyone and determined to end the hurt and pain that threatened to take me under, by wrapping it in a beautifully disguised mask.

I had a steeled resolve to survive this marriage, just as I had endured my childhood. This new state of numbness and isolation would require a controlled mind, with a little help from my obsessions with food, exercise, and listening to music that helped to temporarily soothe the pain of my broken heart.

It was around this time that I entertained a new and dangerous comforter that seemed to momentarily diffuse the ticking bomb of pain that was set to explode each day.

When I became too overwhelmed with my life, my brain was set to a default mode that pacified me with these words, *If life gets too hard, and you just can't take it anymore, you can always kill yourself.*

I spent many alone hours entertaining which form of suicide was a feasible option for me. Most possibilities were out of the question, because they just seemed so scary. There was also the thought that God would spare me from death after a car crash or an overdose, and then I'd be in a far worse condition.

I think back to a night when I crept quietly in the dark from my bed to the kitchen, clutching the sharpest knife from the drawer and placing the tip of the knife on my bare skin...directly over my heart. The slightest pressure of the cold steel pushing against my flesh halted my dangerous experiment. *I wasn't into this kind of pain; I just wanted the depressing emotional thoughts to stop.*

Even though my crazy actions brought temporary relief, the next morning I was filled with more shame because of who I was becoming. Because my trust in people was so damaged, I protected myself by hiding and stopping all interaction that wasn't absolutely necessary. I only remember one person ever questioning the *"new me."*

I was basking poolside, with the music from my headphones pounding in my ears. My sister, Eileen, sat down beside me, motioning for me to take the headphones off.

"What's wrong, Rosie? It seems like you don't talk anymore."

I feigned surprise at her question. "I don't know what you mean," I pretended, "I just love listening to my music."

Eileen made a few more attempts to draw me out, and I politely assured her everything was okay as I adjusted the headphones back over my ears. She walked away with a sad look on her face, and I felt guilty for alienating my sister, whom I loved so much. I so desperately wanted to be real, but I couldn't risk letting my pain and feelings resurface. I wouldn't make it if I opened up with softness and vulnerability. There could be no cracks in my angry, hard as a rock facade, so I turned up the music.

In times of despair, I bolstered myself as I chanted words like the ones from Elton John's song. *"Don't you know I'm still standing better than I ever did…looking like a true survivor, feeling like a little kid. I'm still standing after all this time…picking up the pieces of my life without you on my mind. I'm still standing…yeah, yeah, yeah. I'm still standing."*

I trusted in my own heart and ways, acting like the fool who built his house on the sand. Little did I know that the rain was starting to fall; the floods and winds of a terrible storm were brewing in the distance, threatening to destroy my house…*and great was the fall!*

CHAPTER 16

THE LOVE BOX

"Save me, O God! For the waters have come up to my neck. I sink
in deep mire, where there is no standing; I have come into deep
waters, where the floods overflow me. I am weary with my crying;
My throat is dry; My eyes fail while I wait for my God."

PSALM 69: 1-3

◇◇◇◇◇◇◇◇◇◇◇◇

M y eyes were welling up with tears as the preacher was directing my sister, Eileen, and Gregg, her husband-to-be,
in their vows of marriage to one another. With each new
promise of unending love spoken out loud, I sank a little deeper into
the depressing realization that my marriage was never going to be
the close connection that I desperately desired—it would remain far
from it.

Standing closest to Eileen, as her maid of honor, it seemed torturous
to make any eye contact with Bruce, who stood next to Gregg, as his
best man. I willed myself not to think about the sacred words of matri-
mony, trying hard to stifle the tears streaming down my face, praying
all eyes were on the adoring bride and groom. If not, I was hoping onlookers would think my waterworks were the traditional "tears of joy."

It took every ounce of determination I had to "hold it together," flying under my radar of despair.

It was a relief when Gregg and Eileen faced the packed church of friends and family, and the preacher sent them on their way back down the isle as husband and wife.

Bruce and I locked arms and followed close behind, along with the rest of the wedding party. The atmosphere was filled with smiles, cheers, laughter, and the highest elation to celebrate the beginning of the rest of their lives together. I wanted to crawl into a hole and never come out.

There was a secret place in my heart that was wishing Bruce would be as touched as I was by what we had just witnessed in this house of God. I imagined him taking me aside to express his undying love for me and vowing that our lives together would get better.

As guests headed to the reception hall for cake and light refreshments, eventually, Bruce did make his way over to me to say he was taking off. I don't remember what I said—probably not a lot, as we hadn't been speaking much to each other. I had no idea where he was going, but I acted like his actions didn't matter to me. I was shocked and angry that he wouldn't stick around and at least fake it…if not for me, for Gregg and Eileen.

Bruce was never one to comply with protocol or appearance, even if he was chosen as the best man. I knew I couldn't let him see my vulnerability and pain, to be dismissed as a joke, not one more time. So I acknowledged his goodbye, replaced the tears with my plastic smile, as the cement on the wall of my heart grew harder. I renewed my determination to stay a few chess moves ahead of anything Bruce or life could throw at me. I couldn't let my emotions out of their cage, or I would be destroyed.

When Bruce didn't come home that night, I took it all in stride. He would live his life, and I would live mine. If this was what he wanted for our marriage, I would play that game. I could do this; I had been through far worse in my life.

Although my personal life seemed to be going down the tubes, professionally I was hitting my stride. All the long hours of practicing pitching started paying off. The culmination of speed, strength, and knowledge all came together in my twenties, which was a great thing considering our level of talent was coinciding with our mushrooming popularity.

Daddy was scheduling seven and up to ten games a week. Even now, I think, *How in the heck did I pitch three games in a day?* I guess we can do anything when we're young. Nevertheless, I must admit, it was grueling!

I did notice a pattern. The first game I was as fresh as a daisy and usually pitched well. The second game coincided at about the time a good nap was due, so everyone's performance dipped, including mine. Our drive to the third game always included a not-so-pleasant speech from Daddy, which insured that the last game of our triple-header would be fantastic…tired or not!

On those days, eating was fast and furious—not too much food to make us sluggish but enough nutrients to give us energy.

The tricky thing was calculating the mileage between cities, making sure our appearance was logistically possible, and then hoping for no detours, hazards, or unforeseen forces that would keep us from reaching each destination on time.

Everyone tried to get comfy, catching a few winks, without getting a kink in our necks because of our weird sleeping positions. As we approached each new ballpark, the girls would freshen our make-up and even re-curl hair with battery-operated curling irons. We replaced our dirty socks with clean ones, along with other pieces of our uniform that looked soiled.

When touring was mostly family, we weren't shy about changing our uniforms as we drove, but when I was the only female player, I requested all guys in the van close their eyes for five minutes…hoping they would, but honestly, I didn't even bat an eye, waiting to see if they all complied. In those hurried moments, all modesty flew out the window.

By the end of the night, there were some mighty potent guy smells exuding from our van. The worst smell, by far, came from Lotta Chatter's red curly wig where the sweat never quite had a chance to dry with the short amount of time between our double- or triple-headers.

Take a guess who was given the unenviable task of re-styling those locks before each new game? Yours truly, of course...now that's a task that kept me from getting a big head or feeling too queenly!

In the 1970s, the CB radio became popular with movies like *Smokey and the Bandit* and *The Dukes of Hazzard*. Truckers all across the United States picked up on this new craze, mostly to warn one another about speed traps.

Daddy loved the concept and ended up buying one; but in actuality, he didn't really need a CB for that purpose, as he could talk his way out of any speeding tickets. One season, we counted fourteen consecutive times he was pulled over, with zero tickets written.

To this day, I can be brought to countless tears of laughter by the re-telling of his incredibly successful "get out of another ticket" speech. The moment Daddy spotted that "black and white," with red flashing light on top, signaling us to pull over, he would shout, "Quick...Pass me a booklet." With a huge smile on his face, Daddy always attacked offensively with the first friendly words, "Hi, Officer, I've got the little ball team from California" simultaneously passing him our little red souvenir booklet that we sold each night. If the officer was diverted and started leafing through the pages, then victory was right around the corner, and it was all over but the shoutin'.

I witnessed salesmanship at its finest over and over again. Daddy could sell ice to an Eskimo. By the end of the conversation, the policeman was usually laughing with my dad and excitedly writing down information to have The Queen and Her Court play in his town the following summer.

As we continued on our way, there was plenty of whoopin' and hollerin' in our van; it was like we had won a tough game and Daddy hit a homerun in the last inning!

One of the most challenging triple-headers took place in Central America where, as luck would have it, my first game started with the discovery of "that time of the month" for me which was very challenging and embarrassing, I must say. I have known girls who have been bed-ridden for days, but this was never an option for any girl in our family.

The challenge was being away from our hotel, my unwillingness to involve others into my predicament, the language barrier, and no Seven-Eleven beckoning me to run in and quickly solve my dilemma.

Let's just say that by the end of the day, I had become very creative with rolls and rolls of toilet paper!

One of the biggest surprises came on a tour in the USA when we rolled up to our second game of an exhausting day of driving through winding roads with slow traffic. At 10:15 p.m., Daddy was resigned that our 9:00 p.m. appearance in Cumberland, Maryland was canceled.

All of our jaws dropped to see the grandstands filled with eager fans patiently awaiting our arrival, determined to see The Queen and Her Court.

To be honest, I pictured myself curled up under cozy blankets in bed within the hour. Instead, we quickly rolled into action, getting started around 10:30 p.m. Everyone was so gracious, appreciative, and forgiving, with some of our favorite fans turned into friends for life that night.

After many seasons of touring, we had experienced so many amazing stories of bad situations turning good that we adopted the motto, *"They can't start without us."* Saying that out loud usually helped to ease the tension as we drove like crazy, trying to reach our destination.

When something unforeseen was happening, we always tried to refer back to our motto, along with referencing our first appearance on Long Island, New York. It felt like a beautiful Sunday afternoon drive as we left our hotel with ample time to spare before we reached our 2:00 p.m. game on Long Island. I loved going to places we'd never been before, taking in the beautiful scenery as we drove. Daddy was especially excited to work with a new sponsor that might open up a new series of bookings. As minutes started clicking away without arriving at our destination, everyone in the van could sense the pressure and stress that was mounting.

We were an hour from our starting time, with no ballpark in sight. The directions that were sent to us, ahead of time, seemed unclear. There were no gas stations around to stop and ask for help, no cell phones invented yet to call anyone, and to make things worse, the road we were on narrowed down to one lane, with the heaviest stop and go traffic imaginable. No one in our van dared to peep a sound as minutes passed by very quickly.

Before the popularity of GPS systems, it was our trusty, U.S. Road Atlas that became my best friend, as getting us from one city to the next was one of my side jobs on tour. Every day, I would ask a local how to get to the best road or highway toward our next destination. I would write out all the intricate twists and turns on paper and hand it to my dad to reference as he drove.

On this Sunday afternoon, I kept that atlas glued to my lap, with my eyes peeled, watching the passing signage, and praying I would spot any sign that would help us get to the ballpark.

About five minutes before our scheduled starting time of 2:00 p.m., our van came to a dead stop, as we were sandwiched between a string of stopped cars as far as we could see in both directions. Daddy was fit to be tied.

Thoroughly exasperated, and mostly to relieve his tension of feeling stuck, he jumped out of the van and walked up to people in their stationery vehicles. We assumed there was a horrific accident or road construction ahead.

After about ten minutes, Daddy headed back to our van. I studied his face as he walked back. It seemed the fresh air had helped him. The anxiety was gone from his countenance…he was even sporting a smile. I thought, *Thank you, Lord.*

His next words floored us all! Indeed, there was a major traffic jam. The long line of cars was waiting to get into the ballpark about a mile ahead to see "The Queen and Her Court"! *You could have knocked our socks off!*

All the anxiety rolled off our shoulders as Daddy breathed life into our motto, *"Well, they can't start without us."*

Word spread like wildfire among the people in the long line of cars. Like playing the telephone game, the message reached the front car that relayed the message…The Queen and Her Court are here.

Out of nowhere, a police escort appeared for us, with instructions to follow them as we zigged and zagged around cars, entering the already packed to capacity ballpark.

Even though we were late, the people cheered when we stepped onto the ball field, and the sponsor was elated and didn't mind one bit that we started one hour late. He needed that time to direct the overflow crowd to grass seats only, ringing the outfield.

Unexpected events like that happened over and over, making me feel invincible on tour—reinforcing confident messages to my brain that hardship would work itself out if I persevered. If things went wrong, we didn't give up (Daddy wouldn't let us.). We adapted and overcame all obstacles.

People always asked, *"What would you do if you were injured"?*

This is what we did. I pitched with a sprained ankle so swollen I had to untie the laces to capacity just to get my foot in the cleat. Eileen continued catching my pitches after the batter reached back, swinging his bat, accidentally breaking a bone in her hand. (At a follow-up medical exam back in California, after our three-month tour, Eileen's doctor pronounced that her hand was healing nicely and, in the next breath, he informed Eileen that she was four and a half months pregnant). Norm broke a large chunk of his front tooth while juggling three bats—He finished his routine, picked up the other half of his tooth in the dirt, and continued making the audience laugh for the next hour and a half.

At eighteen, I heard a loud pop in my shoulder as I fired one of my favorite behind-the-back pitches across the plate. The next day, I could barely move my pitching arm. Daddy stopped at the next emergency hospital, as we had just started the first week of a three-month tour. The doctor said, "She has bursitis, which is caused by repetitive movement and excessive pressure." The good news was that my injury was not serious, and it would heal on its own. The bad news was his prescription for recovery... rest, ice, and aspirin for the pain.

With a lifetime of no medical insurance paid out for any of us, Daddy settled his bill, handing over cold, hard cash. As we walked out the door, I thought, *Thanks for nothing, Doc.* We took him up on the ice and aspirin advice, and I continued pitching in agonizing pain for the next three months. The pain was so severe that I couldn't lift my right hand to my right hip. When I pitched, I created motion by bringing my pitching hand up over my head with the help and strength of my glove hand, and letting it drop to create some kind of centrifugal force before I snapped my wrist.

The doctor was right about one thing. Much to my astonishment, I did heal completely in the off-season. As a cautionary result, I never again threw another pitch behind my back. When I resumed pitching, I continued bringing both hands over my head in my pre-motion, as it did help to increase the speed of my pitch.

To reiterate the answer to the question, "What do you do when you get injured?" Well, we have played with broken bones, casts on, stitches, bruises, and sore muscles galore. With Daddy in charge nothing could keep us from performing.

In twenty-five years of pitching with a blindfold covering my eyes, I was hit by a batted ball only twice—once directly in the stomach where the wind was knocked out of me, and the second time on the leg, where I rapidly recovered the ball in front of me and threw the guy out at first base. I quickly learned how to pitch, whip the blindfold from my face with my pitching hand, while simultaneously flinging my glove hand in front of my face for protection. Our mode of operation was "adapt and overcome". I returned from each tour with an elevated confidence. I could be better...I could do better.

I was sure there was some way my relationship with Bruce would get better. I optimistically thought that when two people hit bottom, there's only one way to go, right? Little did I know...we weren't even close to the bottom.

One of the perks of playing on The Queen and Her Court was purchasing my first car, a fiery red, 351 Cleveland, fastback Mustang. It could go from zero to sixty in the blink of an eye. This knowledge got me my first speeding ticket within the first week of driving it as I peeled out into the intersection the moment the light went from red to green. As I sat slumped in the driver's seat, with tears trickling down my face, the police officer handed me the ticket and stunned me with his best wisdom, "Learn to use your mirrors; I was directly behind you the whole time."

This experience describes how I felt when my relationship with Bruce finally hit bottom—shocked, naïve, spiraling down from zero to sixty as we crashed uncontrollably into a cement wall. *Divorce...I never saw it coming! The black and white car was right behind me, and I didn't recognize the danger signs.*

Returning from tour, Bruce and I quickly fell into our "avoiding each other" patterns, even sleeping in separate rooms. I honestly thought that, one day, Bruce would be sick of all this, and we could reconcile and live happily ever after.

My simple thinking changed with the day I received one too many of the same patterned telephone calls. *"Hello."* ...No answer...Click.

If I would have seen a few more *Lifetime* movies, I might've caught on a little faster that something was rotten in Denmark. I nervously rehearsed my suspicions and prepared my most calm and well thought out inquisition, peppered with non-judgmental, soft words hoping to get down to the truth.

I think it was a relief for Bruce to finally admit that the many "hang up" calls were from a girl who he had been secretly seeing. I'm not sure how I managed to keep an outward serenity and composure, as my heart was collapsing, and my world was crashing down, but I was determined to get more details and knew this conversation would shut down immediately if I became agitated or attacking in any way.

The final straw came when he revealed the name of the other girl who threatened to destroy our marriage. She was a supposed friend of mine! My calculated poise crumbled into a pool of unending tears. It's hard to remember words, but I know Bruce tried to reassure me that this person meant nothing.

As the night wore on, unexpected things happened. We extended forgiveness to each other and determined to move forward and make our marriage work. The jolt of this shocking incident helped to snap us out of our complacency.

Putting each other first meant that Bruce would discontinue any contact with the other person, enabling me to build trust with him again, and I made the hardest telephone call to my dad the following day informing him that Bruce and I were having serious problems that might require me to stop touring.

Words surrounding that nerve-racking call are lost in my memory, but the feelings and intentions of that conversation are still with me. I knew Daddy was completely shocked because there was mostly silence and a loss for words on his end. I finished the conversation letting him know that I needed to do whatever it would take to help our marriage and requested his prayers for Bruce and me.

As it turned out, my dad never brought up anything about that dreaded phone call, which was typical of our communication style.

I was shaking all over when I hung up the phone, but I felt peace that I had done the right thing. I knew there was a possibility I might have to give up my career if I wanted to see change and success in my marriage. Looking back, I see good intentions, but a lack of knowledge, wisdom, and commitment. We needed serious marital counseling, and I should have enlisted his entire family as back-up and support. I don't know if it would've changed things, but by keeping things a secret, which was my pattern; this ended up to be the worst thing I could have done.

It was hard dealing with all the feelings swirling around in my brain. Once again, it seemed as if I wasn't good enough. My thoughts ping-ponged back and forth all day long. I was shaming and putting myself down; this led to infuriation and anger towards Bruce. Outwardly, I painted my plastic and well-rehearsed smile on my face and hoped that "magically healed feelings" would follow suit.

My husband betrayed me; my dad was probably feeling the same thing about me; and, the God that I had vowed to serve was probably disgusted and disappointed with me. I was a ball of nerves with all my pretending. *This girl was one hot mess!*

A few days later, I decided to surprise Bruce (or maybe check up on him) at his place of work. As I rounded the corner, I saw "the girl" standing by Bruce's car…putting something under his windshield wiper.

She recognized my fiery red mustang and made a beeline to her car for a quick getaway. I pulled up to Bruce's car, hoping to recover her little note, discovering that whatever she had intended to leave was no longer there.

What happened next still baffles me to this day because it seems like the farthest version of my non-confrontational character, but I guess it's true, *"Hell hath no fury like a woman scorned."*

I flew back to my car and floored the accelerator. My mind was soaring with rage. I was going to catch up and let her have every ounce of suppressed wrath I held inside. It seemed like I was in an out-of-body experience and suddenly became Steve McQueen driving his 1968 Ford Mustang in the famous chase scene from the movie, *Bullitt*. I had no doubt that I could catch her.

Sure enough, my Mustang was gaining ground as we both headed toward the ramp leading us onto the freeway. By now, I could see that she had no intention of pulling her car over and facing the music, so I wasn't sure how this pursuit was going to end.

I just wanted her to know that I thought she was despicable for betraying our friendship and hurting my heart to the core. I laugh to think of this now, but for a split second, my plan was to pull up beside her, so she could see my face and then give her car a little nudge to knock her to the side of the road...just like I had seen so many times in the movies.

Fortunately, my sanity returned, as I couldn't envision denting my prized Mustang. *How would I possibly explain that to people?* I hit my brakes, letting her speed away like a scared little rabbit. I never did confront her, but a couple years later, she came to one of our games and my dad and everyone treated her like a cherished friend, which bugged me. I couldn't blame them...they didn't know a thing. Even though I forgave her, I acted as if she was invisible all night. That was the best I could do under the circumstances as she certainly was no friend of mine.

After that incident, my heart turned cold toward Bruce. I remember thinking, *I must have been nuts to make that terrifying call to Daddy and think that I would actually give up my career for this person whom I would never be able to trust.*

All bets were off, which put us right back to ground zero. A piece of my heart died that day, and my emotions flat-lined into a state of numbness. We both wanted out but Bruce assured me over and over that he would never file for divorce, not wanting the stigma of being the first one in his family to do such a thing. I knew I would never initiate a divorce as the guilt and shame of such an act seemed like an "unpardonable sin" before God and man.

It was ironic that living with such deep-seeded bitterness, anger, and un-forgiveness was okay with me, but divorce was unacceptable. I guess it was all about pretending and appearances—like I thought that keeping the letter of the law would make me more pleasing to God—it was absurd and incongruous thinking!

Bruce and I resorted back to our hellish existence and then I escaped to another tour where life was diverted into a world where people cheered, adored, and admired me every night. It was a three-month reprieve from the daily reminders that I was a failure in my marriage.

I guess, in my pretend world, I thought this lifestyle would continue on indefinitely, but God intervened that following fall and spring and said, *"Enough is enough with Rosie's pharisaical life."*

I was about to discover how real God's faithfulness and commitment was to me. He cares so deeply about His children that He will allow and do whatever it takes to get us back on track in our relationship with Him. It is like God said, "Rosie, I love you so much that I'm going to put you in My Love Box."

When I first encountered God's Love Box, I had a different name for it—The Torture Chamber. Only as I began to see God for who He really was, did I change the name. It felt like all my trials and problems were intensifying, with four un-penetrable walls closing in on me, and no foreseeable way to get around or through those cement walls.

King David describes my feelings in Psalm 139:5—"You hem me in…behind and before; You have laid Your hand upon me. Such knowledge is too wonderful for me, too lofty for me to attain."

Unlike King David, my inability to run from the piercing eye of God's Spirit was anything but wonderful for me at the time. To answer my desperate cries to God for an intimacy that would never run dry would require a breaking of the fallow ground in my heart. He needed me to be still and cease all my striving, so I could hear and see and know Him.

I felt trapped with nowhere to run, and claustrophobic in my spiritual straight jacket as I kicked at the four walls closing in on me. The timing was right. I was on the verge of a complete collapse when lo and behold, I was forced to discover the only way out. There was an opening at the top of His Love Box…I was compelled to look up.

CHAPTER 17

HEALING BEGINS

*"I sought the Lord, and He answered me; He delivered me from
all my fears. Those who look to Him are radiant; their faces are
never covered with shame. The Lord is near to those who have
a broken heart, and saves such as have a contrite spirit."*

PSALM 34: 4,5,18

om sat by my side as I lay curled up on the couch, clutching my head with both hands and writhing in pain. I pleaded, *"Please help me, Momma, my head feels like it's going to explode."* I can't remember the prescribed medication that I had just taken, but it definitely was having no effect. In addition to the bomb that had just exploded inside my head, I was baffled by the clusters of a reddish rash that was marching all over my body, appearing out of nowhere.

Because I was rarely sick, I was genuinely mystified by what was happening to me; but was soon to discover another life lesson coming my way. All the pain, isolation, secrets, and stuffed emotions were screaming, *"No more, no more,"* as they manifested externally throughout my entire body.

Touring was over for the season, and it felt like the four gray walls of winter were closing in on me, with hours and hours of unwanted idleness and solitude, partnered with all my depressing thoughts that my brain would not turn off. For relief, I would obsess on ridiculous plans of escape from life. Even now, it sounds crazy to put such scenarios down on paper.

A constant picture that brought temporary feelings of comfort and peace was one of me curled up in a fetal position in a small, dark, coat closet as you entered my mom's house. These irrational thoughts seemed almost feasible at the time, solving my desire to feel safe, hidden, and my need to disappear off the face of the earth. It felt like I was losing my mind and my grip on reality.

Mom and Eileen did their best to try and talk me down from my emotional ledge with their words of support and love, but there was no way to soothe or comfort my raging nerves or bring normalcy back into a life that was anything but normal.

Through a barrage of constant flowing tears, I begged and pleaded with God for help. At the time it seemed as if my petitions to heaven were falling on deaf ears and bouncing back to me in a loud accusing voice that said, *"You've made such a mess of your life...no one can help you or love you."*

The real truth was God had never left my side. He anguished over every tear that I cried and longed for me to know this deeper, more intimate love that He felt for me. I discovered that He will not usurp His power and authority over His children, but allows each one of us the freedom to choose to love and come to Him. If God removes the choice, then the chance for an authentic, two-way love relationship is taken away also. So He patiently waited until I ran out of chess moves.

Even though I could not see it, from God's point of view, the groundwork for change in my life was colliding with the two key factors necessary for intimacy with God—receptivity and attentiveness.

I was "all ears" and completely open and vulnerable to anyone who could bring real peace to my soul. The timing was right. I was in His "Love Box" and didn't even know it.

I guess my family could see I was going from bad to worse. Unsure of exactly what to do, Eileen came to my house, helped me pack a bag, and offered a place to stay with her and Gregg for a while. There were no objections from me. I was tired, worn, and without any opinions as to what could possibly get my life back on track.

With few words, and in a zombie-like state of mind, I followed Eileen closely to her car and hopped in the passenger seat. As we were driving to her house, a sense of panic began overtaking me. At first, I heard a quiet voice in my brain say, *Just open the door and jump; then everything will be okay.* As the instructions repeated over and over in my head, getting louder and more authoritative each time, I was seized with fear. I was contemplating the possibilities of actually complying with this unknown entity.

In a moment of clarity, I told Eileen exactly what was happening to me. I was stunned by what happened next. She started praying out loud as she drove, *"I command you Satan, in the name of Jesus, to leave my sister alone."*

It was like she waved a magic wand over me. Immediately, the voice stopped, and the most incredible peace permeated my entire body. For the first time in a very long while, I wasn't sure how, but I thought, *everything will be okay.*

Because time has afforded me the opportunity of retelling the happenings of the next three or four months; in retrospect, I have since named and refer to this season of my life as *"The Best of Times and The Worst of Times."* It seemed that the darkness always came before the dawn.

During the first few weeks, it felt unbearable to even make it through a twenty-four-hour day. If you've ever had first-hand experience with such a task, you will understand the tormenting agony of the soul trying to endure the tick, tick, ticking of each hellish second that creeps painstakingly slow, forming the next minute. Sixty of those intolerable minutes have to pass to form an hour, with no relief in sight.

As day would turn into night, I was hoping for a reprieve from all the emotional pain that took center stage in my brain, but sleep eluded me. All my usual diversions, like eating, sleeping, shopping, and sports took the last train for the coast, leaving me alone to face the reality of this mess of a life I was living. I couldn't even turn on the television without something or someone on the screen triggering discouragement and despairing thoughts that would send me further into my hopeless pit. The stifled tears and emotions of the last twenty years burst through to my exterior like the unrelenting waves of the ocean.

It is difficult to describe in words the state of my condition, but when I think about it, I see an image of a little girl whose body is curled up into a little ball, with her knees pulled to her chest...rocking back and forth...weeping...numb. It felt like I was having a nervous breakdown.

Remembering the unenviable task that Gregg and Eileen took on, trying to help me cope and recover, always motivates me to "pay it forward," praying, encouraging, and pointing others to the God of all comfort and hope...the only One who can restore, redeem, give peace beyond understanding. God is in the business of healing and binding up the broken-hearted.

Basically, Gregg and Eileen were my babysitters. I stuck close to Eileen and cried non-stop. I'm sure I was way more than either of them could handle at times, but they never made me feel anything but unconditionally loved and taken care of. Their example was a beautiful model of pairing grace and truth into my broken life.

The first few weeks, I was desperate for relief of any kind and would have given my right arm for a few hours of sleep to interrupt the voices screaming in my head. Eileen suggested that I try a sleeping pill to get me through the night, but it didn't even faze me, so I took a second one—that did the trick and I was out like a light.

The next day I woke up around noon and instead of feeling refreshed, I felt groggy. I offered to vacuum and felt weak and lethargic as I pushed the machine back and forth over the carpet. My mind and body moved in slow motion all day long, and even though my nerves subsided, I had to work hard to process thoughts. I hated the way I felt.

As day turned to night, the effects of the sleeping pill finally wore off. Eileen and Gregg headed off to bed, and I reclined on their couch, wide-eyed, staring at the ceiling, and fully aware that I was destined to experience another sleepless night with only my loathsome, self-defeating thoughts cuddling up beside me, keeping me company.

With no one else to talk to, my thoughts became words spoken out loud and directed to God. I was surprised my words came out so angry, telling Him exactly how I felt. *"I hate the way sleeping pills make me feel, but I've asked and begged You to help me sleep, and You won't help me."*

Deep inside, I figured that God was as disgusted with me as I was and that's why I was getting the silent treatment...but with nowhere else to turn, He was my last hope.

With teeth clenched, I angrily cried, *"If this is what You want, then this is what You get...I won't sleep...I'll stay up all night with You...But I will never take another sleeping pill."*

I grabbed my Bible and began reading...and reading...and reading. *I guess I showed Him.*

Over the years, I had built up so many insecurities, misconceptions, and questions with no answers about my life, and my relationships with people and God. As I read, I was surprised to discover how the Bible uncovered some of these mysteries.

The Psalms were a soothing balm to my open wounds. I loved the way David talked to God, with an authentic openness and honesty that was enviable. David's words bounced from faith to fear, from love and confidence to anger and retaliation.

I felt a twinge of hope for my own life as I realized this anointed and beloved king was not the picture of perfection that I had imagined, and God really loved David even after he screwed up big time…even referencing him as "a man after God's own heart."

It seemed like words were jumping off the pages, directly into my dead heart. As I read the New Testament, I couldn't believe how much Jesus loved people. He went out of his way to love on sinners—now that really caught my attention.

Somewhere during the night, there was a transfer in my brain. The stories of love that Jesus showered on those sinners became personal love messages meant for me. In fact, He seemed partial, going out of His way to have contact with down-and-outers, healing the lost, the hurting, the despised, the sick and lowly, the brokenhearted, the imperfect.

Many verses from Romans jumped out at me. Whether people acknowledged it or not, we were all sinners in need of rescuing…that's why God came down from His throne to Earth. *Wow! All humans, including me, were in the same boat, sinners in need of a savior.* Somehow that brought me incredible comfort to realize that I was the same as everyone else, not some disgusting shameful wretch that was without hope. At this point, the main difference was no one needed to smash a two by four over my head to get me to see my need for a savior. My imperfection and sinfulness taunted me day and night, and felt like a red neon light splashed across my forehead for the entire world to see— Disgusting Failure Approaching.

I read Romans 5:8 over and over. "God demonstrates His love for us, in that while we were still sinners, Christ died for us." *Could this be true? He loved and even died for the very worst version of myself in this life.* The implications of such a statement were life changing for me. My need for perfection to earn His love and acceptance started to melt away into a pool of His promised love as I realized Jesus loved me the exact same, no more or no less…at my best or at my worst.

A strange thing was happening as I read into the wee hours of the night. The minutes that were previously creeping by at such an agonizingly slow pace, now were flying by, along with a sense of hope that seemed to resurface magically out of nowhere. This happened as I began to believe that the God of this universe really loved me just as I was, and He was desperately pursuing me.

All my doubts, fears, haunting and condemning self-talk quieted in my brain as I started accepting the truth of God's overwhelming and unending love for me.

As the sun started peeking its head above the horizon, I spoke these words softly out loud to God, *"If you still really want me, just as I am, you can have me. I'm yours."* Then I closed my eyes and drifted off into a peaceful sleep.

I can't say that when I woke the next morning, I was instantaneously healed and shouting a victory cry; but in the midst of thousands of tears and disparaging, caustic nerves that ruled my life over the next three months, a sense of hope made an appearance a little stronger during the course of each new day.

Not to my credit, but more as survival, I was mercifully thrown into a number of things during this season of my life which resulted in a major transformation. The first being my "love sessions" with the Lord each night because I couldn't sleep. Although this time started off a little rough, it very quickly became my most cherished time of each day...a memory that I now look back on as one of the most special times in my life.

Fortunately, this healing period occurred during my off-season from softball, so I had the opportunity to pull away from the things of this world and focus exclusively on Jesus' life-giving words of truth. For months, I was so nervous and insecure that I never left Gregg and Eileen's home without them...*God bless them both!* Whatever Eileen did during the day, I imitated. Wherever she went, I was the shadow that stuck close to her side. There were invaluable gold nuggets of wisdom that I gleaned each day as I silently observed and walked in my sister's shoes. Gregg and Eileen had an invisible, but very tangible peace and joy that permeated their lives and filled up their whole house. Once I had a taste of this new life, I knew that was exactly what I needed and wanted for my own life.

During any kind of healing process, God uses His people to be His mouth, hands, and feet; and I was given two of the best in His service, Gregg and Eileen. At the time, they were leaders of the youth group at their church, so we all headed to church at least a couple nights a week together.

I recall one very special Wednesday night youth group meeting that profoundly impacted my life that evening and for years to come. I sat in the audience of a spattering of about twelve to fifteen kids and adults as a twenty-four-year-old guy, with a thick beard and a massive headful of curly locks was introduced and casually made his way over to the piano.

Before Keith Green sang his first song, I imagined that he was a little disappointed there weren't even enough bodies in the room to start a good catfight. The embarrassment I felt for him quickly disappeared as he began pounding the piano keys and singing the songs that were soon to be released on his first Christian album, *For Him Who Has Ears to Hear.*

A beautiful filling of God's presence permeated the room, and I felt a strange sense that God was speaking directly to me. The Holy Spirit was the conduit from Keith's mouth to my broken heart. I was transfixed by each word that proclaimed God's complete devotion and everlasting love for me with song's like "You Put This Love in My Heart."

I wept when I heard the words of "Your Love Broke Through."

> "Like a foolish dreamer, trying to build a highway to
> the sky.
> All my hopes would come tumbling down, and I never
> knew just why.
> Until today, when you pulled away the clouds that hung
> like curtains on my eyes.
> Well I've been blind all these wasted years and I thought

I was so wise.

But then you took me by surprise.

Like waking up from the longest dream, how real
it seemed

Until Your love broke through.

I've been lost in a fantasy that blinded me...

Until Your love broke through.

That's exactly how I felt. It was a surprising awakening of God's love breaking through for me. It was there all along, but somehow, in the past, I just couldn't see it or believe it. I sensed a new strength and power like never before, and I knew it was because of God's unchanging and unfailing love toward me. I still had massive problems to work through; and I didn't know what my future would look like, but my deepest desire from that day forward was to devote the rest of my life to Jesus.

Through this night and my "all night love sessions with Jesus," I began realizing that I had eliminated a very important five-letter word from my vocabulary...GRACE.

This undeserved gift of favor was extended to me, and all of humanity, by way of Jesus. It was highlighted throughout His Word and very essential if I was to have the intimate relationship with God that He intended and that my soul had so desperately craved.

God loved me for who I was—His child—and not for what I could do for Him. It seemed to be spelled out so clearly in the Bible...I couldn't believe I had missed it.

Later that night, I discovered it wasn't only a special night for me. The Holy Spirit moved in a dynamic way touching many others also.

Unbelievably, a couple years later, about eight of us drove to the Anaheim Convention Center hoping to experience that powerful night once again, hearing the on-fire evangelist and musician, Keith Green.

With a 7,500-seating capacity, we were turned away, along with hundreds, as it was already packed!

Sometimes you just can't duplicate the special appointments that God sets up for each of our lives!

To honor the impact that Keith and his wife, Melody Green, had on our lives and so many thousands, Gregg and Eileen even named their second daughter Melody.

As for me, and I'm sure, countless others, their music and ministry greatly inspired and encouraged me to continue my walk toward Jesus.

As my emotional stability started normalizing, and I began making my way back to the land of the living, it was still frightening for me to go anywhere alone without crying or feeling like I was going to have a panic attack.

To solve the dilemma of negative thoughts overriding the reality of God's truth, I bought an ever-popular, seventies, eight-track of Keith Green's first album and blasted it, singing at the top of my lungs as I drove.

I did not have any really meaningful conversations with my dad during my recovery and stay at Gregg and Eileen's, but he did secure a divorce lawyer for me and ended up handling almost all meetings and negotiations with both the lawyer and Bruce. While he did this, I numbly went through the motions of ending my marriage. It was all very sad, so I greatly appreciated his help as I spent as little time as possible letting my mind drift in the unsolvable death of my dream.

As spring training for the upcoming season was fast approaching, I was feeling a new strength and more confidence about my life, but there was an overwhelming discontent concerning my purpose and direction. Every day I would have talks with Eileen about my dread and lack of motivation for playing softball another season. My heart was just not in it.

I was passionate about the "Giver of Life," and I wanted to help and encourage others to know Him. My conversations were circular and exhausting, as I knew, in the end, I would have to play softball. *What was the point…just to make a little money and win another ball game?*

Day and night, I prayed and prayed. *"God, you know my heart, I want to share with others the same hope you gave to me, but my path is already set. How can I do this when You know another softball tour is already booked?"*

Not long after I started diligently praying, God replied, as He laid out His answer to me in the middle of the night. The miraculous thing in that sentence is…He gave "ME" the idea directly.

To this day, I find it difficult to come up with creative or original ideas and solutions, but I am a pro at hanging with and following innovative people, duplicating their success and ideas, incorporating the genius I see into my own life. I say that to let you know how miraculous this happening was for me.

At first, it began in a dream. I stood in the middle of a ball field dressed in my Queen and Her Court uniform before a large crowd of people with a microphone in my hand. I felt a great compassion and urgency to share the love of God, but I was unsure of my words. I said to God, *"What should I say?"*

He said two things to me, and I began speaking to the audience. In my dream, the words flowed effortlessly, and I was so excited, knowing I could do this at every game, without the usual selective editing of newspaper and television interviewers each night.

Somehow, I roused myself enough to drowsily reach for a pad and pencil on the floor, beside the couch, and write what I heard Him say. As vivid as everything seemed, I knew I would probably forget everything with the coming of dawn. When my eyes popped open the next morning, I excitedly remembered my dream and knew God had given me my answer. Sure enough, I couldn't remember what He told me. I immediately grabbed the pad, where I was thankful to see two badly scrawled phrases…"Keep it simple" and "Speak the name of Jesus."

I spent almost the entirety of that day on my knees asking God to speak to me about those two phrases, giving me the right words. I so desperately wanted to share the unconditional love that God had imparted to me with the thousands of people I performed in front of every night. I spent most of my life dedicated to perfecting the art of softball, and more specifically pitching; and after all I had gone through during the last months, it felt like my existence would no longer have enough purpose and fulfillment without something more. My life seemed like vanity, unless I could leave the audience with a piece of lasting truth that could possibly change their lives on this earth and the life to come.

The results included the first and simplest verse of scripture that I had ever memorized, John 3:16. This verse states that God loved everyone in the world so much that He sent His only Son, so that anyone who would believe in Him would not perish, but have eternal life.

Within a literal one minute of introduction, I gave each person in the audience a sneak peek into the real Rosie Black, letting them know that I was here to share my talents and abilities for God's glory, thankful to my Lord and Savior, Jesus Christ.

The next time I saw my dad, I explained my new desire and vision, which involved changing the words during my introduction. I was so thankful that he was onboard one hundred percent. Unlike most of the uncertainty of our interaction and communication over the years, I wasn't even nervous. Instead, I approached Daddy with a confidence and surety that God was going before me.

In practice, my attitude about playing softball flipped one hundred and eighty degrees. I approached the upcoming softball season with a new freshness and determination to be the best athlete that I could be, knowing that every aspect of my life would be a representative of Jesus Christ.

I felt restored...brand new...purposeful. I couldn't wait to see what the Lord had planned for the upcoming tour and the next chapter in my life!

CHAPTER 18

SECOND CHANCES

"I waited patiently for the Lord; and He inclined to me, and heard my cry. He also brought me up out of a horrible pit, out of the miry clay, and set my feet upon a rock, and established my steps. He has put a new song in my mouth—Praise to our God; Many will see it and fear, and will trust in the Lord."

PSALM 40:1-3

I t seemed like the upcoming tour was destined to be one of my favorites and, in retrospect, it was.

Although some of my circumstances had definitely changed, the real paradigm shift took place in my heart and mind. I had a new perspective. I saw life and people with a heart that was loved...The King of the universe tapped me on the shoulder with His scepter and pronounced me His own, forgiven, unconditionally loved, and accepted.

It seemed unbelievable to me that just a few months earlier, I felt like the prodigal son returning home as a failure, with eyes cast down and slumped shoulders. I was expecting and deserving the worst only hoping to be connected once again to my heavenly Father. Beyond all belief, God lifted me out of the ashes, putting a smile on my face and a joy in my heart that permeated from the inside out. With one touch of the Master's hand, my life had been reformatted and given a boosted dose of self-esteem, along with a new zest and purpose for playing softball.

Routinely, during our pre-season in California, Daddy arranged non-paying performances in men and women's prisons as well as many juvenile halls. We always felt welcomed and greatly appreciated as a much-needed distraction from the daily grind and routines of life inside these institutions.

The advance preparation to perform behind bars was quite detailed, with extensive background checks on each of us. At first, it seemed kind of scary when we were young teenagers, passing from the front offices to completely secured and locked holding stations, being thoroughly frisked by somber guards who were determined not to leave any stones unturned. Every purposed piece of equipment that we brought in was scrutinized carefully before we could be moved to the next holding station. Everything that seemed questionable, like our metal cleats and the bolts and hammer we used to secure our portable pitching mound and bases, resulted in lengthy discussions of safety before we were allowed to move forward into the next chamber.

I understood and appreciated their need to be painstakingly meticulous, but in the beginning, it's like they knew something we didn't know, with the possibilities of looming danger right around the corner, getting my adrenaline pumping sky high before I even threw the first pitch.

Thankfully, there were only a couple of potentially serious incidents and a handful of stories we laugh about from time to time...like the soon-to-be-bride who was part of our entourage. She was so anxious about her surroundings while watching us perform inside the penitentiary, that she continuously picked and flicked at her engagement ring through the whole game. A few hours later, she discovered her diamond dislodged from its foundation, to be lost forever.

As I have mentioned before, Norm's role of Lotta Chatter always had such an overwhelmingly positive response everywhere we played—prisons were no exception. He always succeeded in bringing fun and levity to even the most desperate and downcast.

However, we all tried to convince Norm to tone down the antics a bit the night we entered a maximum-security prison somewhere in the Midwest. Personally, I felt there was a great chance he would place himself in serious danger if one of the inmates took his humor the wrong way.

As we stepped onto the softball field, within the prison compound, we were alarmed to see a large section of inmates who would be viewing the night's festivities behind a section of caged-in seating on the third base side, with open seating in typical looking bleachers on the first base side for the more trusted prisoners.

Naturally, Norm couldn't contain himself and simply gave his funniest and best, which usually involved zeroing in on one or two distinct players of the opposing team each night. This particular night, Norm directed his running stream of jokes and pranks toward the catcher, who was one of the all-star prisoners chosen to be our opponent.

At first, I couldn't tell if it was my imagination, but I thought the catcher bristled a little as Norm's character, Lotta Chatter, pranked him, while the inmates roared with laughter. Fortunately, as the night wore on, Lotta won his new catcher friend over, and it's like they danced perfectly together, creating comical routines that made for an extremely fun and entertaining night for everyone.

In some instances, ignorance is definitely bliss. As the director of prison activities led us out, he thanked us for coming and expressed his astonishment concerning the amusing interaction between Norm and the catcher.

He said, "I thought there was going to be big trouble for sure. No one here messes with him, because he's a tuff-as-nails hothead, who takes his softball very seriously." Our jaws dropped when he proceeded to tell us that our new catcher friend was a no-nonsense guy who was one of the roughest guys around, serving his sentence for a double murder conviction.

We were speechless and so thankful that all went according to the best-case scenario. That night, underlying sighs of relief passed over each one of us as the guard locked the last gate on our way back to freedom.

Just like clockwork, the opener of our new season would be at Los Padrinos Juvenile Hall about twenty minutes from my home in Lakewood, where the only other near mishap behind secured walls occurred. Because we had been appearing there each spring for a number of years in a row, without incident, the officials knew and trusted us, easing up on some of their rigid procedures. This created a more relaxed atmosphere for all concerned. I guess this lenient ambiance set off signals for a teenage boy who must have been desperate to get back to the outside world. Unbeknown to us, this enterprising young lad tried to make his daring escape by hitching a ride as we exited the juvenile hall after the game. He was holding on for dear life, hidden underneath our van.

As it turned out, he was seconds away from a clean getaway when ear-piercing alarms and whistles started blaring throughout the entire compound just as we pulled up to the last bolted steel gate before our return to the outside.

We had no idea what was happening as guards searched our entire van. Within minutes, they discovered the extra passenger underneath, marching him away as fast as possible. We were stunned! After a few suspicious looks directed our way and some routine questions, we were allowed to leave the premises, thankful to live our lives unencumbered by such confinement and restrictions.

Routinely, our game at Los Padrinos Juvenile Hall was followed by our other annual, local appearance the following weekend at the men's federal prison on Terminal Island, in San Pedro.

These pre-season games were our dress rehearsals before a live audience, getting a good idea how ready we were and what still needed to be worked on. Although we wanted to perform perfectly, it was comforting to know if a ball was dropped or a routine went off track, we wouldn't have to relive our failures again by viewing our mistakes on the sport's segment of the nightly news.

It was like the slogan, "What happens in Vegas, stays in Vegas." Good or bad, whatever happened stayed within the confines of those prison walls.

The morning of our Terminal Island game, I woke up so excited because I knew on this visit, I would be sharing more than skills and entertainment with them. My desire was to leave these men with words of life-changing hope for their future.

To be honest, I felt little twinges of nerves and fear. Talking to teenagers the week before seemed way easier than looking out into the faces of hardened criminals, so I knew I needed to have some alone time with God.

For the prior couple of weeks, my Bible reading had been in Isaiah and Jeremiah. It gave me courage when I read how God called Jeremiah to be a prophet. So I re-read Jeremiah 1:4-8 (Living). The words seemed to resonate in my soul.

The Lord said to me, "I knew you before you were formed within your mother's womb; before you were born I sanctified you and appointed you as my spokesman to the world."

"O Lord God," I said, "I can't do that! I'm far too young! I'm only a youth!"

"Don't say that," He replied, "for you will go wherever I send you and speak whatever I tell you to. And don't be afraid of the people, for I, the Lord, will be with you and see you through."

Then He touched my mouth and said, "See I have put my words in your mouth! Today your work begins, to warn the nations and the kingdoms of the world. In accord with my words spoken through your mouth I will tear down some and destroy them, and plant others and nurture them and make them strong and great."

After reading those passages, I felt the strength of the Lord surging through my veins again. I knew beyond any shadow of a doubt that He had given me a simple message to share and now He was confirming and renewing my courage and confidence to have boldness to look assuredly into the faces of these men, who needed exactly what Jesus died to give them.

The Lord continued to speak to me through His word, giving me what I considered my mission statement, not only for this season, but every year to come.

His word came from the first verse in Isaiah, chapter 61. "The Spirit of the Lord God is upon me, because the Lord has anointed me to bring good news to the suffering and afflicted. He has sent me to comfort the broken-hearted, to announce liberty to captives and to open the eyes of the blind." Another version restated the last line like this: "To proclaim liberty to the captives, and the opening of the prison to those who are bound."

After reading that, I sat quietly before the Lord with a big smile on my face. I knew those words were especially apropos for that day, because I was literally speaking to men bound and restricted within the impenetrable walls of prison. Little did they know that there was a deeper meaning that cut straight to my heart.

God had just rescued me from my prison of darkness and despair, and it had nothing to do with being locked up behind the steel bars of an actual prison cell. The simple message God had given me to share was meant for all those looking for the real pathway to freedom, for those who had ears to hear.

It took us ten minutes to walk through the prison yard, making our way to the softball field, which was a section of a dirt infield and grassy outfield that jetted out and was surrounded by the Pacific Ocean on the far end of the prison compound.

All eyes were on us, as surrounding activities ceased. We were met with smiles, waves from second story cells, whistles, catcalls, blank stares, and "glad-to-have-you-back" greetings from the guys as word spread quickly that The Queen and Her Court had arrived.

In contrast to the juvenile hall, it was not mandatory for prisoners to attend the ball game; nevertheless, it took only a few minutes before we had an army of onlookers following us to the ball field. As we walked, I prayed silently, asking God to bring all those He intended to hear the good news.

The day's events went off without a hitch, including the predictable and anticipated shouts that occurred each year from prisoners volunteering to retrieve every foul ball that was hit over the tall prison fence on the third base side. However, these balls were lost forever into the Pacific blue waters of freedom. A roar of laughter always followed these facetiously helpful and accommodating shouts from the men.

As a result of sharing Jesus, there were a handful of men who approached me and my teammates following the game. They let us know how excited they were to hear that we were Christians too. It was amazing to see how we felt so united with these believers, encouraging and praying for them, until it was time to leave.

The one unbelievable thing, (I can only attribute this to the Holy Spirit), is that from this game on until I retired, every time I spoke into the microphone before each game, proclaiming and honoring Jesus, with only one or two exceptions that I can remember, a supernatural hush would fall over the audience.

When I think back about this, I still shake my head in disbelief. It was uncanny how all loud chatter and commotion would cease from every man, woman, and child the moment I shared John 3:16.

Many nights, it seemed incredibly unnerving. As I spoke to thousands in attendance in packed stadiums, I thought, *It's so quiet I can hear a pin drop.* After I finished and handed the microphone off to others, the loud buzzing of chatter started up again. My only explanation is that this was a display of the power of God.

All summer long, my passion for the Lord revitalized me. Long after our game was over, I delighted in talking with fans until a groundskeeper flicked the lights on and off, graciously hinting that it was time to go.

When we first started touring, we got requests for autographs on all sorts of weird things, including money and body parts. Initially, we said yes! It felt exciting and rock-starish, but later we had to set some boundaries in case it was illegal or just plain creepy and uncomfortable.

On this tour, if someone wanted an autograph, but didn't have our team picture, booklet, or other sports memorabilia, I pulled one of my favorite tracts about God from my coat pocket, signed it, and told them to read it when they had the chance.

Because we usually played a game in a new city every night, moving somewhere else the next night, I felt like my calling was one of planting the seeds of God's word, praying someone else would water it, and counting on God to make it grow.

Following our games, I headed back to my hotel room to wind down from the night's festivities by spending time alone with God. If I was still amped up, I would walk the halls, (usually everyone was asleep by this time) praying as I passed each room for whoever was in there, and sometimes sliding a gospel tract under their doors.

My faith was soaring. I didn't have to know each person I was praying for, because I knew God knew them inside and out. I believed He would visit each room by the power of the Holy Spirit and touch their lives as I prayed, according to His own plans.

It seemed so dreamlike to me that a few short months ago, I desperately wanted to avoid life, sleeping as much as I could, using this as a strategy for survival. Now I was living an adventure, praying everyone could know the love, joy, peace, and freedom that was available for the asking. Sleep was only a necessity.

Every once in a while, God encouraged me with a letter or verbal exchange from someone who received or rededicated their life to Him as a result of hearing the Good News at our game. As time went on, more people started bringing their family and friends to our games, knowing that there was no way they would get them to set foot in any kind of church. Additionally, I was truly blessed to hear many say that because I was bold enough to share my faith on the softball diamond, it encouraged other believers to do likewise…in whatever areas God had gifted them.

On the flip side, every once in a while, my dad would receive a few negative comments complaining about the offensive "preaching." That is when I first pulled out the ole stopwatch and timed the "long" (*being sarcastic*), one-minute sermon that so infuriated our onlooker.

I always tried to respond to every piece of correspondence, good or bad, with honesty and a willingness to "agree to disagree." By now, I was well aware that no matter how perfectly I pitched or what I said or didn't say, I was never going to please everyone. Besides, every time I flipped on the television or read a magazine, many high-profile celebrities were referencing Buddha or Mohammad, even changing their names…so why couldn't I share my beliefs? Honestly, I didn't really take it personal as the Word of God even describes Jesus as a stumbling block and a rock of offense to those who rejected Him.

There were a handful of times Daddy came to me before the game and let me know that our sponsor requested that I eliminate my testimony before their game. I didn't take this appeal lightly, but prayed all afternoon until I felt I had God's direction on the matter.

I deviated only once that I remember. I began praying many weeks in advance, when I saw our schedule, making note that we were playing at an all-Jewish community center in the Bronx, New York. My intent was not to purposely offend, but to share God's love. As a result, I decided to eliminate John 3:16 from the New Testament and instead, I chose a scripture from the Old Testament…Proverbs 8:17. "I love those who love Me, and those who diligently seek Me will find Me."

I wanted everyone listening to know that, above all, God loved them, and was waiting to have a relationship with anyone who would pursue Him in sincerity and truth.

I certainly don't know all that God was doing behind the scenes, but I could sense more was happening in the spiritual realm than I could detect. Before the game even started, there was a huge commotion on the first base side. The next thing I saw were paramedics…a man died.

The mood was somber as I shared my faith on the microphone and like normal, except for my voice, the silence throughout the crowd was deafening. Following our game, I prayed that God would make Himself known and comfort all the people who were greatly impacted by the night's unexpected happenings.

For years, one of my favorite places to play each year was on the army base at Fort Dix, New Jersey. It became a greatly anticipated destination, as we rolled up to the guard post in our maxi-van.

Following an identification check, they issued us a visitor's pass and directed us to the motel where we got to stay right on the base. It wasn't long before we knew our way around; it was a well-organized little city within a city, with a hospital, restaurants, PX, etcetera. Everything we needed seemed within walking distance, including a beautifully manicured softball field with bleachers that could seat six thousand spectators.

Times have changed but years back, it was especially exciting for the female members of our team to perform at Fort Dix because the six thousand seating capacity was filled with ninety-nine percent male recruits. It was like going on a USO tour. Every small gesture, smile, or talent from Eileen or me brought thunderous applause from the many male onlookers who zeroed in on our every move.

I cannot speak of Fort Dix without sharing one of The Queen and Her Court's "timeless classics." Over the years, Eileen's retelling of this story, which she experienced firsthand, has since turned into a comic routine that never fails to leave us grabbing our stomachs in fits of laughter and tears rolling down our cheeks. This might be one of those had-to-be-there stories, but the following is directly from Eileen..

> *"Before the inning started, I was standing behind home plate talking to the umpire. Out of nowhere, I felt an explosion of excruciating pain coming from the female region of my body, six inches below my belly button.*
>
> *My pain coincided with a loud crack that echoed through the atmosphere, followed by all six thousand mostly male fans letting loose in perfect unison, with an audible agonizing groan, as they witnessed what I was still trying to process.*
>
> *Dazed…I couldn't figure out what happened. I thought, since we were on an army base, maybe we were being attacked, or perhaps, a low-flying airplane has hit me. [That's my favorite line.]*
>
> *After a few seconds, I was shocked to see a softball trickling a few feet away from my body. The mystery was solved as I looked straight ahead and saw the sick look on Rosie's face.*
>
> *Somehow, she thought we were ready to start, pulling her blindfold down over her eyes and firing one of her blazing fastballs as a perfect strike!*
>
> *As bad as it hurt, I knew this was one injury I was going to have to shake off, as rubbing the pain away from this precarious spot was not an option with so many eyes watching.*

My sister took it like a champ. For some unexplainable reason, I pulled that blindfold down, thinking we were ready to go. I was in my "pitcher's zone" and fired away.

Even though I never did that to Eileen again; over the years, this story did provide proof positive to skeptics who were certain that the reason I could throw strikes was because I could see through my blindfold. Not a chance!

Besides this unforgettable happening, it seemed like everything was always spot-on when we played at Fort Dix. The excitement and adrenaline started pumping through our veins before the game even started, as squadrons of soldiers from all over the base marched in unison, calling cadence, just like I had seen so many times in the movies. This continued until all the bleacher seats were filled.

Each appearance there was a competitive duel, with determined opponents, and free-swinging batters aiming for the fence, hoping to be the ones to finally beat The Queen and Her Court. I always felt an extra appreciation and respect from our opponents, as well as our audience, and they rewarded us all by their applause and laughter.

This summer I couldn't wait to play there, knowing that I had so much more to give the men and women of Fort Dix than just my softball skills. Following our game, I could not believe the response to sharing my faith, as lines of guys stood waiting just to say thank you. Some even shared how hard it was to be away from home and the ones they loved. It was a blessing to be a reminder to them that God was here with them that night, even on the softball field.

I have taken the time to elaborate about our experiences and memories at Fort Dix, so you will know how I felt when we returned the following summer, and were told to eliminate what I said about Jesus. If I didn't, we would never be invited to come back again! I was devastated and completely torn as to what I should do. Even though it felt like an incredible decision and burden on my shoulders, it meant so much that Daddy gave me free reign, leaving the verdict up to me on whether to share my testimony or not.

I was always baffled by this, since giving up control seemed so contrary to his character. I have concluded that my dad was an evangelist at heart, and I believe he did not want to quench those stirrings in me.

I went to God and the answer seemed simple, as I remembered the many young men and women who were greatly encouraged the year before.

Sure enough, as promised, we did not receive an invitation to play at Fort Dix the following season. I was incredibly sad to think we would never be back, but I had put this decision in God's hands a year ago, and I was not going to take it back.

It felt like rejection, but I brightened to think, *I must be doing something right…I was in good company. Jesus was rejected. Did I think it would be any different for me?*

I have since learned a million times over that nothing is set in stone or over until God says it's over!

A few years later, we just about fell over when Fort Dix was back on the schedule. I was jumping for joy! God moved. The person who pronounced our fate was gone, and everyone there couldn't wait for us to return, including us!

As a renewed confidence and hope for my future returned, it seemed like my pitching talents soared. Spiritually and professionally, I felt unstoppable. It didn't hurt that three top-notch athletes, who were equally as proficient in their positions, supported me.

Eileen and I had grown very close on and off the field. She knew my mannerisms and read my eyes and body language so well that people were surprised to discover she could skillfully handle all my pitches, without a signal.

As my brother, Norm, got taller and stronger, he started to hit his stride as a talented athlete, in addition to being an incredible entertainer. He put those two assets together so effortlessly that I'm sure he never got enough credit for the degree of difficulty he effortlessly delivered to thousands of fans each year.

Rounding out our team and returning for his second season as shortstop was Eric, who was one of the most gifted athletes I had ever seen. He brought an added athleticism to our team as he wowed audiences with his rifle-like throwing arm, power hitting, and world-class running speed, stealing bases at will each night a la Jackie Robinson style.

I often thought, *What a nightmare for opposing pitchers to have to face Eric every fourth batter in our rotation; sometimes three or four times per inning.* At times, he seemed super human. I was just happy he was on my team. He brought a new confidence and assurance, spurring each of us to raise the level of our game, as we patterned our skills to resemble his expertise. Needless to say, my dad was all smiles.

In addition to all Eric's exceptional athleticism, I admired his low-key mannerisms and humility, never letting the accolades go to his head. Together, the four of us formed a combination that was hard to beat, making tour life more fun than work.

As the summer progressed, it seemed natural when Eric and I grew closer to each other, with mutual romantic feelings that I thought had possibilities of turning into something long term for the two of us. Because of my renewed relationship with the Lord, I now had purpose pitching, using the talents that I had worked so hard to perfect, to glorify Him. I began envisioning many more years of softball as a career.

Also, I couldn't help thinking, *With Eric touring by my side, all my dreams might still come true.* This was the fairy tale that I was looking for...the one that ended with everyone involved living happily ever after!

CHAPTER 19

GREAT EXPECTATIONS

"Hope deferred makes the heart sick, but when
the desire comes, it is a tree of life."

PROVERBS 13:12

◇◇◇◇◇◇◇◇◇◇◇

I couldn't believe what I was hearing as I gazed blankly into my dad's eyes. I felt trapped and vulnerable sitting directly across from him, separated by the huge executive-style desk in his office that enhanced the chasm between us.

This should have been a fabulous visit to his office. It was payday, following one of the best seasons ever. Unfortunately, these end-of-the-summer wrap-ups were exactly the same every year—a day I always dreaded, sitting quietly, listening to Daddy, and feeling like a "little girl" no matter what age I was. As he summarized my tour performance, he made me feel that I never seemed to live up to his expectations or achieve the high marks of perfection that I hoped would make him pleased with me.

To be honest, I don't remember much of what was said because my brain shut down automatically as soon as I heard Daddy say, "Eric will not play one more season if you pursue a relationship with him."

When the sound of Daddy's voice ceased to ring in my ears, I knew he was expecting a response to his mandate. With tears running down my cheeks, I muttered meekly, "It's too late, I already love him, so do what you have to do. Eric and I will just have to figure it out."

I'm sure that was not the answer he was expecting, but with no confrontation on my part, our meeting ended. It would have served no good purpose to debate him on any topic, much less this one. From previous talks, I knew my "no rebuttal" strategy probably eliminated an extra hour of listening to another monologue that would have surely ensued.

Looking back, I wished we could have had a dialogue about the pros and cons of jumping into a new relationship so soon, leaving the freedom to choose in my court. It may or may not have made any difference in my decision; but as I left that day, I knew Daddy highly disapproved. I was in the "doghouse" and that was a heavy burden to carry around in my soul.

Eric and I continued seeing each other through the fall and winter, awaiting his verdict. Nothing much was said, which was typical of our family's communication dynamics. All of our family got together for holidays at Daddy's house. We ate, played games, and put on smiles, avoiding any kind of conflict at all cost.

Then spring training rolled around, and Eric was not dismissed! I was elated! We had talked of marriage and even though both of us had recently divorced, I saw no reason to put on the brakes. In retrospect, this was pretty naïve thinking, especially considering the fact that the divorce rate for second marriages is between sixty and sixty-seven percent!

Eric was mature, responsible, disciplined, and easy going. He loved God, and it was a blessing to see how easily he blended with my family and church friends. I never had to worry that Eric would say or do something that would offend anyone, leaving me in a perpetual state of anxiousness. I didn't have to try to make amends, offer excuses, or continually smooth things over. It seemed I had found someone who could flow with everybody, including my dad.

Our mutual love of sports and competition occupied the off-season as Eric and I had great fun entering mixed doubles tennis tournaments, usually coming out on top in winning fashion. It felt like we had everything in common, including the same psyche, that probably started with the fact that we were both the first-born of five children, each having two brothers and two sisters.

I wondered if the puzzle pieces of a successful marriage were finally coming together for me? Because Eric was a schoolteacher, his summers were available to tour. *I didn't think it could get any better.* I was certain that God was answering my prayer for someone to love and protect me, making the touring life seem more normal, with a husband by my side.

With this kind of thinking in the forefront of my brain, all systems were "Go." Eric and I moved at lightning speed, throwing our small church wedding together, right before we left California for the upcoming summer tour in June.

I could not have been happier. Each night, I was overjoyed to look over my shoulder and feel Eric's strength and support as he covered the shortstop position, as well as a large radius that included third base, left, and centerfield. I felt proud when the audience would ooh and aah as Eric would dive and make the impossible catch or steal bases at will.

The same union and harmony between Eric and me carried over as we shared life's daily tour routines off the softball diamond. Our relationship seemed easy as a flowing river, with barely a flicker of conflict between us. I thanked God daily. All was right in my world, and I was sure this was how marriage should be. I felt safe and secure.

By this point, all family members were used to the rigorous ways Daddy pushed us to be our best. Each season, we all waited to see what new idea, fad, or invention he would dive into to make us better. Some of the activities and agendas he utilized would become permanent, helping to raise the level of success for The Queen and Her Court, while others would disappear until a new idea popped up.

One thing I knew with certainty; if Daddy was incorporating something new into his life, everyone around him would be required to be thoroughly immersed in it too—doing likewise—no questions asked.

I can recall some comical images of twenty-something year old guys, who played on our team, being required to eat only lighter, milder foods like vegetables, fruits, eggs, and oatmeal following our night games, just because Daddy did. The look on their faces when they were told not to order a good ole steak or cheeseburger was priceless. Daddy pronounced that these foods were bad for digestion right before going to sleep…so that was that. Fortunately, for the guys, that mandate only lasted one season.

Another season, I thought anarchy was brewing among the new recruits, as I heard all the private grumblings increasing at a feverish rate, when Daddy insisted that every player take a dip in the swimming pool before each game to loosen all stiff joints that resulted from riding for hours in the van. Once in the pool, Daddy gave instructions on a series of water calisthenics that were to be followed to a tee. I had to conceal my amusement at all their whimpering and whining. I wanted to give them the "tip of the century" and say, *"Guys, just do it. You'll be in and out of the pool in fifteen minutes, but if you fight him on this, double or triple that time."*

I completely understood how they felt after driving all day together, cooped up in our twelve-passenger maxi van. We all wanted a little space and quiet time, stretched out on a bed, before our appearance that night.

That being said, I did find these water exercises to be extremely beneficial, especially as I got older, having to pitch every night. Daddy's idea was a good one. On my own, I took it one step further by routinely taking a dip after each game in pool water that was usually very cold; followed by a hot-as-I-could-stand-it bath in my room. This cold/hot treatment worked the best for me, helping to reduce the soreness in my pitching arm, as well as all my other joints. To this day, I still include a number of these water exercises.

As a teenager, I recall one year that Daddy was heavily into bodybuilding and all that goes with it. He even bought a tanning apparatus for maintaining a golden tan during the winter months at home. This was before the media alerted everyone to the dangers of excessive sun on people's skin. I was totally on board, giving Daddy's new activity the big "thumbs up." *Whose legs don't look better with a little tan?*

That summer Eileen, Debby, and I loved that we had his blessing, lathering our bodies with baby oil, as we lounged by every pool possible, soaking up each glorious ray of sunshine, in search of the perfect bikini tan.

We loved it, that is, (*remember the days of trying to be a cool teenager?*) until the time the three of us were reclining poolside, and heard the cluster of girls right next to us, who were chatting with us earlier, giggling and simply aghast as they pointed out the man in the skimpy white speedo and shaved body, standing on the second balcony.

I cringed. I didn't have to even look. There wasn't a doubt in my mind that the girls were gawking at my dad, who was all oiled up, and scanning the pool area, looking for us. Not an eyelid would have fluttered at Muscle Beach in Venice, California, or maybe sunning in the south of France, but not here...not in this little mid-western town.

My cheeks flushed. I could feel Eileen and Debby's thoughts shouting in unison with mine, *Please, please, please...don't see us, and please don't come down those stairs!*

But you know that didn't happen. I don't know who was more embarrassed—us or those giggly girls who never uttered another word to us, sitting in silence after Daddy plopped himself right next to us. *Oh, the perils of being a cool teenager!* I think all of us breathed a sigh of relief when the speedo was out and regular swim shorts were in.

One season, Daddy spent hours in our garage, completely disassembling a softball, filling it with lead, and then sewing it back up himself. He was always thinking how to improve our skills, and sometimes his ideas were genius. I will have to hand it to him, because that weighted softball became one of the best strengthening tools, helping to increase the speed of my pitches. It weighed about one pound, being the perfect weight to use while practicing my rise ball and fastball, without injuring my wrist. Later Daddy negotiated an advertising/ sponsorship deal with the deBeer Softball Company, to make one- and two-pound softballs, exclusively for The Queen and Her Court. On tour, I used a weighted softball in my warm-ups before every game. After flipping it for a few minutes, a regular softball seemed like I was pitching with a wiffle ball. It made me feel like "SuperWoman," no matter how tired I was.

Daddy's intentions were good, but sometimes the end results were not worth the toil and strain it had on all those participating. This is the case the time we were on one of our foreign tours, and he called us all together during our rest time in the afternoon. Our task was to start a daily reading aloud of the entire American Softball Association (ASA) rule handbook, cover to cover.

It was grueling and especially nerve-racking for my sister, Karen. At the end of each chapter, Daddy would ask multiple-choice questions to make sure we understood each ruling. Karen wasn't as quick with her answers, which frustrated Daddy, so his voice got louder. As his voice got louder, all of us could see her brain shutting down, which made everyone in the room tense, knowing the situation could escalate.

Everyone felt Karen's desperation. When Daddy wasn't looking, Eileen and I were secretly mouthing the correct answer to Karen, but she was so panicked by then that she could never focus in on the questions...or us.

Every day, we dreaded this meeting. It was more mentally exhausting than any ole ballgame, but there was light at the end of the tunnel.

All of us breathed a collective sigh of relief, knowing that we were finally coming to the last chapter. When that day came, we were all smiles, quietly rejoicing with one another. I'm sure you can imagine how shocked we were when Daddy called us all to his room the next day and announced we would be going through the rule book a second time. Our hearts sank. I couldn't believe what I was hearing. This needed to be a joke, but it was not. I was angry, but kept my feelings well hidden. He just didn't get it. Too much was too much!

As a newlywed, I guess I was hoping Daddy wouldn't add too much more to our agenda beside the actual performance and competition that each day presented, traveling all day to a new city, with the pressures of squaring off against a new team every night. This daily routine, along with each of our added chores to keep our well-oiled machine in tip-top shape, presented a unique challenge of its own. However, in an effort to keep our dialogues fresh and exciting, Daddy gave each person the assignment of coming up with two new ideas, phrases, or jokes that could potentially be added to our routine.

Every day, en route to our next city, we would have a team meeting where each person, without exception, was required to participate with two new ideas. Fortunately, our contribution didn't have to be jaw dropping or spectacular, just something that showed we made a valid effort. After we had exhausted every last quip of our own, we spent any free time during the afternoon scouring the sport's page, magazines, and any comedians or sportscasters on television, hoping to catch a joke or some creative commentary to use the next day in our meeting.

Eric watched a lot of sports, so he was always on the lookout; and when Eileen's husband, Gregg, came out on tour, he was like fresh blood, making it a funny game as he collected extra sayings for Eileen, taking care of many future team meetings.

We brought humor to this new drudgery by making it a game between us. Of course, if one of us turned up shy of the required two quips, we all contributed, bartered, and paid each other back, so no one would get in trouble. This actually bonded us together as family and teammates.

Once again, we breathed a thankful sigh of relief when Daddy discontinued this extra-curricular activity, moving on to a different agenda the following season. Unfortunately, the grueling, daily team meetings were here to stay. Even if my previous night's performance didn't require too much feedback, those meetings were always so draining, just listening to Daddy critique everyone else. On the days that his comments felt like dripping water on my skin, I slipped on my most opaque sunglasses and willed my brain to drift to more pleasant scenarios. Even though he couldn't see my eyes, it was imperative to keep my body language in an appropriate state of acknowledgement, affirming his statements by shaking my head up and down behind those dark glasses. These strategies helped me cope and keep my sanity.

Unfortunately, Eric did not have this "blocking out" ability. I could see the strain and discouragement of the daily negativity sweep over him, smothering his self-confidence like a heavy blanket. I genuinely felt like this tour would be one of my best ever, but after three or four weeks on the road, I sensed some warning signs brewing up close and personal.

While I know my dad would be the first to acknowledge the excellent and added athleticism that Eric brought to The Queen and Her Court; for some reason, he could not settle or be content with all that Eric brought to our team. At our team meetings, Daddy began focusing on Eric's lack of showmanship, which included smiling and over-exaggerated gestures, like waving and blowing kisses to the audience. Eric did his best, but the things my siblings and I learned early on to keep peace, did not come easy for Eric's reluctant and introverted personality.

Every day I could sense Eric's "I can never be good enough for him" mentality and frustration growing deeper and deeper. During our daily team meetings, Eric's attitude was quiet and respectful as Daddy would drone on and on with negative comment after negative comment concerning Eric's performance.

I wondered, *"Where is this coming from?* Daddy was all smiles and compliments to Eric the summer before, but now that we were married, he didn't hold back. *Couldn't he see that his continual unmerited hammering away at Eric was having the same adverse effect on him as it did for my brother Marvin?*

When we were alone, I tried to encourage and lift him up, but I could see the destruction of Daddy's words were winning over mine.

The real topper came as Eric executed one of his famous headfirst dives, jamming his hand into the base and breaking a bone. Injuries in sports are nothing new, especially if you are a person who doesn't hold back. For other professional teams, the solution is simple...just pull a substitute from the eager bench of players dying to get in the game. For The Queen and Her Court...not so simple as most years we had maybe one substitute.

Unfortunately, this particular season there was no one to replace Eric, so he sat on the sidelines in his cast, feeling frustrated and chomping at the bits, while we recruited someone from the opposing team to fill in for him each night.

It was a hard blow to our team, and for Eric personally. A cloud of depression seemed to hang over our marriage.

Even before the cast was off, Eric convinced my dad to put him back into the offensive line-up, where Eric would either bunt or hit one handed. Because of his speed, ninety percent of the time he would successfully make it to first base regardless of where the ball was fielded.

My "dream tour" certainly did not go as I had planned. Once we were home again, I was sure the bad feelings would disappear and spirits would be renewed. Home would alleviate the pressure of walking that fine line through a path of eggshells, trying to make my dad and Eric happy at the same time. Ironically, I do remember having that fleeting thought—*different husband...same dilemma... impossible task!*

My stomach had that same familiar tightening as I noticed storm clouds forming long before the cloudburst. The coffin was sealed shut when Eric went in for "payday" and found out that Daddy docked his pay, fining him for every game he didn't play.

When I think of that, I wonder how some athletes today would take the news that their million-dollar contracts were deemed null and void because they were out for the year with an injury...*court dates would be set and heads would roll!*

Needless to say, Eric informed my dad he would not be touring again. When I heard the news, my heart was shattered and gripped with agony and fear at the thought of spending our summers apart.

To endure such a scenario, my mind went into Scarlett O'Hara mode. *I can't think about that right now...I'll go crazy...I'll think about that tomorrow...After all, tomorrow is another day.*

Just as Daddy had changed his mind about Eric touring; come spring, I was confident I could help Eric erase the trials of the past summer from his mind. Some way, somehow, I would find a way to help reverse this unbearable decision, and keep my hopes and dreams alive.

CHAPTER 20

DANCING WITH THE DEVIL

"Therefore, let him who thinks he stands, take heed lest he fall."

I CORINTHIANS 10:12

"Be strong in the Lord and in His mighty power. Put on all of God's armor so that you will be able to stand firm against all strategies of the devil. For we are not fighting against flesh-and-blood enemies, but against evil rulers and authorities of the unseen world, against mighty powers in this dark world, and against evil spirits in the heavenly places."

EPHESIANS 6:10-12

I should've seen the handwriting on the wall…but I didn't. Marriage number two was over almost before it started. I was certain that divorce would never cross my path again. I would have bet my life on it. When my marriage crumbled so quickly, it sent me into a tailspin that kept me reeling in shame for years to come. I likened my slow fade and eventual outcome to an anecdote that I heard a few years earlier on "boiling a frog."

The premise is that if a frog is placed in boiling water, it will jump out, but if it is placed in cold water that is slowly heated, it will not perceive the danger and will be cooked to death.

Metaphorically speaking, I would have never submitted to the boiling water of divorce, but I made naïve and undiscerning spiritual and personal choices as I slid into the tranquility of the soothing, warm water around me, believing no harm would come.

Just like the hot-as-I-could-stand-it baths I would take after every ball game, I adjusted to the increase of the temperature. By the time I recognized the danger, being fully immersed in the lethal boiling water that was upon me, there seemed to be no turning back. I discovered my strength was gone, and I was too weak to jump out. The results were swift and fatal. I was cooked!

Because the effects of a second divorce were so shocking and devastating to me, both emotionally and spiritually, I have spent years of my life retracing and analyzing thoughts, choices, and events that contributed to such an undesirable outcome, hoping that more understanding would help me avoid other future pitfalls.

I dread the writing and vulnerability of recreating this chapter of my life, but, I am forging ahead as I cling to the promise from Psalm 34:5 that says, "Those who look to Him for help will be radiant with joy, and no shadow of shame will darken their faces."

Following Eric's earth-shattering decision not to tour, I collected my emotions, making it my number one objective to change his mind. Like most women after childbirth, I was sure I could help Eric forget the labor pains of the past summer, renew, and be ready to go again by the time spring training rolled around.

I threw myself into this goal, trying all conceivable methods. I displayed every emotion, tactic, and strategy possible with countless heartfelt conversations, punctuated with lots of tears, pleading, and begging, practically promising him the world if he would just do this for me.

With the reasoning of a seasoned lawyer, I presented a logical case, showing Eric how the pros far outweighed the cons, financially and personally. One minute I was pouring on the guilt for not being a good husband, and the next minute I was full of praise, hoping he loved life with me so much that the thought of being without me for a single day would be unthinkable. I attempted every form of manipulation, both good and bad, hoping that something I said or did would break through the cracks and find a way to his heart.

Then, of course, I pulled out the "big guns." I was sure that changing Eric's mind would be no match for the power of God, so I prayed my guts out, believing that the One who loved me the most and knew me the best would surely understand how being apart from Eric would be detrimental for our marriage, ripping my heart out in the process.

At times, it felt like déjà vu…always pleading, coercing, and trying to be worthy enough to win the love, care, and protection of both God and man.

During these months, a seed of doubt made its subtle entrance into my brain, as I tried to figure out what was so horribly wrong with me that all my cries for help could be so easily dismissed by all the male figures in my life, who professed to love me the most?

Along with the doubt, I was willingly drinking cups of the spiritual poison called bitterness on a daily basis. The Bible has a lot to say about staying on guard concerning the dangers of bitterness springing up and causing insurmountable trouble, with the power to defile unsuspecting lives. (Hebrews 12:15)

The bubbling fountain of bitterness that I harbored underneath the surface in my soul day after day seemed small, as long as I was able to regulate the presumed more deadly overt sins, like anger and hatred, that were begging to spring forth, along with many other unsuspecting allies.

I believe my inability to recognize the danger, as well as my unwillingness to repent of this elusive sin, was the first step in allowing the devil to have a foothold in my life. I was deceived.

As spring training began, reality smacked me right in the face. Eric would not be touring with me. My heart hurt like crazy, but there wasn't a thing I could do about it. To eradicate the pain, I dusted myself off, blocked out, numbed out, shut down, put a smile on my face, and determined to make this the best, most fun tour ever. With or without Eric, I vowed to be happy.

I remember saying to God, *"Well, it's just me and You again. I love you, and You love me...and that's all I need."*

My thought patterns were slowly hardening as I cemented the belief that there was no man alive who could be trusted with my heart. Outwardly, I assumed a fabricated posture of spiritual strength. Inwardly, I vowed to need no one. I would make the best of my life with a false bravado—it was me and God against the world.

Shortly, I was to discover that the spiritual foundation I was laying for myself was structurally unsound. I was building my house with bricks of lies, deceit, doubt, unforgiveness, and bitterness. It was never going to be possible to maintain a loving relationship vertically with my heavenly Father while shutting out earthly, horizontal relationships with those around me. Later I would understand the error of such thinking as this relational principle is clearly spelled out in 1 John 2:9-11 where it says, "Anyone who claims to live in God's light and hates a brother or sister is still in the dark. It's the person who loves brother and sister who dwells in God's light and doesn't block the light from others. But whoever hates is still in the dark, stumbles around in the dark, doesn't know which end is up, blinded by the darkness" (The Message).

I thought I could eliminate the pain of feeling unloved by stuffing all of the unwanted emotions, keeping mankind at a distance, and refusing to bare my life and heart to even one more person who would surely stomp it flat. It was immature to think that I could live each day without loving others, while continuing to maintain a vibrant, authentic relationship with God.

Fortunately, my heavenly Father knows me better than I know myself. I was an expert at fooling those around me with all my phoniness, but I didn't fool God for an instant. In truth, He saw what I would not acknowledge out loud—I was angry and didn't trust Him either. I was a walking, breathing, ticking time bomb…heading for disaster. It took every ounce of energy to maintain my dysfunctional charade, but this was nothing new, as I had been rehearsing and perfecting this lifestyle since childhood.

My marriage was one of outward cordiality, just going through the motions, and as more time passed, my relationship with God seemed about the same. Inwardly, I was appalled and saddened with my behavior and life and was sure God felt the same. By this time, there wasn't much to say to God, which made me very melancholy, since it wasn't that long prior to this that I had enjoyed an intimacy that was the joy of my life, talking to Him about everything.

To subdue the perpetual state of guilt and shame, I chastised myself with demeaning words 24/7. I did this as a way of doing penance, I suppose. My debasing self-talk played like a broken record in my brain without a turn off switch.

As my second marriage was beginning to crumble, it was hard for me to maintain that intimate "God and me" relationship. The thoughts and sin in my life were crippling and acted as a snowball rolling down a mountain, getting bigger and bigger, gaining unstoppable momentum and speed.

Like Adam and Eve, I decided to hide and run from God even though I desperately needed Him more than ever; but I was too ashamed, afraid I would see disgust and rejection if I looked directly into His eyes. I was convinced God and I agreed on one thing…I would never be good enough. My life was one big disappointment!

I look back on this time in my life and can see how subtly truths became blurred distortions and outright lies. Somehow my "fun tour" was turning into a nightmare of uncontrollable nerves. My only reprieve was the few hours each night that I threw myself into pitching and competing. Pitching was the part of my identity that always gave my brain a much-needed boost of encouragement, acting as my ally, always applauding and lavishing me with unconditional accolades, assuring me that I was worth something in this life. For those brief hours during games, pitching felt like a friend wrapping their comforting arms around me, whispering words of affirmation in my ear. It was what I did best, so I clung to that little bit of self worth that pitching brought me each night.

Following each game, the thought of going back to my room alone, with just my screaming thoughts as companions, brought on anxiety that turned into panic attacks. At times like these, I remember foolishly thinking, *Wouldn't it be great if I was into alcohol, drugs, or something to dull the repetitive messages to block the assault in my brain.*

Instead, I tried diffusing these attacks by grabbing my earplugs, turning my music up to deafening decibels, and running for miles and miles, late into the wee hours of each night, until my body was ready to drop from exhaustion.

Where did the girl from last summer go? The glorious peace and joy that I had experienced on the previous tour; walking the hotel halls and praying over the people in each room was long gone.

I continued to share the gospel before each game, believing that truth was still truth and the hearer would still have the opportunity to choose eternal life, even if it came from a life that was turned upside down. Even though I was falling apart, I managed to maintain an outward professionalism, keeping my emotions in check, pasting on a winning smile for the audiences each night and in front of my dad during the day.

I maintained a false strength and even prided myself for sustaining such a fake bravado, withholding every honest emotion from Daddy. I felt that I had given him the only thing he really wanted—Superstar pitcher, Rosie Black.

Inwardly, I was scrambling to plug up the holes in my life, to keep the dyke from bursting, determined to keep Daddy from seeing any emotional cracks in my armor. July 28, 1982 was one of the few times that I can remember removing the mask that I held so firmly in place. I was emotionally caught off guard when I heard the news from home that the musician, Keith Green, along with eleven others, including his three-year-old boy, Josiah, and his two-year-old girl, Bethany, died in a plane crash on their private airstrip in Texas. I was horrified to imagine the pain his wife, Melody, who was six weeks pregnant at the time, must have felt receiving the shocking news at home with their one-year-old girl, Rebekah.

I crumbled into a pool of tears. I cried and cried and cried for days. I could not possibly explain how I felt, nor did I even want to try. Daddy would never understand. It didn't have anything to do with softball, so why even bother trying to explain the depths of my grief over the death of this Godly man whose music had been my constant companion, and how his life impacted my life in such a profound way. After about three days of uncontrollable visible mourning, I knew I had better pull it together, as I could see Daddy's face change from sympathetic to "enough is enough."

However, in my alone time, the sadness continued and God got the brunt of every raw emotion I was thinking and feeling. My sadness turned to anger. I was more confused about God than ever. My biggest question was, *"Why, why, why would You take this Godly man who was on an unstoppable mission to touch lives for Your kingdom and leave a wretch like me…a nothing…a failure?"* This whole thing seemed like such a waste. There were no answers that made any sense, so I filed my hard questions away deep into the recesses of my heart.

The only one that I thought I could depend on was God, and now it seemed I didn't really know Him at all. In light of all these unanswerable questions, I decided to stop talking about it with God, shelving my feelings. After all, it didn't seem like it would be right to be angry with

God, so I buried all the unsolvable queries and pretended nothing was wrong between us, just like I did with everyone else.

I returned home that season in a fragile state of mind but without all the pressures of touring, I managed to resume an acceptable robotic dance with Eric. I'm pretty sure both of us thought everything would stay the same in our marriage, as long as we didn't cross the boundaries into dead-end discussions of him touring, or my broken heart. We kept a vigilant silence in these areas.

Although I ended every tour physically and mentally spent, I always felt a spark of excitement and anticipation when the new season began. Daddy would pull out a brand-new Rand McNally Road Atlas of the United States and Canada (no Google Maps yet), and highlight a skeleton tour for me. Daddy's enthusiasm was certainly contagious as he kept everyone posted on the newly added cities to our schedule.

The summer tour of 1983 was packed, and after spring training, it looked like we would have a strong team of ball players who would help make it a winning season. Even though we exhibited strength on the ball field, being the only female remaining left me feeling unsupported emotionally and spiritually.

All my teammates were returning players, except for the one new recruit, Bobby, who looked like he was going to have oodles of potential offensively and defensively, filling Eric's former position at shortstop. My baby brother, Norm, who captured the hearts of the audience as Lotta Chatter handled the first base position with expert proficiency, and the catcher was my good-natured and very talented Canadian, Doug, who was returning for his second season. Doug took the place of Eileen who had given birth to Sara, and was pregnant with her daughter, Melody.

Because most of us knew the routines already, practices seemed extra smooth. Over the years, I always pushed myself and practiced hard; I felt like my work ethic was finally paying off in great dividends, not only in my pitching, but also in Daddy's attitude toward me.

It seemed like he was more lighthearted, even easier on me than the guys. I don't know if his more lenient approach with me had to do with his confidence in my pitching skills, no husband around to compete with, or perhaps getting older was helping to mellow him…maybe it was a little of all of the above!

Nevertheless, practices seemed more enjoyable. The atmosphere was relaxed with smiles and laughter as each of us bonded as teammates and worked with diligence to perfect our craft for the coming season.

One practice in particular, I recall breathing in all the beauty of the ball field that was nestled up on a hill in Rolling Hills Estates just a skip and a jump away from my dad's house. The warmth of the sun seemed to energize my soul, and I felt happy for once…optimism flooded my being.

As the guys were practicing fielding drills, I ran my usual conditioning laps around the circumference of the park. The second time around, I was mesmerized by the hundreds of snails that lined my running path and came out of hiding, following a light rain the previous night. I was zigging and zagging to miss crunching their shells with the steel spikes from my cleats. The third time around, I, uncharacteristically, deviated from my no-nonsense work ethic and decided to scoop up as many snails as I could, stuffing them into my light windbreaker jacket. By the time I finished my laps, I conjured up a wild plot to unload my bulging pockets, filled with my mollusk treasure, into the brand-new size thirteen athletic shoes of our newest recruit, Bobby.

At the moment, it seemed like a brilliant idea to test his sense of humor. As practice was coming to an end, I began to regret my carefree mindset, hoping my fun-loving prank wouldn't bite me in the butt with a scolding from Daddy.

As I purposely hid behind our van, packing away equipment, and watching the scene unfold from afar, I heard Bobby yell out, "What's the goo in my shoes?" All the guys roared with laughter as Bobby demanded to know who would stuff his newly purchased shoes with snail guts?

Gulp! I was the clear culprit, as I stood with eyes bulging like a deer caught in the headlights.

"*Sorry, Bobby, I'll buy you another pair,*" I muttered quickly and quietly...hoping Daddy wouldn't realize what I had done. When Bobby comprehended that I was the prankster, he softened. "It's no big deal." He chuckled, "I think I can get them out, but I might have to get you back."

I smiled all the way home, *I have an ally...life is looking up.*

In the midst of preparing for this tour, there was an unexpected happening that caught us off guard. It was a shocker for me, as well as everyone else in our family, when we found out that my dad and brother, Marvin, had somehow reunified after many passing years without a single word of communication between them. Their coming back together after so much time had elapsed felt like a downright miracle.

Even though I know there were no apologies or healing-inspired discussions of the past from either of them, I couldn't believe what I was seeing. One day Marvin was out, and the next day he's in. Daddy invited him to join us at our practices; and before I could blink, he asked Marvin to be a part of our summer tour as an extra player.

Their relationship resumed with smiles and hope, but unfortunately it turned sour within weeks, both returning to the father/son dynamic that they ended with years before. Nothing had changed...It was what it was.

Even though it was sad to witness, I breathed a sigh of relief when Daddy sent Marvin home after the first game of our tour. We weren't even out of California, but I knew it was the best decision for all concerned...before they stopped speaking altogether.

I knew ahead of time that this summer, especially the first half, would be packed with lots of excitement and an abundance of tough opponents because of the geography.

Our troupe had about a weeks' worth of games heading up the coast of Northern California, Oregon, and Washington. I figured that was just enough time, with not too tough of competition, to hone my pitching skills on live opponents before I had to face a month of hard-hitting teams in Canada every night. I was confident and at the top of my game, but I certainly didn't factor in an incident that happened within that first week. Later, I would reflect on this happening as pivotal. It was certainly one-hundred-fold more deceptively damaging than it appeared at the time.

Before each game we entertained the fans with a pitching demonstration, ball-handling skills, and juggling routines that were crowd-pleasers throughout the years. All the routines in our pre-game show were successfully completed when I accidentally stepped on one of the yellow juggling softballs that had been discarded after our routine.

I cringed with a moment's worth of pain as my ankle rolled sideways over the ball, and I continued to take my position on the mound. It was time to play ball. With adrenaline surging through my body, I barely noticed the throbbing. After all, I had turned my ankle many times much worse than this without any repercussions at all.

Heading into the last inning, the pain in my left foot increased ten-fold. I couldn't wait to get that cleat off! Following the game, the telltale sign of the true condition of my ankle was written all over the faces of my dad and teammates as they bent over to take a closer look.

It was more than a concerned expression as Daddy shouted with a sharp edge of urgency for one of the guys to get some ice immediately!

The extent of my ankle injury was hard for me to access under the ballpark lights, but I knew it wasn't good when I rose to walk to our van and crumpled back down because the pain was so acute. I grabbed the arms of my teammates on either side as they ushered me off the field.

There are some memories that have stayed with me over time, and this is one of them. Everyone met in my motel room to access the situation. Sitting on my bed, I couldn't believe what I was seeing. I thought, *No wonder I wanted my cleat off.* My ankle was screaming for an escape, as it ballooned beyond recognition, with black and blue bruising spreading across my whole foot.

The pain that was shooting through my ankle wasn't even close to the dread I felt in my soul...unsure of how I was going to navigate through the next three months of contracted ball games. I instinctively knew from past experience that the question wasn't *"if" I was going to pitch...it was "how" could I pitch with a sprain so bad that I couldn't even stand on my own?*

With everyone circled around me, Daddy led us in a prayer for my healing and complete recovery...then came the hard part. One of the guys emptied out the plastic trash container in my room and filled it up with mostly ice and a little water. That was the beginning of five to six, foot-immersing ice treatments that I had to complete daily over the next month...but the first one was the hardest.

Tears involuntarily rolled down my cheeks. In an attempt to lighten the mood, my wacky, but wonderful brother, Norm, announced that he would go first with his foot to show me how it was done.

He let out a squeal of shock as his foot slid into the swirling ice. With a smile plastered on his face, wondering what he had gotten himself into, Norm knew he had to complete the task with grand bravado if he was ever going to convince his sister to follow suit. Although it didn't make it any easier when it was my turn again, he did make me laugh in the midst of my crisis and instill a bit of courage to do what I had to do.

After a fitful, anxious night alone in my motel room, the new day brought no miraculous healing as the guys collected my suitcase and helped their crippled queen hop to the van, heading to our next stop later that night.

With permission, we took the wastebasket filled with ice, and I forced my left foot into the frozen tundra fifteen minutes of every hour as we traveled. The remainder of time, I kept it elevated, still hoping it would feel normal by game time.

I cried in my room, wondering how I would get through the night and the nights to come. Looking back, I can recall the logistics and details of jamming my gigantic foot in my cleat with no laces tied. To complete a pitch, I planted my sprained left foot in front of my body, trying to keep the pressure of my weight on my back foot. *Of course, that was an impossible task.* From that stationary position, and no leg power from my normal leap forward off the mound, all my concerted effort went into whipping my pitching arm and snapping my wrist as quickly as possible…hoping to create enough speed to get it by the batter.

My pitching wasn't pretty. The pain was intense and by the night's end, I was physically exhausted as I headed back to my room with a throbbing foot. Some days were harder than others, but we managed to finish most nights successfully. For the most part, the fans were understanding and gracious; and my teammates picked up the slack, lightening my load, with their talents, brawn, and humor.

From day one, Bobby took on the task of wrapping my foot with an ACE bandage, getting ice, and in general…playing nursemaid to my every need. During such a hard time, it felt good to have someone so attentive and caring each day.

Long before the swelling in my ankle decreased, I could feel my mind crossing dangerous boundaries as our bond and familiarity grew stronger, until my heart and actions finally followed suit.

Guilt weighed heavily on me. I asked myself many times over, *How could I have yielded to this temptation?* Silently, I wondered if the enticement of this relationship had anything to do with the secret happening that I held in my heart…an incident that occurred a few months earlier?

Eric was already asleep. I was restless and feeling anxious. I couldn't sleep. It was around midnight. To find relief, I grabbed my jogging shoes and headphones, heading for a run. As usual, my mind was racing with hopelessness and defeat.

I don't know where this line of thinking came from, but I thought, *I wonder how powerful Satan really is?* With music blaring in my ears, I said aloud, *"If you are real, then make Bobby appear right now."* It felt more like a game to distract my thoughts, knowing nothing would happen.

Five seconds later, I quickened my running pace as I sensed someone chasing me. I let out a blood-curdling scream as a hand touched my shoulder. My Walkman flew out of my hands, yanking out both earplugs as my body flailed uncontrollably, trying to regain balance to keep myself from exploding onto the pavement.

I looked up, terrified to see Bobby. He had no idea the words I had just uttered to the "evil one." I felt like my mind went into shock mode, as I stared back at him...speechless. Bobby was completely unaware of the real reason I was gasping for air. He stood there like a proud peacock, laughing his head off, so elated to pay me back for the snail incident.

"What are you doing here, Bobby?" I muttered. "It's almost one o'clock in the morning!"

With a shrug of his shoulders, he nonchalantly proclaimed, "Oh, my buddy dropped me off at the corner...just been dancing...I thought that was you...what a coincidence!"

I smiled weakly as I uttered, "Yeah, what a coincidence."

With eyes wide open, I was naively dancing around a fire, with an opponent who was playing for keeps.

CHAPTER 21

THE LONG WAY HOME

"When I kept it all inside, my bones turned to powder, my words became daylong groans. The pressure never let up; all the juices of my life dried up. Then I let it all out; I said, "I'll come clean about my failures to God." Suddenly the pressure was gone—my guilt dissolved, my sin disappeared.

PSALM 32: 3-5 (THE MESSAGE)

◇◇◇◇◇◇◇◇◇◇

As the tour was coming to an end, I had every naïve intention of making the transition from my "tour bubble" and returning to my off-season home life, switching from Bobby to Eric, without any hiccups...just like in the movies. I was delusional! *Did I really think my indiscretions would remain a secret, and my emotions of living such a double life could be turned "off and on" like a light switch?* Apparently so.

The insanity of such blurred thinking was about to collide with reality. In truth, this reasoning was a perfect indicator of my life. I was spinning wildly out of whack, while priding myself on being in complete control! The ugliness of my life was not going to be wrapped up in a neat little package with everything returning to normal. Eric discovered the truth.

With the luxury of looking back, I can thank God for allowing the truth to surface, even though it was incredibly traumatic. I was certain the consequences of my sin would surely take me under this time…with no possibility for recovery. I was hitting rock bottom…AGAIN!

The phrase "hitting rock bottom" strikes a very different cord now than it did back then. Since then, I have seen great benefits from such a negative sounding posture. Coming to the end of self makes way for the possibility of a "real hope" for solutions to emerge. I have secretly prayed many prayers for some of my dearest friends and loved ones to "hit rock bottom," like I did. My hope was that they would release that "thing" in their life that has falsely held the promise of bringing them happiness. Even though the choices are still in our court, hitting rock bottom can be the beginning of one's miracle. Being in this devastating position holds great promise of receiving "God's best thing"—Himself. Of course, it would be quite a while before I could fully embrace the hidden blessing of hitting my bottom.

My first inclination was to "run for the hills" and disappear from everyone. In fact, that's what I did. I drove with no particular destination in mind, checking into a motel, hoping to escape, and imagining that my unsolvable problem would magically disappear. However, the fact remained—no matter where I escaped to, I couldn't escape me. My thoughts held me captive. There was no peace, rest, or solution. Fear was strangling me. I was sure I would go mad this time, and someone would have to put me in the nuthouse.

In the midst of this craziness, I left my motel room and went to the closest pay phone. My one sane thought prompted me to call my mom. It was a cry for help. Plus, with all the hurt I was causing so many, I couldn't bear the thought that she would worry where I was.

The call was brief. "Momma, I've screwed everything up, but I'm okay…please don't worry." Mom's voice was gentle and loving, "Everything will be alright, honey. I'm here, if you need me. I love you and God does too."

With tears rolling down my face, I said, "I love you too…and please pray hard." After I hung up the phone, Mom's love gave me a moment of clarity and courage. I knew what I had to do. I had to go back and face the music!

I couldn't go home, so I did the only thing I could think to do. I called Eileen and asked to stay with her. Once again, Gregg and Eileen were gracious to take me in.

The long road back was not an easy one. The emotional pain had taken on a deeper intensity than the last time I had stayed with them. The shame and humiliation of my life had me questioning if I would really ever be normal again. *How many times could I mess up, before the trauma would take me down completely? How many times would I disappoint and fail God?* Here I was again, three years later, in the same situation…only worse… with another impending divorce staring me in the face.

The first couple of weeks were characterized by non-stop crying, accompanied by unsuccessful attempts to silence the screaming voices in my head. On one occasion, I endeavored to subdue my pain by repeatedly striking my head on the wooden door jam in Eileen's living room. For a few brief moments, I exchanged my raw emotions for a methodical, controlled physical penance, exchanging one pain for another.

Within seconds, I discovered I had the little eyes of Eileen's toddler, Sara, intently watching her Aunt Rosie, in bewilderment. She was just learning to talk, and putting words to her impressions. She said, questioningly, *"Sad face, sad face?"*

I was jolted out of my trance as I quickly brushed away my tears, putting on my biggest smile. "Oh sweetie," I chuckled, "No, it's a happy face, happy face!" Oh, how I wished those words were true!

Over the next few weeks, I returned back to the basics that I knew to be true…but it wasn't as easy as before. Because I was God's child, I knew He promised to love and forgive me…no matter what! Somehow, I believed those promises were true for everyone, but me. Many days, it felt like a wrestling match to accept those truths. *How could I receive such love when I couldn't even love or forgive myself?*

Eventually, I had to make a choice to discard my thinking and accept the gifts that Jesus made possible by His great sacrifice on the cross. He wanted me to have these gifts, His love and forgiveness…a new identity.

Once again, I concluded, *What was the point of His horrible death if I didn't believe Him?* By refusing to take God at His word, I was nullifying His great purpose for leaving His throne in heaven and coming to earth.

This was my starting point in moving forward but over the years, I discovered my resistance to these gifts was all wrapped in deep seeded emotions that lurked right below the surface and seemed to be dictating my behavior.

My learned life pattern and inclination was to earn everything that I received, so I could be IN CONTROL. But two realities were slapping me in the face—I will never be good enough to earn God's love and forgiveness, and after thirty-one years on this earth, doing things "my way" left me reeling like a spinning top…wholly "out of control." *It was time to surrender my foolish thinking.*

Even though my faith was low, and I struggled to reconcile my life with His truth, it felt good to be talking again…to be honest and open, confessing my sin, and surrendering my life to a loving Father who loved me so unconditionally.

When I focused on God's words, I felt very emotionally centered. But the moment I thought about what I had done (my past), or tried to imagine how to solve problems in the days ahead (my future), then it felt like the walls would come crashing in on me. Clearly, God was trying to teach me that the only way to make it in this life was to live in the present…one day at a time…as prescribed in Matthew 6:34.

I spent my days trying to figure out how to incorporate these truths into real life. It all seemed so confusing. I had so many questions. *Why didn't my actions match what I truly believed? How did things get so messed up? How do I keep my spiritual life steady when my whole existence on this earth has felt like a spinning top.. out of control all the time?* When my deepest desire had been to make Jesus the Lord of my life, it was beyond baffling to think that that desire had disappeared in such an incredibly short period of time.

Once I started talking again, I detected an underlying anger toward God that seemed to surface out of nowhere. It sounds absurd now, but I felt God unfairly had me over a barrel.

Daily, I hounded my sister with complaints that sounded like this. "Eileen, I tried my best and failed...God has clearly made this road too hard to walk...but I believe that only Jesus provides the way of salvation, so it seems God has put me in an impossible situation...between a rock and a hard place. My dilemma is beyond frustrating...I want what I cannot seem to attain."

Thankfully, she took our conversations in stride and displayed great patience, allowing me to come full circle and remember the truths of God's grace, love, patience, and forgiveness. As my faith and thinking were renewed, I allowed His strength to undergird my life, so that glimpses of joy and stability started to emerge again.

It seemed as if the Holy Spirit etched this phrase into my brain, which I still speak out loud today when life seems tough, *"Rosie, you don't have to be perfect...You just have to keep moving forward in this journey with Me. I will give you the strength to do this."*

Even now, my whole body relaxes as I acknowledge, "My Christian walk is not about a perfect me...it's about a perfect Him."

It was clear that I had much to learn, but I was greatly encouraged to persevere as I read about each of Jesus' disciples. They walked and talked with Him, witnessing miracles, and receiving words straight from his mouth. They swore their allegiance to Him, only to fail, just like me. But they repented, learned from their mistakes, and continued following the Lord. *They didn't give up, and neither would I.*

As my faith grew and my walk got stronger daily, I was to learn another very important spiritual principle. Even though our sins are forgiven the moment we ask God, the consequences of sin remain, and sometimes leave a trail of destruction and grief that doesn't disappear overnight.

Eventually, Eric and I had to talk. When that day came, I'm sure my words sounded hollow and insincere to him. There was no way to ease the pain of the situation. I felt incapable of giving him any great answers when I couldn't even understand the "whys" myself?

After so many years, most of our conversation escapes my memory, with the exception of Eric's two conditions that needed to be in place if we were even thinking of trying to move forward in our marriage. The first one was to stop seeing Bobby and the second was to quit touring.

In my heart, I silently acknowledged that that is exactly what needed to happen for any chance of repairing our relationship! Instead, I said, "Eric, I will stop seeing Bobby, but please don't ask me to stop touring... You know I just can't do that!"

Eric didn't say another word. The conversation was over...There was no more discussion...That was that!

Over the years, I have replayed this scenario many times in my head. I have spent countless hours of guilt and regret over the fact that I didn't have the courage to do the right thing. Back then, I just didn't have the emotional maturity that it would take to stand up to my dad and fight for my marriage.

After that conversation, zero time elapsed for any chance of having a change of heart or mind. I received divorce papers immediately. Eric and I didn't even hire lawyers. With only a few years of marriage under our belt, and no children involved, we amicably took whatever we brought into the marriage, and our life together was over.

When Eric moved out, I left Gregg and Eileen's house and moved back into my home, with a new determination and focus to understand God and myself. I was thoroughly exhausted from living a life of ping-ponging emotions—high and exuberant one minute and crashing to new lows the next.

My earnest prayer was to have a life of steadiness and consistency with God, no matter what circumstances came my way. Also, I threw myself into a heavy regimen of scripture memorization as a tool to ward off the lies that continuously attempted to attack my soul and wage war in my brain.

I posted note cards with God's truth all over my house as constant reminders. I kept one card written from Psalms 119:31-34 on my refrigerator for at least ten years. I read it every day as a reminder of where I had been, where I wanted to go, and who would help me accomplish the goal I had set for my life. "I cling to your commands and follow them as closely as I can. Lord, don't let me make a mess of things. If you will only help me to want your will, then I will follow your laws even more closely. Just tell me what to do and I will do it, Lord. As long as I live I'll wholeheartedly obey" (Living Bible).

After two divorces, it was a no-brainer to realize there was some kind of change and re-wiring that needed to take place in my thinking. So I turned to Proverbs, which was loaded with wisdom and discernment regarding relationships of all kinds. Each chapter was full of insights, revealing the character of all types of people. I was desperate for knowledge and understanding in the area of relationships, and I was sure God would give me direction and answers if I continued on this path.

I wasn't sure what the rest of my life would look like, but in going forward, I made a decision to set a few boundaries around myself that I would uphold if I were ever considering the option of marriage again. These nuggets of gold from Proverbs became the first of many new guidelines.

Proverbs 12:15 "A fool thinks he needs no advice, but a wise man listens to others" (Living Bible).

Proverbs 15:22 "Without counsel, plans go awry, But in the multitude of counselors they are established" (NKJV).

As I looked deeply into my soul and began speaking my thoughts out loud to my circle of wise, Godly, confidants, I discovered that I had developed an immense distrust of people. This made it easy for me to shy away and shrink back from being authentic. I had become a master at presenting only what I wanted people to see. Deep inside, I felt that no one would accept or love the real me. Even though this wasn't true, the only thing that would convince me to peek out of my turtle shell again was the realization and assurance that God's love for me was unconditional. It was a forever kind of love. The time had come for me to willfully choose to depart from this pattern that kept me shrinking back to my non-threatening world of isolation, which was a major step contributing to my downfall. Isolation is always the beginning of a sure-fire spiral down to the depths.

So, I vowed two things: I would fight my tendency to close off from others and isolate myself, and I would not entertain the idea of marriage again, unless I had a "thumbs up" from the handful of trusted family and friends who had my best interests at heart.

As weird as it is, looking back, having this bit of wisdom firmly in place, and sticking to it, probably saved me from a third devastating marriage."

With our summer tour fast approaching, I tried pushing down anxious thoughts over seeing Bobby again on a regular basis. I wanted to take things slowly, but that seemed like an impossible task, as we had already taken our relationship way past the beginning stages. Nevertheless, I instinctively knew to keep our connection on the down low in front of my dad.

As I pressed in toward God and truth, I began to feel more significant and secure in my own skin. Slowly, some of the blinders covering my eyes were peeling away, allowing me to make observations and have vulnerable conversations about some of the red flags that were present.

Inconsistencies and confusion were always present in my and Bobby's relationship. This was probably due to the fact that our foundation was unholy and cracked from the beginning. Still, it seemed like Bobby had an equal number of positive characteristics, so I kept dismissing my nagging thoughts, hoping he was just in the process of maturing.

In keeping with the new goals I had set for myself, I stayed accountable, open for input, and was determined to wait on God until I felt His abiding peace, along with the "much needed approval" from my circle of loved ones around me. That was my protection, because I wasn't at a point in my life where I could trust my own decisions.

Along with two marriage proposals from Bobby, I experienced a lot of pain and heartache before I managed to tear myself away from this relationship that I believe was designed by the evil one to destroy me.

Sometimes I feel foolish that I let almost four years pass before I could sever the ties completely, but those thoughts disappear when I am able to help other gals who are experiencing the same thing I did, pointing them to truths that sustained me. Then I know nothing is a waste in God's hands.

As we left California for the summer, I knew this was going to be a different kind of tour. After twenty years, I was the only remaining member of my brothers and sisters to be playing on The Queen and Her Court. It seemed strange, like a new era had begun. I rolled with the punches, trying to push down sad and lonely feelings. In retrospect, my dad was probably feeling some kind of sadness concerning this new era and the future too, but I couldn't tell as our relationship was not one of authenticity and vulnerability. Instead, with his usual exuberant confidence and infectious optimism, Daddy introduced a new book that would be required reading in our team discussions that summer. The book was *Tough Times Never Last, But Tough People Do!* by Dr. Robert Schuller. He was the lead pastor of the largest glass building in the world, The Crystal Cathedral, where millions viewed his telecast each week on "The Hour of Power."

Robert Schuller's book, filled with positive and inspiring stories of turning problems into possibility thinking, was very uplifting to me at the time. Things weren't perfect, but I felt a shift in my thinking...*just maybe the ominous cloud over my head was finally lifting.*

Following our summer tour, Daddy bought each member a copy of the book, and, as a group, we made our way to the city of Garden Grove to visit this magnificent glass structured church, The Crystal Cathedral.

I cherished the words Daddy penned on the front cover of my book:

> *To our Precious Rosie,*
>
> *The birth and existence of 20 years of The Queen & Her Court is more of an outstanding example of Possibility Thinking than the Crystal Cathedral. This book has been a timely treasure from God to bless and encourage us all. Memorize and live these principles!*
>
> *Love, Your Daddy*

His words represented a special affection and bond between us. It felt like an acknowledgment from my dad, letting me know that I was a big part of helping to achieve his incredibly unique dream. Every time I eyed my personalized book, it symbolized his love and appreciation for me. My self worth soared to the heavens...*I was finally "good enough."* I let myself hope again for all the possibilities of a bright future to unfold.

I could never have predicted that in five short months, the sweet aroma in my spirit would be quenched by a foreboding darkness that was meant to destroy everything and everyone in its path.

This was the end of an era...Daddy and I would never tour together again.

CHAPTER 22

FADE TO BLACK

"Fear not, for I have redeemed you; I have called you by your name;
You are Mine. When you pass through the waters, I will be with you;
and through the rivers, they shall not overflow you. When you walk
through the fire, you shall not be burned, nor shall the flame scorch you."

ISAIAH 43: 1-2 (NKJV)

There was an urgency in Eileen's tone as she emphasized each word, *"Rosie, Daddy hasn't been doing very well."*

"What do you mean?" I asked.

"He's been feeling light headed and passing out. The other day he was seeing spots, so he bent over, putting his head between his legs, hoping that would help. Instead, he fainted, falling down on his head. Daddy went to the hospital, but the doc couldn't figure out why this was happening to him." Eileen continued, "Getting no answers only made matters worse. He seems really down and depressed about his health… and life in general."

"Well, Eileen, you know Daddy feels depressed every winter."

"I know, but it seems different this time. Maybe you can give him a call."

"Will do, sis. I'll call him as soon as we hang up. Thanks for letting me know."

After seeing Daddy, I had to agree with Eileen. His mood resembled his customary winter blues...only worse. He acted like he was in a deep, dark pit, with no hope of getting out. I did my best, along with Eileen, Carol, and others, to pull him out of that pit but all our efforts were in vain. It seemed like a cloud of negativity was overpowering Daddy, so I did the only thing I could think to do to try and help him. I packed up some clothes and took up temporary residence in my old bedroom. As it turned out, I spent the night during the week for over two months, going home on weekends and then returning each Monday.

As difficult and discouraging as this time period was, I know now, what I never suspected then. This time spent with my dad was an appointment from the hand of God.

In retrospect, most all the warning signs and symptoms of suicide were present, but I never had a clue that such a shocking act was on the horizon. I could see that Daddy was having a hard time eating and sleeping, which didn't help matters; but I was sure I could make him happy if we had time together, talking about future plans and details for our upcoming tour. This was a sure-fire remedy for lifting his mood in the past.

But nothing worked. It seemed like he had lost all interest in the things that usually got him excited.

During my two-month stay at Daddy's house, I only saw one spontaneous burst of joy from him. We captured this memory in a photo, as he got down on his hands and knees and gave my three-year-old niece, Jeralynn Joy, a piggyback ride, as she squealed with delight.

Most of the time, Daddy's thoughts centered on his unbearable pain, but physically speaking, we weren't quite sure what that entailed. So we persuaded him to see another doctor, hoping there would be answers to solve the mystery. After running many tests, the doctor suggested medication to help with Daddy's severe depression. His response was decisive, "I will not take any medications, because I am not depressed. Don't let me hear any of you saying that I am depressed!" *The message was received.* That made him so upset that no one dared to peep that word in his presence, even though I was sure that an ominous cloud of depression was hovering over him, and maybe causing some of his physical symptoms and pain.

Years later, as I searched for answers, I felt strongly that most of his life, Daddy was probably struggling with a severe depression turned inward, manifesting in the form of anger and control. We made suggestions to go for counseling, but the closest Daddy came to that was meeting only one time with a pastor on staff at his church…and talking with his brothers.

Hoping that exercise would clear his head, I coerced Daddy to go to the gym and on walks with me, like we used to do together. When it rained, I suggested we just take our walk inside the mall.

I knew he wouldn't have done these things if I hadn't pushed, but I tried to keep things upbeat and positive, assuring him that everything would get better as he continued these routines. With spring training fast approaching, I was confident that this strategy would pay off.

I felt flickers of hope, especially when I would witness a scene like the one of Daddy struggling to get through his water calisthenics at the gym. One minute he was lethargic and minutes later, I was shocked to hear him enthusiastically sharing the good news with a stranger on how to know Jesus and have eternal life. Inwardly I smiled and thought, *that's the person I know…it won't be long until he's back to normal.*

I racked my brain to think of things that would help. One day, I excitedly suggested that Carol, Daddy, and I go to the Bible bookstore and buy a New King James Bible. His other Bibles were worn from all the use and markings. I proposed the idea that a new Bible would help him start fresh, and God would reveal answers, with reminders and promises to help. Of course, he had to be persuaded, but I was excited when he agreed. I was hopeful that God would use this act as a springboard to help Daddy center his thoughts back on the promises of God.

At times, I felt sure that Daddy would recover. I thought, *in some ways, this trial is causing him to change for the better.* This idea was especially apparent when I heard that he had talked to one of his sisters whom he hadn't spoken to in years, making things right between them.

Eileen and I both made a mental note that even though Daddy never came right out and said the words, "Please forgive me for abusing you kids," he acted kinder and gentler with us. In one conversation with Eileen, he fumbled with his words but hinted at a couple of regrets. He said, "I felt bad a couple of times, when Marvin got me so upset that I went overboard, taking it out on you, Eileen."

I was stunned to hear the second regret that Daddy felt bad about. He said to Eileen, "Maybe I could've handled things differently when Rosie and Eric were married." Of course, these acknowledgments were not presented as the perfect apologies, but we received those words from our dad as a salve of consolation over our wounds. *We knew that it was a miracle for him to take any kind of responsibility… this was the best that we were going to get, and it was certainly better than nothing.* In the end, Daddy's making amends and visiting and calling on family was just another danger sign that he was getting his affairs in order. The most obvious warning of Daddy's impending suicide came directly from his own mouth, but ironically, his words never penetrated my brain because of my learned ability to deflect pain by blocking out whole monologues that threatened to bring me unwanted stress and anxiety.

This story sounds as unbelievable to me now as the first time Eileen spoke it aloud, following our dad's death.

I said, "I can't believe Daddy killed himself…I never saw it coming. Did he ever say anything to you?"

Eileen glanced my way with a shocked look on her face, "Are you being serious?"

My eyes widened and my heart started beating faster. "Of course, I'm serious," I replied.

Eileen continued, "Don't you remember? Daddy told us both."

I was emphatic, "There is no possible way I ever heard Daddy speak of suicide!"

She said, "Well, do you remember when he called you, me, and Carol into your old bedroom for a talk?"

I paused for a moment to think back. "Yes, I do recall that...but Daddy never said a thing about suicide. I remember him being very negative and pessimistic. I cried the whole time he was talking."

"Well, that's when Daddy told us, that if it gets too bad, he was going to have to take his own life," Eileen said.

I sat there *stunned*. If this were coming from almost anyone else but my trusted sister, I wouldn't have believed it. I knew I needed to be healed in this area, but I was alarmed that I could actually block out an entire thirty-minute conversation.

As I collected myself, I said, "Daddy must've said something pretty scary. Once I started crying, I didn't hear a word. What did he say?"

For the next few minutes, Eileen laid out the gist of his conversation. The first half was about the pain he felt, stating that something was physically wrong, but he couldn't keep living like this. He said it was hard on Carol and everyone else, and that it would be better if he was not around.

I interrupted her, "I think I remember him saying that, and that's when I started crying."

Eileen continued, *"Well, after that, Daddy said something like this: If it gets too bad, I'm going to have to take my own life."*

I was speechless as Eileen's words penetrated my mind. It seemed inconceivable that our dad would have uttered those words. He was always so strong and invincible. My whole life, I firmly believed that my dad would probably outlive us all.

Eileen continued, "When I tried to talk sense to him, he continued his talk with more subdued words, so he wouldn't upset us, basically laying out details that were written out about the house, the team, and how he'd want all other affairs to be handled, in case things got too bad for him."

After Eileen had conveyed all that she could remember, I said, "Well, I guess we both left his impromptu meeting that day pretty devastated...only I barely heard a word he said!"

During this time period, I entered into a season of immersing myself into the word of God. I came across a scripture in Matthew 17 where Jesus rebuked a demon, and it came out of a little boy. Later, in private, his disciples asked Him why they could not cast out the demon. In verse 20, Jesus said to them, *"Because of your unbelief; for assuredly I say to you, if you have faith as a mustard seed, you will say to this mountain, 'Move from here to there,' and it will move; and nothing will be impossible for you. However, this kind does not go out except by prayer and fasting."*

After hearing those words, I was more determined than ever to have enough faith for both of us to see the impossible take place in Daddy's life. Jesus' words were like a shot of assurance in the arm...my faith soared after spending time with God. Following my quiet times with the Lord, I always tried to encourage Daddy with whatever God disclosed to me. Although I did not see any big changes in his attitude, I was determined to stay the course, with unwavering faith and patience for God to move, in His own time.

Privately, I decided to re-double my prayers, believing God would heal Daddy completely. Also, even though it was never one of my strong suits, I fasted from food for three days. I was bummed that I could not fast for longer, but I continued in faith, not letting it get me down. I was sure of one thing...Daddy was not going to come out of this doom and gloom without a miracle from God.

I felt like the Holy Spirit directed me to pray in a very bold and direct way, which seems strange as I write it now. My prayer was for God to heal Daddy...body, soul, and spirit, or take Daddy to be with Him... one or the other. A supernatural confidence and peace came over me each time I uttered this prayer. I promised God I would not doubt Him, even if His answer was to take Daddy. I kept this prayer between me and God...not letting Daddy know, as it seemed pretty black and white.

Without really seeing much of a difference in Daddy, I decided to head back to my house. I must admit, it was easier to have faith for Daddy's healing when I didn't have to witness his downcast behavior. I made it a priority to call him daily and relay the same incredibly powerful and encouraging words that God was revealing to me.

Daddy always thanked me for sharing, but as I hung up the phone, I could tell by his voice that the things that were strengthening my faith were probably not having the same impact on him. Nevertheless, I stayed positive, even if I didn't see an instant change. As far as I was concerned, I would continue until there was answered prayer.

In an effort to *"pray without ceasing,"* I tried to sleep as little as humanly possible...refusing to go to my cozy bed at night. Instead, I got a blanket, books, and my Bible, and set them up on the floor, by a wall furnace next to my bedroom endeavoring to pray all night...interceding before the throne of God...pleading on behalf of Daddy.

When I prayed, I envisioned myself clinging to God, refusing to let go of Him, in the same way Jacob did when he wrestled all night with the Lord at Peniel (Genesis 32:24-32). I was determined to hold on to God until I got my answer.

On another night of praying, I was encouraged to persevere by reading a story Jesus told to his disciples about a widow who appealed to an evil judge for justice. The judge ignored her for a while, but eventually she got her justice. "Then the Lord said, 'If even an evil judge can be worn down like that, don't you think that God will surely give justice to his people who plead with him day and night?' Yes! He will answer them quickly!" (Luke 18: 1-7 Living).

Nighttime was approaching again. I had been praying and reading all day...God seemed silent. There were no specific words of encouragement...no revelations to lift my dad's spirit. It was a big fat nothing!

I felt disappointed and a little panicked. I begged God, "Please, God, speak to me. I have nothing encouraging to say to Daddy tonight. How can I call him with nothing to say?"

For minutes, I sat in silence in a heap on the floor. In the stillness, I heard God's voice. *"Tell him that you love him."*

God's voice was not audible, but very distinct. I knew I heard correctly, but I still felt hesitant. I spoke aloud, *"Of course, I will tell Daddy that I love him, but he knows that already…I need something more profound from you, Lord."*

I waited. Silence…so, in obedience, I began to dial Daddy's number.

"Hi Daddy. I've been praying for you all day…and I don't have too much to say, but God told me to call and tell you that I love you very much."

Our conversation was uncharacteristically short. Daddy thanked me for praying and told me he loved me too…and then we said goodnight.

Over the years, I have never been more thankful that I was obedient to God. More than anything, that call and all the quiet times of prayer that the Lord and I spent together was more of a merciful provision for me, than for my dad.

Daddy and I never talked again. He took his own life the following night. In ways that I did not know at the time, God was preparing me for my walk through the valley of the shadow of death. His grace and mercy covered me in so many ways that I reflect back on. God was constantly whispering in my ear, *"Fear not, my child, for I am with you."*

CHAPTER 23

TREADING WATER

"And the Lord said, 'Simon, Simon! Indeed, Satan has asked for you, that he may sift you as wheat. But I have prayed for you, that your faith should not fail; and when you have returned to Me, strengthen your brethren.'"

LUKE 22: 31-32 (NKJV)

◇◇◇◇◇◇◇◇◇◇◇◇

There are no adequate words to describe the torment of the person left to survive their loved one's suicide.

Daddy was dead, leaving behind those who loved him, to die hundreds of deaths daily, playing horrific scenes over and over in their minds, and trying to come up with some kind of understanding to the whys.

From the time of Eileen's pronouncement of Daddy's death at my house and for at least one year straight, I cried every day. My emotions were like a light switch...and the power to flick the switch off and on was given to a two-year-old just discovering the magic of electricity.

It felt like I was thrown into a permanent abyss as I grappled my way through a very intense and complicated grieving process, brought on by Daddy's unexpected plans to take matters into his own hands.

Because of the specific prayer I was led to pray beforehand, I trusted that God would give me the strength to emotionally handle a natural death; if it wasn't God's will to answer my prayer for Daddy's complete healing. However, I was shocked and knocked completely off balance with the news that he didn't die quietly in his sleep, for example, but that he intentionally murdered himself, which is the true definition of suicide.

In the midst of the unending tears, suffocating sadness, and waves of pain that threatened to take me under, I recognized the Lord's abiding presence was sustaining me throughout each day. This cup of suffering was not going away any time soon, but, daily, I witnessed evidence that God wanted me to know His love and care for me would be constant, especially during this most difficult trial.

Family and close friends were a vital part of God's provision for me. As we prepared for the funeral, I stayed the first two weeks back at my dad's house. At first, I was kind of spooked to walk by Eileen's old bedroom, which is where Daddy shot himself. I guess I was afraid of what I might see or discover. Even though, my old bedroom and other rooms were available, some of us took pillows, blankets, and sleeping bags to the den, we found comfort being together with loved ones who were feeling the same emotions...especially as nighttime lurked.

For a while, I was deathly afraid to fall asleep, but after hours of crying, my mind and body became weary, and I would eventually doze off. Each time I woke up, the reality of Daddy's suicide would terrorize me anew. This frightening scenario happened over and over, leaving me disoriented and exhausted.

Another thing that kept me fearful and vigilantly attempting to fight sleep were the nightmares that began occurring in the form of two different scenarios. One image was Daddy putting a pistol to his head and then pulling the trigger. The other image was similar...putting the gun in his mouth and doing the same, as I helplessly watched in terror. I'd awaken shaking and so nervous that I wanted to jump out of my own skin.

At first, I didn't seek details of Daddy's suicide, because it felt easier not to talk about things, remaining in denial. Eventually, I couldn't take it anymore; the nightmares were all-consuming. Even if the knowing was painful, I knew I needed to ask for more specifics surrounding his death.

Eileen confirmed that it was a gunshot to the head. Each new detail was agonizing to hear, but I guess it was part of the mourning process. I silently thought, *"This horrible mental image will never go away...I just want to remember Daddy as he was before this whole mess!"*

Plans for my dad's funeral had to be made, but I wasn't in any frame of mind to be of any help. While my brother, Norm, took on the unenviable task of calling hundreds of family and friends, informing them in a very non-descript manner concerning Daddy's sudden death and funeral arrangements, I spent all my energies just trying to survive each day. I was trying to wrap my head around everything that had transpired.

The day after Daddy's death, I remember being in the den with other family members, when my dad's wife, Carol, came in for an impromptu update on plans and details that would take place in the next couple of days. I listened quietly in my comatose state, as she tried to walk us through the upcoming events.

All her words were preceded with, *"It is your dad's wishes..."* It was hard to concentrate on what she was saying. I didn't want to hear anything. My brain was pounding. My thoughts were exploding with each new mandate that Daddy gave Carol to pass on to us from the grave, no less.

I recoiled thinking of the impossible task ahead to grant his wish of making his funeral a "day of celebration."

Oh, sure Daddy, I thought. *I'll just push a button to stop the sadness and tears and pretend I'm celebrating!*

Then came his instructions concerning what to tell the hundreds of friends, family, fans, and media concerning his death. His words were some vague medical jargon, which certainly mentioned nothing about suicide.

The volcano within erupted. I thought, *The insanity must stop NOW!* I interrupted, "Carol, I cannot say that, and I will not lie, especially if relatives and close friends ask me point blank." She did not contest. Carol was just the messenger. I understood. We all did what we were told our whole lives to please Daddy.

It was an odd feeling that day. I could actually speak up for what I believed in, without any repercussions. It took me awhile to sort out the newly awakened freedom within. Some days, I felt guilty for rejoicing in this freedom that I had gained with my dad's passing. But as the years of grieving disappeared, I discovered that I now had sole responsibility for accepting or rejecting God's direction for my life, without any interference, or feelings that I was disappointing Daddy.

As it turned out, the local newspaper posted a small notice stating Daddy's death as a suicide, despite what was reported. Except for family and close friends, I chose not to speak in detail concerning the particulars; I kept the shameful truth in hiding. That being said, few people knew what really happened.

A few days later, I learned a chilling story that would have rocked the media, surely making headlines, if not for God's intervention.

I could only listen to Eileen in disbelief as she shared a shocking account that occurred one month before Daddy died, with the mysterious details confirmed by Carol after his death.

Eileen began, "The warmth of the sun felt soothing as I walked from my car into Daddy's house to do office work. I was feeling happy and light-hearted as I entered Daddy's front door."

"Bam!" she said. "The moment I headed down the hallway, it felt like a ominous black cloud covered me. Rosie, there was such an eerie darkness and evil oppression all around me as I saw Daddy and Carol

sitting at the dining room table. The first words out of my mouth were, 'What's going on in here?'"

Eileen chuckled, "I was surprised at myself...like I would ever say anything like that to Daddy!"

"Daddy had an inexplicable look on his face and said, 'Oh, nothing.'"

Eileen continued, "I could never get that scene out of my head. After Daddy's death, I asked Carol what was going on that day? She said, your dad was writing out a double suicide pact, and I was signing it!"

Listening to this unbelievable story, I sat there shaking my head in horror. It was hard to take in all that I was hearing. Finally, I found my voice, *"Obviously, that didn't happen...what changed?"*

Eileen resumed, "Carol said that a couple days later God told him that it wasn't right."

My mind was whirling...so many thoughts...so many questions. *God saved Carol, but why didn't He help Daddy come to his senses, and save him too?*

It was stories like this that cemented my belief that God was not caught off guard by Daddy's suicide, but there were no clear-cut answers to all my "whys." After all this time, God still felt so mysterious.

Nevertheless, even though unanswerable questions remained, I recognized God's abundant grace sustaining me as I muddled through each hellish day. Along with his abiding presence, He revealed many insights that only come as one passes through the fire. For years, I had felt uneasiness about the "dos and don'ts" as I fumbled for ways to comfort those experiencing the pain of losing a loved one. Now, I had first hand knowledge of this school of hard knocks.

I made a mental note as I observed that each family member grieved differently, so discerning what comforted them might not have been right for me. I was touched with the thoughts and prayers of everyone who sent cards; and even though I didn't feel like eating, I noticed close friends preparing food for our family, just in case. That was comforting. Although I didn't want to talk much, I was strengthened to feel a quiet presence of close friends in the same room. When too many people congregated, I recall being overwhelmed, retreating to hide in one of the bathrooms for an extended period of time, waiting for the well-wishers to leave.

During this time, it was not beneficial to hear loved ones quote a lot of scripture, or try to come up with answers for such a catastrophic happening. The only exception to the previous statement was this. If the person had experienced some kind of unexpected tragedy in their life, I was "all ears," listening for any nuggets of wisdom that came out of their mouth.

On one occasion, as I was popping my head out of the bathroom; I saw my Uncle Dallas, who was the brother closest in age to Daddy. I asked him to tell me some stories about my dad. I always remembered that was one of the things that brought me solace, even making me laugh a little.

The day before the funeral, arrangements for a private viewing of Daddy's body were made for family and close friends who wanted to say their last goodbyes…the funeral was to be a closed casket.

I told Eileen, *"I don't think I want to go. Are you going?"* I was already having such a hard time with all the unpleasant visuals in my head. I couldn't bear one more shocking sight. Eileen's response was decisive. "I need to go, but you do what's right for you." I thought for a few minutes and said, "It seems kind of scary, but if you're going, then maybe we can go together. If I decide I can't handle going in to view his body, I'll just wait outside."

Maybe I was just feeding off of Eileen's courage, because every part of me wanted to run away. Instead, without hesitation, I followed her into the room to view my Daddy's body for the last time. Although his body looked swollen and fake with pounds of heavy make-up, I was relieved to view his face all intact, unlike the nightmares that plagued me. Silently, I thanked God that I could not find any trace of a bullet hole in his head. I felt my strength draining rapidly as my eyes quickly scanned the lifeless shell that used to be my Daddy. Sadness overpowered me as I walked away.

That day presented a new life principle of healing that I cemented into my brain. *Sometimes we have to dip down into more pain to eventually be healed from the already devastating pain at hand.*

With every fiber of my being, I did not want to walk through that experience, but in doing so, it was the way that God answered my prayers for relief from my horrific visuals, and now, I only remember Daddy as he was in life.

Following that day, the nightmares of being in Daddy's presence, watching him commit suicide, became extinct. It was one of the first of many answered prayers from God that moved me closer to healing.

I couldn't wait for Daddy's big "day of celebration" to be over. I say that sentence with tongue in cheek, wrapped in a bouquet of sarcasm. The sanctuary was packed with loved ones as my brothers and sisters and I sat up front in our brightest attire (no black was allowed), doing our best to rejoice and commemorate our dad's life. My heart was not into it, but we all did our best.

Like so many times before, amidst tears, I plastered on my finest winning smile to honor Daddy that day. There were many bygone nights that I pushed my own demons and thoughts of suicide away, fearing the outcome of my eternal security. Now, without any concrete and absolute answers from the Bible on the subject, I had to choose to believe that Daddy was in the presence of God. It was either that or be devastated for the rest of my life. I could not allow my thinking to entertain any other options.

I reasoned that suicide, like any other sin, was not the unpardonable sin, as revealed in the Bible as blasphemy of the Holy Spirit…a continual unbelief or rejection of Christ, after truth has been revealed by the Holy Spirit. Therefore, I made a conscious decision to rest on the mercy of the Lord, trusting in the constancy of His Word and believing that He is the same…yesterday, today, and forever (Hebrews 13:8).

Somehow Daddy's suicide triggered an overload of thoughts surrounding this subject. In the coming days, I would spend hours debating the issue of suicide in my head. I had to have some answers and come to concrete conclusions to move forward.

As one who knows the feeling of being left to pick up painful shards and pieces from this most selfish act, I felt that I had received the cure, by way of experience, to never again consider suicide as a plausible option for myself, knowing the agonizing heartache it caused others.

Because I was so dogmatic in my new stance on suicide, I was secretly shaken that I couldn't instantly get rid of the suicidal thoughts that still popped up out of nowhere. This left me feeling off balance and scared.

A startling thought kept repeating continually...*You are like your dad in so many ways...You will probably end up doing the same thing he did.*

It was time to put a stop to this dark, satanic kind of thinking, by bringing my thoughts to light. Once I began sharing these dangerous conversations out loud to loved ones around me, all thoughts of suicide disappeared from my life forever.

Amidst the sadness and grief, God's overwhelming presence sustained me. It seemed unbearably difficult to make it through each day; but looking back, I recognize His mercy and grace were tangible in every detail, big and small. During this time, the word of God was my lifeblood, giving me strength, comfort, and the courage to make it through every new twenty-four hours...and yet, if I'm honest, some scriptures caused an unwelcome stirring in my soul. In an effort to press forward, I made a conscious decision to put any confusing thoughts and scriptures that clouded my thinking, on the back burner. I would take up these unresolved and perplexing conversations with God again at a later time.

Spring was right around the corner when an uninvited and pervasive issue grabbed hold of me, and kept re-surfacing continuously for many years. About three months had elapsed since Daddy's death when Eileen shared a recent talk with our mom. Eileen gently slid into a conversation with me by saying, "The other day I was talking to Mom. and she asked if all of us kids were taken care of in Daddy's will?"

My ears perked up to see what she was going to say next. Because I was single, I did have thoughts and concerns regarding my financial future; but up to this point, neither of us had given any thought to the subject of a will. As Eileen formed her next words, I secretly hoped she was going to say something positive. Daddy had made such an effort in planning every detail of his passing…maybe, just maybe, Eileen was going to say that Daddy showed me and my siblings how much he loved us by leaving some kind of tangible provision.

Eileen continued, "I told Mom that Daddy left everything to Carol."

I remained expressionless as I took in each new bit of information. Truthfully, I wasn't shocked by what I heard, but inwardly, I could feel a flood of hurt and disappointment overtaking me. I wanted to shut down, but I forced myself to be present with my sister.

"What did Mom say when you told her that?"

Eileen said, "She was horrified! Mom continued to tell me that although they didn't sign anything following the divorce, Daddy convinced Mom not to pursue the court's mandate requiring him to give her half of the money and half the value of the house. He would've had to sell the house to come up with the cash he owed Mom. Instead, he appealed to her motherly instincts…you know, let's do what's best for the kids. He assured her, in the end, it would go to the kids anyway."

I snickered, *"Convinced Mom? More like, told Mom. I'm sure she didn't really have a choice."*

While I sat stunned with this new revelation, Eileen resumed, "Anyway, Mom doesn't want to say anything, but she suggested we should at least talk to Carol." After a few more conversations and prayer, Eileen and I decided to let Carol know what Daddy had promised Mom.

As a result, Carol handled the situation with the utmost fairness and integrity, no questions asked. She moved swiftly, obtaining a current appraisal for the Rolling Hills Estates house; issuing a check for half of the property's worth, representing our mom's half, which we split five ways.

I took two thirds of my portion and handed it right back to Carol, completely paying off the balance of my home in Lakewood that my dad had purchased in cash about ten years earlier. Then, I took the remaining amount and bought a new car, as my 1970 Mustang was requiring more mechanical problems than I felt capable of handling...*that's the last thing a single gal wants...car problems!*

Although all the money was gone, I was relieved and thankful to have this bit of financial security, with no house or car payments. There was no doubt in my mind that through this outcome, I was witnessing the merciful hand of God, moving through Carol. God was making His presence known...He had the last word.

My trust and confidence in God grew by leaps and bounds. Through this act, I felt like He was reassuring me that He would always take care of me. God's intervention felt like He had applied a soothing salve to the cavernous, gaping wound in my heart. However, even with such favorable results, I had to intentionally allow God's Spirit to move in my heart, consenting to take the necessary steps to find peace and healing for my father-wound. This process took years.

The big question for me was, *How do I really forgive my dad when he was no longer alive? If I couldn't tell him how badly he hurt me, would it ever be possible to feel completely healed?*

If this was strictly a money issue, I could have let it go; but it wasn't. It went so much deeper, cutting into the core of my being.

In the months before Daddy's passing, I felt like I was just starting to reconcile the events of my scary, abusive childhood. Even though there were no apologies from him, I had decided I just wanted to be free from the past and forgive. Now it felt like I was back to square one on this crazy emotional merry-go-round. Daddy's latest actions represented his lack of love, care, protection, and loyalty to me.

I felt like I had loved and been loyal to him to a fault, putting him above every relationship...maybe even God. He said that The Queen and Her Court was God's will for our lives, and I believed him. I wanted desperately to ask him if he thought leaving me with no husband, no career, no future, and in financial quicksand was part of what he considered "God's will" also.

After putting twenty years of my heart and soul into his dream, forsaking any other direction or plans for my life, Daddy opted out, leaving me with nothing. Some days, I sarcastically reasoned, *If he would have just treated me, not like a daughter, but like the loyal employee who stayed after everyone else was long gone, maybe I would have received some kind of a pension or at least a gold watch!*

During the first year of Daddy's death, I was so overcome by sadness and grief that I didn't fully realize how much anger was percolating inside of me. But as time went on, I witnessed my deep hurt bubble up and explode into angry words, as I yelled to Daddy, only to have my words bounce off the silent walls and return back to me empty. I couldn't help but think...*What if I would have done that to him when my life turned upside down? Was there another girl out there who could've taken my place on The Queen and Her Court, and been willing to put up with all his demands for these last two decades?* I was convinced the answer was a resounding "no"!

I had honored him with my loyalty my whole life, and when the dust settled, it was beyond hurtful that my dad did not reciprocate. For the longest time, it seemed no matter how hard I tried to forgive and believe that Daddy loved me, the same negative conversations would overtake me, playing like a broken record and cutting deep into my soul. In life, Daddy's words were powerful, and I trusted him, but his actions kept screaming from the grave, always persuading me how little I really meant to him.

I desperately wanted to please God by extending forgiveness to Daddy, just as the Lord had graciously granted forgiveness to me, promising to blot out every transgression of mine as far as the East is from the West.

By faith, I would speak the words "I forgive you, Daddy," out loud… only to take them back every time I felt the pain and hurt of trying to pick up the messy pieces and move forward in my life of uncertainty. It would take years before I could say those words and mean it, without the sting of his actions waging war in my soul.

Somehow, I needed to figure out how to reframe my dad's suicide and gain a new perspective from the Lord, so I could heal. I tried my best, but unfortunately, the healing and freedom of forgiveness wasn't going to happen for me overnight.

After reading the book of Job, I sometimes imagined Satan confronting God concerning my faith in the Lord, saying, "If just one more tragedy occurs in Rosie's life, surely she will walk away from you."

God took up the challenge, allowing Daddy's suicide. It seemed God had a plan, with an abundance of confidence in me…a whole lot more confidence than I had in myself. I hoped I had the courage not to disappoint Him. I had the benefit of knowing Job's story from beginning to end, where the unthinkable happened. He lost all his children; his empire collapsed, and boils spread all over his body. Yet, he remained faithful and, in the end, God restored everything, and Job was blessed more than in the beginning.

Like Job, I wanted to be able to say, "Though He slay me, yet will I trust Him" (Job 13:15). More importantly, I wanted to learn to trust and know the wisdom of God, even when my life was falling apart.

In the midst of all the grief and suffering, there were moments I had a strong sense that things were going on all around me…certainly much more than meets the eye…some kind of spiritual warfare. I would have a hard year ahead of me. My life was about walking a dark path and hoping there would be light to shine on me up ahead. I just wanted the sadness to lift, and the dagger in my heart to be removed. I was furiously treading water…hoping to survive.

CHAPTER 24

THE SHOW MUST GO ON

*"Fear not, for I am with you; Be not dismayed, for I am
your God. I will strengthen you. Yes, I will help you. I
will uphold you with My righteous right hand."*

ISAIAH 41:10 (NKJV)

◇◇◇◇◇◇◇◇◇◇◇◇

The summer tour of 1985 was both a blessing and a curse. I was a thirty-three-year-old grieving mess with a recently buried dad, two divorces under my belt, financial uncertainty, and a perplexing relationship with Bobby that was as inconsistent and unstable as my emotions that bounced from high to low many times during the course of each day.

Any moments of clarity that I had entertained concerning my current relationship were pushed aside as the shock of my dad's death threw me back into Bobby's arms…even though I knew better.

Right before Daddy's passing, I received one of the best pieces of wisdom on how to discern whether pursuing this relationship was advisable. I have never forgotten my sister's words, and have shared them over the years, in one-on-one conversations with countless gals experiencing my same dilemma.

"It just seems so confusing, Eileen. Bobby and I aren't able to move forward in our relationship, and yet I remain." I continued, "Some days, I think it could work with Bobby…but then other days I know he's not the right guy for me. I guess it's hard to let go, because I see that he has so much potential."

Eileen smiled, "Well, Rosie, Adolf Hitler, one of the most evil men that has ever lived, had a lot of potential too, but you certainly wouldn't want to marry him."

We both laughed out loud. Her point was well taken. *Hadn't my past mistakes reinforced the fact that it could be disastrous marrying a person while hoping they would change…hoping all that potential would transform into the man I envisioned?*

Eileen's words made sense. I knew our impending end was right around the corner. However, with all that had just happened, I did not have the necessary strength and courage to face the idea of going on our summer tour feeling alone and unloved. So I continued on in our fated relationship, ironically, feeling more unloved which only added to the pain and heartache that I was already experiencing.

Before taking off for three summer months on the road, I received two cherished items from Carol. She had five Bibles that my dad had used throughout his life, and she wanted to let each sibling pick one. When she laid them before me, I selfishly wanted them all…anything that reminded me of him, I wanted. I vacillated between the worn, black, Living Bible with hundreds of his highlighted markings and the New King James Version that I had helped him pick out at the Christian bookstore a few months before his passing.

Although the Living Bible was more sentimental to me, I chose the other one. There were a few select passages, mostly in Psalms, highlighted in blue. By reading these sections, I was hoping to interpret what he read in his last days and gain some kind of insight into his thinking.

There were no profound discoveries, but over the years, I did make this Bible my own, using other highlighters, avoiding blue, so I would always know which markings were his. Every few months, I would go searching for all the words in blue and think of Daddy.

As Carol started cleaning out Daddy's closets, I made a special request, which seems strange and even kind of comical now, but I was living in strange days back then. I asked if I could have my dad's faded navy blue sweatpants. If there was anything that reminded me of him, it was those sweats that he wore lounging around the house and to every softball practice. The part that makes me laugh now is that I began wearing those sweatpants to every practice when we started spring training. It's not like they looked good on me either. I pulled the drawstring tight, cinching them around my waist. Because my legs were longer than Daddy's, the elastic bottoms were hiked up about three inches above my ankles...think dorky floods. It was not a good look!

This wasn't like me, but it was a good reflection of how "out of it" I was. It was difficult to embrace the sudden and permanent ending of Daddy's life on this earth. Somehow, wearing those pants brought me comfort, helping me feel close to my dad when he was no longer around.

This tour was going to be like no other. I desperately wanted "normal" in my life. It probably wasn't a good idea to be away from my family and the support and stability of my church and close friends so soon; but after twenty years on the road, this life was all I knew. It provided finances, a purpose, and above all, a well-established identity...the feeling of being normal.

When I began the tour, I didn't realize how so many things would trigger memories of Daddy, reminding me that he was permanently gone from this earth.

As we piled into our twelve-passenger maxi van, I slid over to my regular seat in the first row, right behind the driver's seat. I burst into tears. I had logged thousands of miles staring at the back of Daddy's head. It seemed like every little thing reminded me of my dad. We'd go miles out of our way if he saw an "all you can eat buffet" sign or if a café posted anything about "Mom's home cooking." White rail fences, winding around a ranch house, horses, and cows were scenes that always inspired Daddy. Early on in our touring days, he never passed up an opportunity to teach us to distinguish between all the different breeds. As I passed through landscapes without Daddy, tears would come gushing if I spotted a lone jersey cow or palomino horse on a hillside.

Swimming pools, specific hotels, favorite towns, and even certain songs that he hated reminded me of Daddy switching the channel immediately and monologuing on the evils of that song. These memories made me sad.

Every night, I dreaded heading to another ballpark where I would no longer be able to look over and see Daddy on the sidelines or hear his southern twang on the microphone. That being said...amazingly, once I arrived, setting foot on each new softball diamond, I became Rosie Black, fearless softball professional. Each night I propelled myself into giving my best. Performing was my respite from sadness. Pitching was my happy place.

Preparing for the first pitch, I gazed into a sea of faces that came to see me and felt blessed. As I blazed pitches past batters, I felt powerful, invincible, and in control of my life. When I was on the pitching mound, all the grieving and sadness turned into passion and determination to conquer and move forward in victory. If I struck out the town's softball hero, strength surged through my veins...as I silently whispered to Daddy...*look what you just missed*. For a few hours each night, I was "normal" again, forgetting the nightmare of Daddy's suicide.

Once I got back to my hotel room, I wondered where my courageous spirit had disappeared to? It was back to sleepless nights, sadness, and tears. One night, following our game, I felt extra agitated and restless. I was rooming with Carol, who was excitedly chatting long distance on the phone with the brother of her best girlfriend from church. (She would end up marrying Norm, who has been a gift to her and a blessing to all of us.)

Admittedly, I was extra annoyed. She was so happy, and I was so sad. Also, Bobby and I had been extra disconnected during that time, making matters worse. I was becoming nervous and frantic. Walls were closing in on me. I had to get out of that room…fast! I grabbed my Walkman and earplugs and took off running blindly, with tears streaming down my face for I don't know how long. Through the tears, I spoke to God, *"I just can't take this anymore. My life is just too hard. I wish I was dead."* I just kept muttering short little phrases, *"Where are you? I need you…Help me, God."*

Finally, I could feel my body tiring and my spirit relaxing a bit. Up to this point, I had been oblivious to time. As I slowed to a walk, I glanced at my watch and couldn't believe one and a half hours had passed.

I thought, *I'm exhausted and so far away from our motel. It's after 11:00 p.m. I'll never make it back to the room by our midnight curfew.* I glanced around. I had no idea where I was.

I never liked breaking rules, and I didn't want anyone to worry; but I couldn't figure out what to do. There were no cell phones back then, and I had no money with me for a pay phone. I was racking my brain for solutions when a carload of loud guys and girls saw me walking and pulled over to the side of the road, asking if I needed a ride?

It felt a little sketchy taking rides from strangers, especially late at night, but they seemed innocent enough, so in my desperation, I smiled and yelled out, *"Thanks"* as I headed over to their car. As I reached for the back seat door handle that was slightly opened for me, the car jolted and sped away…everyone erupted into roars of laughter. At first, it startled me; I felt humiliated. But soon a smile formed in the corners of my mouth…those punks got me good!

After a minute, I noticed their car was stopped up ahead again. They were still laughing and calling out sarcastically to me.

I wasn't going to fall for that again, and wanted nothing to do with them. I was a little nervous that they weren't driving on, especially after I had motioned that I no longer wanted a ride.

I started taking notice of my surroundings in case I had to quickly dart away. I had been walking along the grassy edges of a dimly lit park. Just before I dashed off in another direction, I witnessed a scene that has stayed with me for years.

As four boy's heads were sticking out the car windows, mocking and jeering loud taunts back at me, the timer for a row of very high-powered sprinklers from the park automatically turned on, spraying their faces and drenching the inside of their car.

With shocked looks on their faces, they didn't know what hit them. All the heckling ceased, as their car sped off! The joke ended up being on them.

I hadn't laughed that hard in quite a while. I couldn't have planned that any better if I tried!

I made a right turn onto a big boulevard, heading back in the direction of our motel. As I was chastising myself for running so far away, I noticed a group of college kids in a parking lot. I quickly scanned their faces and approached a guy who was just about to hop in his car. I made a snap decision, determining that he looked safe enough. "Hey, if you're heading that direction"...I pointed..."could I get a ride for a few miles?"

"Sure," he said. "My buddy and I will be taking off in a minute."

"Thank you so much," I responded.

The driver hopped in and motioned for me to jump in too. I felt slightly uneasy and foolish as I got into the front seat, but all those feelings amplified when his buddy slid in right next to me.

Why in the world didn't he jump in the back seat, where there was more room?

Every internal warning signal went off. I felt very vulnerable and unprotected, being sandwiched between these two strange guys in the front seat. *What had I got myself into?* I didn't want them to see how scared I was, so I became "Chatty Cathy" talking my head off.

I described my predicament, and the driver indicated that he knew exactly where the motel at the top of the hill was. I was hoping, maybe these were two nice guys, who were lending me a hand. That is…until the driver's talk and demeanor changed, and he slid his right hand on my left thigh.

I was freaked out but very playfully, took his hand and placed it back on the steering wheel. I scolded, "Two hands for safe driving." The driver continued talking sleazily to me, and I could sense he was up to no good. *This was not heading in the right direction.* I silently pleaded for God's protection, like never before.

Immediately, I diverted all my attention to the quieter guy to my right and asked, "Do you play any sports?" Then, I proceeded to do what I do best…I told them all about The Queen and Her Court and how we had just played in their home town.

The quiet guy bit my hook and started asking questions while I relayed every unbelievable softball story I could think of. It worked! It seemed like we arrived in minutes at the bottom of the hill leading to my motel.

I said, "Guys, I have to run, so I can make curfew. You can just drop me off right here." As I looked directly to the quiet guy on my right, motioning for him to let me out, I bolted out of that car as fast as I could, yelling back, *"Thanks so much for the ride."* I sprinted as fast as I could up the incline without looking back. I prayed that my jelly-like legs would not give out on me. An overdose of adrenaline continued pumping throughout my body, hours after I entered my dark room and slid quietly into bed.

I silently prayed, *God, I felt an evil presence in that car tonight, and I know you saved me from something bad. Forgive me for taking my life for granted, and thank you for always being with me.*

After that night, I had many more tears throughout the summer, but through that experience, I realized that no matter how difficult life got, I wouldn't purposely put myself in dangerous situations anymore. I didn't want to die…I wanted to live. Each day, I tried to remind myself that I was passing through a season of grief. I needed to have courage, and one day, this season would pass.

Just as I had assumed, most of the fans who came out to see The Queen and Her Court each year, didn't really press me for details when they noticed that my dad was missing from our entourage. If they asked, I gave them my succinct pat answer, which usually sufficed, especially when they could see my body language change from pleasant to sullen and distressed. For the most part, everyone was very respectful of my feelings and privacy, and they changed the subject.

The one exception I can recall happened at one of my favorite tour stops. After the first appearance on the nationally televised PTL Club (which stands for Praise the Lord), founded by then televangelists Jim and Tammy Faye Bakker, we became a regular attraction each summer at the newly built Heritage USA.

This spectacular Christian theme park opened in 1978 and by the late eighties, became one of the most popular vacation destinations in the United States, right behind Walt Disney World and Disneyland, with millions of visitors each year. There were manicured grounds, a water park, a skating rink, amphitheaters, campgrounds, and more.

We were paid a flat fee for our two-hour appearance, so any visitors for that day could watch The Queen and Her Court for free.

One of the highlights for me was staying in the deluxe accommodations of their 501-room, Heritage Grand Hotel, which was of the highest quality, housing an indoor shopping complex and "Main Street USA" on the lobby level. I loved my window-shopping excursions every time we were there.

The morning following our ballgame, I was scheduled to make a television appearance on The PTL Club. It only took a few minutes for Carol and me to drive to the lavish production studio, which was also built on the Heritage USA grounds.

Most of the time, my television segment was with Jim Bakker, but today I found out it would be with Tammy Faye. Over the years, I had done so many interviews that it didn't really matter if I talked with a male or female. Rarely, did an interviewer ever ask me a question that I hadn't heard hundreds of times before. But knowing that Tammy Faye wasn't really into sports, I wasn't sure what her line of questions would be like.

Carol, Tammy Faye, and I said our hellos and talked briefly before the cameras were to roll. She asked where Royal was and Carol explained that he passed away suddenly, giving a brief explanation. We requested that there not be a prolonged conversation about my dad, as this was still a very sensitive subject because it was so recent.

Everyone gave us their looks of sympathy, nodding their heads in total agreement. Even though it was unsettling to talk about Daddy right before we went on, I was relieved that this subject was discussed, and we were all on the same page. I felt a little weepy, after all their condolences, but I was determined to bolster some courage and act as a professional.

Cameras were rolling. A packed studio audience applauded as we took our seats on stage. Tammy Faye introduced us, launching right into our segment with the one topic that we asked her not to talk about… Royal Beaird.

I was stunned, but sure she'd move on quickly with something else. I was wrong! The majority of our allotted time was dedicated to remembering my dad. I felt as if I were sitting across from Barbara Walters. It felt like Tammy Faye was purposely pushing me hard for tears. *Was she deliberately doing this, even though she could see it was painful for me?*

She didn't know what she was getting into…if it was tears she wanted, I could certainly oblige. Once the waterworks started, they didn't stop until I was off that stage.

Tammy Faye made a few attempts to draw a response from me. But my grief was full blown, mixed with anger at her insensitivity to me…I set my jaw tight, refusing to respond to a word she said.

Carol ended up answering all my questions, finishing out the interview. Reflecting on that day, I had mixed emotions. It was the first time I had ever done anything like that. I chastised myself for not being able to push my feelings aside and complete the interview...but another part of me felt justified. Maybe, in some kind of way, I was making a point. You can't disregard and disrespect people without consequences.

Weeks later, we received two random letters sent to our home office that felt like God's voice speaking to me, making me feel better.

Both letters expressed their kindest condolences and prayers for me. Both letters stated how seeing me on television that day really touched their lives, and that they could feel the presence of God. I was very surprised by their response to the interview...especially since I was completely mute.

Wow...could this be true? Could I let people see the real me? Could God still use me if I didn't portray perfection? What was God trying to say to me? Daddy had always taught me that "the show MUST go on" ...but now he was gone. Would life be okay if the show didn't go on?

It seemed like there was a seismic-shift taking place in my brain. The real question was not "What does Daddy think about my life, my decisions, my behavior? But instead...what does God think?"

Maybe I was starting to see the bigger picture.

CHAPTER 25

CROSSROADS

"And though the Lord gives you the bread of adversity and the water of affliction, yet your teachers will not be moved into a corner anymore. But your eyes shall see your teachers, your ears shall hear a word behind you say, 'This is the way, walk in it.' Whenever you turn to the right hand or whenever you turn to the left."

ISAIAH 30: 20,21 (NKJV)

◇◇◇◇◇◇◇◇◇◇◇◇

It was surreal. The grandstands were packed as I purposely tried to embrace this memory, taking in every detail. *Was this really the last game I would ever pitch for The Queen and Her Court?* My stomach felt sick and a cloud of dread hovered over me. After twenty-one years of touring, I couldn't envision what my life would look like after this night.

I knew one thing…I had to discontinue this line of thinking, or I'd be a blubbering mess in a matter of minutes. I fired the first pitch between my legs for a strike. The stunned batter seemed mesmerized as the ball whizzed past him. He shook his head in disbelief, and the crowd erupted in laughter and cheers. I silently thought, *If this is it, I'm going out with a bang!*

But let me back up a bit…

It was good to be home after the first summer following my dad's death. With the familiarity of family, church friends, and the consistency of sleeping in the same bed again, I regained a healthier focus. I knew in my heart that I needed to pull a permanent plug with Bobby, but our relationship lingered. I guess the big problem I had was trying to visualize taking steps backwards into the "friendship zone" and continuing to tour together. *That seemed like a torturous scenario.*

Also, in the back of my mind, I felt sad to think if Bobby wasn't to be a part of my future, then no guy from this day forward would probably ever understand or know the real me if they had never met my dad. The only thought that helped to combat that thinking was what my sweet mom said to me about a year earlier. At the time her statement cut deep, but in retrospect, she was imparting a bit of realistic truth.

As we were saying our goodbyes following lunch together, I said, "Mom, don't forget to pray that God will send me a husband."

She replied, "I will, honey…but I don't think you can have a successful marriage as long as your dad's alive."

I was floored. I said, "Well, that's not good news, especially since Daddy will probably outlive us all."

Her words haunted me for the longest time. Now I was wondering if they were prophetic.

I was trying to honor God in all aspects of this relationship with Bobby, hoping to receive some clear-cut direction…but He seemed silent…even confusing at times. For example, one Sunday I decided to fast and pray all day, asking God for a specific sign concerning the relationship. I alerted Eileen to my plan and let her know that I did not want any interruptions, so I would not be answering my phone. I said, "Eileen, if there is some kind of emergency, or you want to talk to me… ring once, hang up, and then call back and I will answer."

As I prayed and read my Bible, an incredible sense of peace flooded my being. I felt an overpowering presence and confidence that God was with me. He knew all the intricate details of my life. He even knew I was going to fast and pray today before it happened.

A new strength that wasn't my own surged through my body. I was asking for His help, and I was certain His answer was coming.

Around 4:00 p.m., my phone rang, cutting through the silence. I didn't budge from my spot on the couch, expecting a series of rings… but it only rang once.

I welcomed the thought of hearing my sister's voice as I walked over to my phone and waited for it to ring again. With a chuckle in my voice, I said, "Hey Leenie, what's up?

Bobby blurted out, "I've been trying to reach you all day. Where have you been?"

My mind was reeling, and it took a few seconds before any words would come out.

I stammered, "Did you just call a minute ago and hang up?"

"I guess so," he replied. "I thought something was wrong with the phone."

I paused to collect my thoughts. I wasn't sure what to say. We hadn't seen each other for the last three weeks.

Finally, I continued, "Why did you call?"

Bobby said, "Can I come over so we can talk?"

"Bobby, we've said everything there is to say. We're just not moving in the same direction."

"I know I've been a jerk, but I want to change."

I was trying to stand my ground. It felt like I had heard all this kind of talk a million times before. I said, "Bobby, I've got to go now. I was planning on going to church tonight."

"Please can I go too?" Bobby said. "We can go as friends."

It was hard to think straight. All I could think was, *I can't believe God allowed him to break the phone code, so Bobby could get through and talk to me.* It seemed miraculous. *Was this my sign from you, God?*

I conceded.

Before the night was over, Bobby said everything I needed to hear, with a heartfelt apology and new commitment to me, along with a renewed desire to seek God for his life...putting Him first in our relationship.

I was sure that this shift in Bobby's thinking would change everything. After the unbelievable chain of events that Sunday, I opened a piece of my heart that had been well guarded, shielding and protecting me from being hurt again.

Because of the circumstances surrounding my day of prayer and fasting, I was convinced God was leading me to move forward in this relationship, so I intentionally opened my heart to trust and be vulnerable again. That was scary for me.

Three weeks later to the day, Bobby went back to his inconsistencies, and I was in complete shock, confused, and so, so very angry with God for letting me be duped again. With all sincerity, I had waited on God asking Him for direction. All I wanted was what He wanted. I couldn't figure out why He would let this happen, letting me sink to new depths of pain?

At the time, it seemed like a very cruel joke that God would allow me to be sucked back into the relationship, only to experience a deeper hurt than ever before. I went round and round with God. I couldn't figure out how to move forward in our relationship if I couldn't trust Him.

However, I was sure what to do with Bobby...*Sayonara*!

If I could have inserted a microchip into the frontal lobe of my brain flashing "danger, danger" as a reminder of my resolution with Bobby, I would have.

Instead, I wrote out a detailed list of proven facts as to why I should never again be a part of this relationship. Many of the reminders consisted of lying and trust issues. At the bottom of my list, I signed, dated it, and kept it in plain view on my nightstand to review each day.

As far as my relationship with God, I made peace with Him and decided to trust Him whether I understood Him or not. As much as

Satan hoped that I would shrink back, I could not deny God's great love for me and did not want to live my life without the Lord. Instead, I concluded that just because I do not understand what He's doing doesn't change the truth of His character…trustworthy, holy, all-knowing, omnipotent, perfect, loving, consistent, and faithful to His children, even when we are faithless.

In retrospect, God knew it would take every ounce of strength I had to remove myself from such a toxic relationship, especially when Bobby dangled my illusive dreams of marriage and a happy life touring together in my face. Even if the truth of Bobby's character were as plain as the nose on my face, it would take a miracle for this relational bond to die.

I believe God knew a disastrous third marriage was impending if I didn't feel acute pain over and over again in this relationship. God allowed me to repeatedly experience the full impact of deceit and lies from a person who professed otherwise, until I finally got the message. Somewhere along the line I did start to get the message, praying, "God, do whatever it takes, but don't let me get into another bad marriage." I didn't get out of this relationship without experiencing immense pain, but God was faithfully answering my prayer.

As we started gearing up for our next tour, I was about to discover the reality of my prayer for "God to do whatever it would take" mixed with a merciful dose of His love and faithfulness to me.

I knew it was coming when Carol married Dr. Norm, and she decided not to tour. I envied her decisiveness to go back to school and pursue her dream in interior design. Once again, I was happy for her, but sad and confused about my life. I was not looking forward to traveling with all guys, especially while trying to keep up pleasantries and a high quality of softball gamesmanship with a guy whom I was trying to sever all ties with. Keeping my distance was especially hard when my job required us to be with each other the entire summer, 24/7.

I had no idea how this was going to work. It was going to be a lonely summer. In over twenty years of touring, something happened that had never occurred before. Normally, once we hit the road, leaving California, we were gone for the entire summer, coming back in August or September. This summer was going to be different. No matter how hard we tried, there was one week surrounding the Fourth of July that didn't get booked.

Because we were close to O'Hare Airport in Chicago, Carol decided it would be cost effective to purchase round trip tickets, flying the team home for the week, instead of hanging out for the next seven days in some random hotel.

Hallelujah…that was fine by me! I considered this a much-needed reprieve from all of Bobby's manipulation and emotional abuse.

This unexpected break in the action was exactly what the doctor ordered. I hadn't realized what a toll the last month of touring had been on my nerves. I felt like I was tip toeing on eggshells around Bobby.

With four days until our flight back to Chicago, I accepted an invitation to help my friend with her young son's birthday party. Following that, she also invited me to an informal gathering of their adult friends for an after party that would take place in the evening.

It had already been a long day, and I was exhausted. As adults started arriving, I slipped into the kitchen and pre-determined to do some cleanup before I made my exit. I listened to the chatter of voices as the adjoining living room started to burst with people.

A loud uproar of greetings and laughter filled the room as I looked over my shoulder just in time to see two strapping guys walk in the front door. Everyone seemed exuberant to see these guys…John and "Big Dan."

Eventually both guys made their way to the kitchen and food area, introducing themselves to me. As they entered the kitchen, I did make a mental note that the tallest guy with the handsome face and soft brown eyes dipped his head just under the door jam, with about an inch of clearance above his head.

I chuckled silently to myself. *Well, he's certainly tall enough Lord. I could wear any size heels and still look pint size next to him.*

Instead of going back with his friends, Dan grabbed a towel and began drying the dishes as I washed. Our conversation flowed easily, with me asking questions and Dan doing most of the talking. Somewhere during our exchange, I said something about prayer, letting him know I was a Christian. I was sure that would be a conversation-stopper, and then I would leave.

But much to my surprise, Dan replied, *"I'm a Christian too!"*

At this time in my life, I was pretty cynical when it came to the entire male species. In my books, all males fell into one-category...liars, users, and jerks!

I'm sure I had a smirk on my face as I challenged Dan. "What is your definition of a Christian?"

I knew my question sounded blunt, and I might be putting him on the spot, but I was just so sick of the games.

Unbelievably, Dan's answer rang true as he let me know he had received Christ in his teens, had fallen away, and had recently made a new commitment to the Lord.

Because my trust level in guys was at an all time low, it was hard for me to take his words at face value, but this new guy definitely piqued my interest.

Time flew by. The next time I glanced at my watch, I was shocked that it was past midnight. Before I left the party, Dan's friend, John, asked me if I was available to go to a dance the next night.

His words took me off guard, as I hummed and hawed. I thought, *This is awkward. Surely, he's seen me talking to Dan all night.*

After a couple minutes of uncomfortable, non-committal stammering on my part, John finally said, "Ah, come on. It'll be fun. You and Big Dan...my girlfriend and me. We'll pick you up at 8:00 p.m."

I accepted.

All these years later, I chuckle thinking how someone else asked me out for Dan on our first official date. The next night Dan seemed genuinely disappointed to learn that I was leaving town for the next month and a half, asking if he could write. I was pretty sure that his gesture to write was all talk, but I gave him a list of our scheduled mailstops on tour anyway.

True to his word, there was a letter from Dan every week at the designated post offices across the United States. This was a very non-threatening and romantic way to get to know him.

In retrospect, I'm amazed at God's miraculous timing bringing Dan and I together just when I needed it the most.

Back on tour, I learned in an undeniable way that Bobby had been cheating on me. Even though I knew we were over, it cut me to the core, making me feel like a fool for ever trusting him. My self esteem would have gone completely down the toilet had it not been for those cherished letters I received from Dan.

I knew full well in my heart that even if nothing materialized between Dan and me, this unexpected happening in the middle of our tour was part of God's mercy toward me.

With a couple weeks before returning home, I was disappointed when I didn't receive any more letters from Dan. I sighed, *"Well, it's just me and you Lord."*

I found out later that he lost our list of mailstops. However, he did continue faithfully writing letters and sending them to my home address, which I didn't find out about until I returned home.

I figured Dan had moved on, and I scratched him off my list of possibilities, focusing on counting down each day until I was home again and nowhere near Bobby.

Even though the last two years had left my head and heart reeling, and my self worth the size of a pea, somewhere deep inside I could feel my strength and hope for the future building momentum. Like never before, I sensed the presence of God empowering me to be the best I could be each day. New courage surged through my being as I realized even if I felt lonely, I was never alone. I was standing at a crossroads in my life, needing to make changes.

Before our last game, I let Carol know ahead of time that if The Queen and Her Court continued another season, I would never again travel with Bobby.

As it turned out, Carol was making decisions for a new direction in her life, and it did not include setting up another tour for The Queen and Her Court.

All the cards were showing. All family members had moved on. After twenty-one years of touring, I could sense this season of my life was coming to a close. I was filled with emotion as the last game of our 1986 tour came to a close. Part of me resisted leaving the ball field. I didn't want my career as a professional athlete to be over.

Behind the smile that was pasted on my face was sadness, combined with a blind hope for what was yet to come.

As each fan excitedly requested my autograph that night, I tried to reciprocate their love with a cheery countenance to match their exuberant presence. They represented a lifetime of people who came out to see The Queen and Her Court year after year, giving me the most unique catalog of memories any person could ever hope for. At that moment, I had plenty of question marks concerning my future, but my foundation was on solid ground. One day at a time.

On that day I did what I did best….I gave an autograph and a queenly smile.

EPILOGUE

When I started writing this book, I knew there was one last thing I had been intentionally avoiding since my dad's death, over thirty years ago.

Recorded on a ninety-minute Memorex cassette tape was Daddy's one minute and twenty-five second farewell message.

Even after I received the cassette from my Uncle Dallas, I couldn't seem to make myself listen to it for two years. Every time I eyed it on the shelf, my stomach would tighten, a nervous dread overtaking me. I was afraid to hear his voice. *What would I feel? Would I discover traces of unforgiveness still lingering in my heart? Would I become so consumed with sadness, giving depression an opportunity to take me down? Did I have the strength to re-live such a painful time?*

Nearing the completion of my writing, I knew I had the courage to hear Daddy's voice again and be okay. My heart was beating loudly, and my stomach was so nervous that I relieved myself in the bathroom a couple of times while Dan and I listened to and transcribed each word. I tried to remain detached and emotionless. I cried briefly, regrouping and steeling myself to complete the task, fearing that the tape was so old that it might snap before I got to hear it all the way through.

Daddy's voice was calm, methodical, unemotional, and emphatic to relay details of his suffering, stating, *"My wife and my real neat family have done all that they can do for me so...so please don't hold any of them responsible for my actions."*

I repeatedly listened to his last minute and twenty-five seconds recorded for me. I allowed myself to feel each of his words, crying and even chuckling over his Texas twang pronouncing the word "wrestled," saying "wrastled." After the shock and anxiousness of hearing his voice again faded away, I was surprised when I began responding to his words...as if we were having a two-way conversation. When Daddy said, *"It will come as a shock and terrible strain to them."* I replied aloud, "No lie, Daddy. It just about did me in." When he said, *"Sorry for the inconvenience,"* I couldn't help my spontaneous sarcasm, "Yes, Daddy, just a wee bit inconvenient...my whole life was in shambles." With his very last words, *"Thank you for understanding,"* I wanted him to know that even after twenty-nine years, the pain wasn't as acute, but there would never be a perfect understanding. Only trusting God and surrendering over my lack of understanding has helped me to rise up from the ashes of this destruction.

After the exhaustion of this completed task, I felt closure and an overwhelming peace. I knew that the forgiveness and love I felt for my dad was genuine, and I wished he could have been a part of my journey post softball.

Actual forgiveness was a much longer process than I thought it would be, but I refused to give up. First, I acknowledged that unforgiveness was wreaking havoc, emotionally, and would take me down a path of destruction. This sin would eat me alive. I was drinking the poison that I brewed daily for my dad, and it wasn't working. So, I determined to forgive and align myself with God's will, knowing that this prayer may not come easy, but it would be answered.

I researched all scripture on forgiveness, soaking in the truth of the words of Jesus. Passages like Matthew 18:21, 22: Peter asked, How often should I forgive someone who sins against me? Seven times? No, not seven times, Jesus replied, but seventy times seven! Jesus then spoke a parable that made it clear what God thought about forgiving others and the repercussions to follow if they didn't forgive.

Matthew 18:35: That's what my heavenly Father will do to you if you refuse to forgive your brothers and sisters from your heart.

While I had the head knowledge of scripture pointing the way, I couldn't seem to do what He asked. It was a heart issue.

How do I change my heart, Lord?

My healing boiled down to a few key things that my heavenly Father probably had to emphasize repeatedly in various ways until it went from my head to my heart.

I focused on the fact that my specific sin had put Jesus on the cross. He was perfect, did nothing wrong, and loved me so much that He willingly died an excruciating death to pay for and cover all my sins… past, present, and future.

When He rose from the dead three days later, that horrible day turned into the best, most victorious day of *my* life and for all those who accept His free gift of grace. Jesus' resurrection assured all who believed in him a passage into heaven for eternity.

There it was!!! The Holy Spirit touched my heart with knowledge I had known since the age of eight years old. I could not refuse a request from a love so great! He gave up everything to have a relationship with me. My heart was flooded with overwhelming love and gratitude. I knew I could forgive, and I did.

While life will always be filled with ups and downs, I discovered that God had many unexpected surprises waiting for me following that last ballgame in 1986.

In the spring of 1987, Dan and I married and have been walking together through life's wild ride for the last thirty-five years. He has been the faithful, committed partner that I prayed for the Lord to send me…a man dedicated to God, and always maintaining the promise he gave me on our wedding day. In his words, *"God sent me to treat you like the queen that you are."* What girl wouldn't want that!

The first summer that I didn't tour, I felt like a cat on a hot tin roof…restless and out of place. I wanted to be anywhere but at home.

My sweet sign contractor husband tried to make things better, convincing me that he could sure use my help at work. Although I ended up doing his bookkeeping for twenty years, I must admit that making the transition from professional athlete to working in his office was not the easiest thing I've ever done.

I have etched in my brain the memory of my first non-touring summer with poor Dan trying to think of things at his office to keep me busy. One day he saw that I had nothing to do, so he cheerily asked if I could pass him a pencil about five feet away, acting as if I was doing him the greatest service. I burst into tears and ran out of the room. Bitterly, I thought, *Gee thanks, Lord. It wasn't all that long ago that I was on national television striking out Johnny Carson, and now I'm nothing, with the highlight and biggest accomplishment of my day passing my husband a pencil. This is not exactly what I had in mind.*

Clearly, I had a lot to learn, and the next decade was to be an intense course in finding my true identity...not in the things I accomplished, but in who I was as a child of God.

It only made matters worse when it seemed like the only thing every well-intentioned person could think of to ask me about was softball. Since I wasn't touring anymore, that was the last thing I wanted to talk about. I desperately fought off tears each time. The conversations were as excruciating as the single gal listening to all her married girlfriends chatter happily about their marriages, or the gal who so desperately wants to have children just like all her other friends, but is not getting pregnant.

As hard as this time period was, I can look back and acknowledge that God extended an abundance of patience and mercy to help me along the way. The most surprising happening occurred that fall when Eddie Feigner, owner, pitcher, and the male version of The Queen and Her Court contacted me, stating that he would love to get together in our hometown of Long Beach.

After treating Eileen and me to a delicious dinner, Eddie proceeded to ask what our future plans were for touring. Eileen and I hadn't given touring any thought, so we just listened as Eddie threw out a number of possibilities of joining him, or booking a tour for us.

Eileen and I thanked him for the night, told Eddie we'd think over his proposals, and would get back to him.

We talked all the way home. The more we thought about it, the more excited we became. Between Eileen and I, we knew that we had been more than equipped and trained for the last two decades to book our own tour, put a team together, and tour again if we wanted. With Eileen and I raring to go as pitcher and catcher, half of The Queen and Her Court was already in place.

So that's what we did for the next two summers, and it was a blast!

Many times, we wished Daddy could see how smoothly things were, without all the stress and anxiety that co-existed when he was alive. It felt more like a paid vacation…doing the thing I loved the most. Instead of booking every possible day, Eileen and I planned a few relaxing days here and there, so our bodies could recuperate.

After the completion of two very successful tours and a third summer halfway booked in advance, we both knew the Lord had spoken to us. We were not to tour again, so we canceled the dates that were already booked.

It's hard to quit something when everything is going great, and you are still at the top of your game. But, then again, as years passed, I've always been thankful that my last memories as a professional athlete were good ones, winning and retiring on top.

Looking back, we know that God honored our obedience in this area and has blessed us for putting Him and our families above our desire to continue this career in sports. These extra two tours were an immense blessing, helping me transition and move forward to other things in life.

Satisfying our desire for competition, Eileen and I started playing tennis in the amateur world, as a doubles team. With many tennis lessons, and the same determined focus that we learned in softball, we joined our local college tennis team and were thrilled to win the only tennis State Championship to date for men or women in Long Beach City College history.

We joined the USTA (United States Tennis Association) winning many 4.5 level tournaments together, and after years of honing our skills, we won a USTA National Championship at the 4.5 level. Even though I was not getting paid, the exhilaration of winning in this new sport felt exactly the same as did my wins as a professional athlete.

After five years of marriage to Dan, I sensed my heart and head changing in regards to the subject of children. After years of playing on The Queen and Her Court, I think I was resigned to the fact that touring would be my life and kids were not in the cards for me.

At the time, a more pressing subject always took center stage. More than having children, my future objective was singular. I was determined to be in a successful marriage. My mind would not allow me to entertain any other scenarios beyond that dream.

Although I knew Dan would love to have children, I let him know in the beginning of our relationship that I felt the exact opposite. If he married me, children would not be in the equation. He acknowledged the reality of such a statement and was true to his word, never pushing or pressuring me in this area.

When I realized our marriage was secure and forever, my viewpoint concerning children flip-flopped, doing a one eighty.

God helped things along by planting this seed of change in my heart when my sister, Karen's little girl, Jeralynn, came to live with Dan and me as a kindergartner. Like her middle name, which is Joy, she filled our world with love, fun, purpose, and lots of joy. I loved being "a mom," and I was crushed when she left our home after a year.

From that point on, I prayed daily that someway, somehow God would bring us a child, and I could be a mother again.

Because I wasn't getting pregnant, Dan and I started looking into adoption. I remember the day a manila envelope from the state of

California arrived in the mail. I eagerly ripped open the one-inch-thick envelope that was our return response from an introduction meeting Dan and I attended inquiring about adoption.

After skimming the first few pages of fine print, I realized this process would involve filling out page upon page of detailed questions, background checks, and many other hoops to jump through, with no guarantees of adoption. At the time, this mountain of paperwork left me discouraged and dazed. I was overwhelmed, bursting into tears. This wasn't going to be my answer. The thick packet was filed in my trash basket, and I continued to pray, *God, if You want me to have a child, you are going to have to do it, and send someone to help me with each step of the way.*

God's answer was a supernatural miracle through a private adoption from His hand alone with many details specific to my prayer. I hoped I would have the support of someone who would walk me through each step of the adoption process, that it would be financially feasible; and if possible, I could experience motherhood with a newborn. He answered these particular prayers and so many more.

At thirty-nine years old, I was a neophyte, wide-eyed with anticipation...ready to embark on this exciting journey called motherhood. Dan and I buckled up our newborn baby boy in the brand-new infant car seat...ready to head home from the hospital with our precious Luke Daniel Schoepf. We giggled like two little kids, hoping we had fastened Luke in the car seat properly. *Ready or not, here we come!*

Not too long after this, Dan and I were shocked when I discovered I was pregnant, and equally saddened when I miscarried at ten weeks.

Although I probably didn't realize it at the time because I was a new mom, Luke was a very easy baby. He slept eight hours through the night at five weeks, progressing to eleven hours. Because of his sweet nature, I felt compelled to start praying for God to send us another child...a brother or sister for little Luke.

Just before Luke turned two years old, we all went to pick up a cute little wide-eyed toddler from the foster care offices. I wish I had a video of that day. When Michael, who was only four and a half months older than Luke, spotted Dan, he reached both hands toward him and said, *"Daddy."* Our mouths dropped open! Although I believe God ordained him to be our son on that very day, Michael Thomas Schoepf legally became our very own son three years later.

The blessings didn't end there. Our family kept growing. Both Jeralynn and her younger sister, Janelle, came to live with us until they were adults ready to move out on their own. As I was learning to relinquish control over how I thought my life should be, God never ceased to amaze me with answered prayers, putting together our family.

I also became involved in two programs that poured as much blessing into my life as I was trying to give out. The first was Release Time Education, an after-school program where I taught the Bible, for fourteen years, to fourth and fifth graders from a local elementary school in Long Beach.

The second, and most current, ministry Eileen and I have been blessed to be part of is working as counselors with the counseling program at our local church in Long Beach.

I felt a special call from God as I had the opportunity to meet with many gals, one on one, making a space for them to share their emotions and vulnerability, while directing their hearts to the only One who could truly heal, restore, and bring hope for their future.

As I listened to so many stories of heartache and pain, I suddenly became incredibly thankful for every hard thing that God had allowed to touch my life. Each week, I silently whispered fresh praise, as I marveled over the way the Lord had brought me through everything, just so I could exude His quiet confidence and hope to these hurting women when they needed it the most. During these moments, I wouldn't have wanted to change a single day of my life. I knew that each day, the good and the bad, had been a part of shaping me into the person that God had intended me to be. This opportunity to serve others also acted as God's redemptive process for my life, as my passion to encourage and help others had been born out of all the pain and "whys" in my past.

So far, life still seems like it's moving at a pretty fast pace. I can't even imagine what the next season will look like, but with God, I know the best is yet to come.

ACKNOWLEDGEMENTS

As I started writing my manuscript, I thought this was certainly the hard part. Little did I know that the gargantuan task of getting my book published would require a very special person to come alongside Eileen and me to see this project come to fruition.

Words can't express our heartfelt gratitude to Erik Seversen, speaker, author, adventurer and educator, who took up the mantle in helping us cross the finish line in getting our book published. We are so very thankful for his expertise in editing along with his generosity of time and knowledge.

To our two biggest cheerleaders, our husbands Dan Schoepf and Gregg Francabandera, thank you for always allowing us to reach for the stars in all our wild adventures. We couldn't have done this without your love and support.

Throughout the years, we have been blessed with unbelievably talented athletes on our team. A special thanks for the contributions you have made to the success of The Queen and Her Court.

Lastly, we want to say "thank you" to our friends and fans who have supported and followed The Queen and Her Court for 25 years.

DID YOU ENJOY THIS BOOK?

If you enjoyed reading this book, you can help by suggesting it to someone else you think might like it, and **please leave a positive review** wherever you purchased it. This does a lot in helping others find the book. We thank you in advance for taking a few moments to do this.

THANK YOU

CONTACT THE AUTHOR

Contact Rosie Black Schoepf and Eileen Francabandera directly at:
Email: thesisters7777@gmail.com
Instagram: thesisters7777

Made in the USA
Las Vegas, NV
05 May 2023

71619325R00168